THE CHALLENGE OF CROSS-CULTURAL INTERPRETATION IN THE ANGLO-INDIAN NOVEL:

The Raj Revisited

(A Comparative Study of Three Booker Prize Authors:
Paul Scott, *The Raj Quartet,*
J.G. Farrell, *The Siege of Krishnapur,*
Ruth Prawer Jhabvala, *Heat and Dust*)

SALZBURG UNIVERSITY STUDIES

IS A PROGRAMME OF

THE INSTITUT FÜR ANGLISTIK UND AMERIKANISTIK

PARIS LODRON UNIVERSITY, SALZBURG

THE CHALLENGE OF CROSS-CULTURAL INTERPRETATION IN THE ANGLO-INDIAN NOVEL:

The Raj Revisited

(A Comparative Study of Three Booker Prize Authors:
Paul Scott, *The Raj Quartet,*
J.G. Farrell, *The Siege of Krishnapur,*
Ruth Prawer Jhabvala, *Heat and Dust*)

Gerwin Strobl

THE EDWIN MELLEN PRESS
LEWISTON, NEW YORK / SALZBURG AUSTRIA
1995

The author asserts moral rights and copyright to the material in this volume.

Cataloguing information for this volume is available from the Library of Congress, Washington, D.C.

SALZBURG ENGLISH AND AMERICAN STUDIES
Volume 3

EDITOR: JAMES HOGG
INSTITUT FÜR ANGLISTIK UND AMERIKANISTIK
UNIVERSITÄT SALZBURG, A-5020 SALZBURG, AUSTRIA
Fax N° 0043 0 66 2 80 44 613

TO ORDER: ISBN: 07734-4190-5

Europe and the Commonwealth: The Edwin Mellen Press, Ltd.
Lampeter, Dyfed, Wales
United Kingdom SA48 7DY

North America: The Edwin Mellen Press
Box 450
Lewiston, New York
USA 14092-0450

Printed in Great Britain by Antony Rowe Ltd, Chippenham, Wiltshire

For my parents

in gratitude

Table of Contents

	page
Introduction	3
I. 'BEYOND MARABAR' - PAUL SCOTT'S RAJ QUARTET	6
1. Scott and India	6
2. 'The Road from Dibrapur': An Introduction to the Theme	21
3. 'Mayapore': The End of Liberal Humanism	48
4. 'Pankot': Twilight of Paternalism	90
5. 'The Situation': Truth and the Quartet	134
6. 'An Imperial Embrace': Fiction and History in the Quartet	157
II. 'A MOMENT OF HISTORY': J.G. FARRELL'S THE SIEGE OF KRISHNAPUR	188
III. 'AN ATTEMPT TO REMAIN STANDING': RUTH PRAWER JHABVALA'S HEAT AND DUST	221
Conclusion	257
Bibliography	260

INTRODUCTION

"Anyone who has ... entered a bookshop in the last few months will be aware that the British Raj, after three and a half decades in retirement, has been making some sort of comeback." [1] This is Salman Rushdie writing in 1984. It is the opening shot in a now famous essay in which he blasts away at what another literary voice from the subcontinent had called "the rage for the Raj". [2] 'Rage', of course, sums up neatly Rushdie's own feelings about it. And it is almost in an effort to calm himself that he dismisses the renewed interest in the old Indian Empire as " ... the phantom twitchings of an amputated limb." [3]

Whatever the merits or shortcomings of Rushdie the polemicist, he is surely right in linking the revival of interest in the Raj with the name of one novelist above all others, that of Paul Scott. When Scott started in the late 1950s to write novels set in, or dealing with, the East, India was very much out of British minds. Kipling, though officially 'rediscovered', remained on the periphery of public interest, the lesser Anglo-Indian novelists had, deservedly, been banished from the nation's bookshelves, and as for E.M. Forster, he was rapidly turning into something of a living literary relic: honoured, venerated even, but very much an anachronism. The subject matter itself seemed to have vanished in the mists of history. Forster, in fact, was moved to add an almost apologetic note to the 1957 Everyman edition of *A Passage to India*, warning his readers that Chandrapore no longer existed. [4] Small wonder then that early reviewers tended to remark on Scott's 'surprising' choice of subject. As late as 1975, with the *Raj Quartet* completed and wider recognition at last forthcoming, a *Times* "Profile" on Scott speculated that " ... possibly the real reason why he is so little known is not that he

---

[1] Salman Rushdie, "Outside the Whale". *Granta* 11, p.125.
[2] cf. Anita Desai, " The Rage for the Raj". *New Republic* 25 November 1975, pp.26-29.
[3] Rushdie, p.128.
[4] cf. E. M. Forster, *A Passage to India*. (Abinger Edition 6) London 1978, p.313: "Assuredly the novel dates."

makes himself so little known but that his subject is one that people are unwilling to take on". [5]

Events were soon to prove the critics wrong. Only two years later, in 1977, Scott received the Booker Prize for what was to be his last novel, *Staying On*: a late personal triumph but also confirmation of a wider breakthrough. For this was the third time within a few years that the prize had been awarded for a novel with an Anglo-Indian setting - J.G.Farrell's *The Siege of Krishnapur* and Ruth Prawer Jhabvala's *Heat and Dust* having received the same accolade in 1973 and 1975 respectively. British India was once more firmly on the map of the literary world.

This study, then, aims to investigate the revival of the Anglo-Indian novel as it took place in the late 1960s and early seventies. To do this, it will look at the novels which at once produced and epitomized it - six in all, written within a span of less than ten years. Four of them are by Paul Scott and make up his tetralogy *The Raj Quartet*. Though they were published separately as *The Jewel in the Crown* (1966), *The Day of the Scorpion*, (1968), *The Tower of Silence* (1971), and *A Division of the Spoils* (1975), and can be read as self-contained novels, they are nevertheless clearly intended as a larger unit and will be treated here as such. [6] J.G. Farrell's *The Siege of Krishnapur* and Ruth Prawer Jhabvala's *Heat and Dust* complete the list. [7]

Some twenty years separate us now from the time when these novels first appeared. Much has changed. Two of our authors, Paul Scott and J.G. Farrell have died, and Ruth Jhabvala has moved to another country and new fictional worlds. Yet the six novels with which we are concerned have weathered the years well. Unlike much that was published in the sixties and seventies and lavishly praised at the time, they have never gone out of print, are widely read, and have attracted growing critical attention.

---

[5] Moorhead, Caroline: "Getting Engrossed in the Death-Throes of the Raj." *The Times* 20 October 1975.

[6] *Staying On*, which shares with *The Raj Quartet* its setting and several of its characters will not be considered here since it deals, as its title implies, with post-Independence India only.

[7] Farrell died in 1979, while working on a second novel set in British India. This fragment which has since been published as *The Hill Station*, is too obviously incomplete to merit discussion here.

Criticism tends to focus on individual authors, and this has also been the case here. Only a handful of scholars have worked on more than one of our writers, very few of them in the same book or article. Of our three novelists, Paul Scott has perhaps been the most popular with the critics. In fact, his stature and critical reputation have grown remarkably. Twenty years ago his name was a blank page in most literary journals; now scarcely a year goes by without a respectable crop of new articles on his work, and there have even appeared a few full-length critical studies. This is in marked contrast to the fate of J.G. Farrell, who, though he has attracted little hostile criticism, continues to suffer scholarly neglect. Perhaps this is due to the pronounced heterogeneity of his Empire Trilogy. It does not fit neatly into the traditional pigeon holes and has therefore remained on the margins of critical debate. Ruth Jhabvala's fiction, lastly, has always had a large number of admirers - and also of vociferous detractors. Most Jhabvala criticism, however, has been devoted to the full range of her 'œuvre', or aspects of it, rather than to individual novels.

This study, then, is not intended to represent a comprehensive survey of critical thought on each of our authors; nor can it claim to cover every aspect of the novels it will examine. Its aim is more modest: it will look at the portrayal of the Raj and at the reasons why three novelists with widely differing backgrounds should all have turned to it. And it does so in the belief that these six novels do not represent "the phantom twitchings of an amputated limb" but the not altogether painless treatment of a long-ignored wound.

I. 'BEYOND MARABAR' - PAUL SCOTT'S RAJ QUARTET

1. Scott and India

Surveying the literary scene in Britain and despairing of the usual diet of "... muffled curses at the welfare state and ... the exhausted records of adultery in Hampstead", Anthony Burgess once remarked that there had been since the days of

> ... the Victorian giants ... only ... one block-busting theme, and that was the rise of the British Empire. It's a theme that's been merely nibbled at, Kipling who could have written an Anglo-Indian *War and Peace* - being the most shameful nibbler of them all. [1]

It is doubtful whether Paul Scott ever saw the Empire in quite those terms, that is to say as a potential 'block-buster'; and if he did decide to take up the theme and duly went on to write something rather like the Anglo-Indian *War and Peace* Anthony Burgess had been hoping for, it was not due to a conscious decision. Certainly, he did not originally set out to become what, in the eyes of many, he has in fact become: the chief chronicler of the 'Decline and Fall of the Indian Empire'. Indeed he might never have written about India at all had it not been for the lasting impressions of that country gained when he was sent out to defend it during the Second World War.

The usual story then: an impressionable young Englishman, exposed for a few years to the magic charms of the East, who spends the rest of his days gushing forth about tiger-shoots, plucky young memsahibs and Peace at the Khyber. Well, not so in Scott's case.

To begin with, India itself did not, at first, charm him greatly. Unlike the other writers (and scribblers) one usually associates with the East, Scott, of course, had not gone out to take up a promising career, nor had he stepped off a P&O ship as one of the usual tourists, armed with letters of introduction, sketchbook and gun-case. Not for him the

---

[1] Anthony Burgess, "On Lengthy Matters". *The New York Times Book Review* 14 Dec. 1975, p.39.

reassuring certainty of a welcome as 'one of us' wherever he would go; nor could he afford to scorn the company at the club, secure in the knowledge of power and influence of old Cambridge acquaintances who would always come to one's rescue if the worst came to the worst and, meanwhile, of a maharajah, no less, offering a temporary haven from the vicissitudes of life. Inevitably, Scott's India was very different from that of the Kiplings and Forsters. He never had to ask for a chance to see the 'real' India - Army life thrust him right into it; as deeply as any novelist might wish for, considerably deeper, in fact, than the young Scott cared for at the time.

The resulting culture shock was violent indeed: much more serious than that experienced by most Western visitors, who were usually well-shielded from the more offending sights and smells of the native towns; all the more so, as nothing in the young man's previous experience of life - limited as it was to the prim and respectable middle class world of suburban London - can have prepared him for this assault on his senses, his mind and his system. The descriptions in *A Division of the Spoils* of Army life in Calcutta, and of the trials and tribulations of the ill-fated Captain Purvis in particular, capture something of what Scott must have thought and felt at the time.

Assuredly, India was neither beautiful nor, for that matter, very mysterious; it was just filthy, squalid, and in every respect preposterous beyond belief. It cannot have gained much in attractiveness either by the war then raging at its gates, and the ubiquitous scars left by the suppression of Gandhi's "Quit India"- campaign. Not surprisingly, Scott was, at first, utterly dismayed, as he recalled in an interview some thirty years later: ". . . I looked at the place, and I said, my God, what a mess it is. I don't know a thing about it; I don't want to know anything about it".[2]

---

[2] Francine Ringold, "A Conversation with Paul Scott". *Nimrod* 21 (1) 1976, p.28.
It is perhaps with these lines in mind that Janis Tedesco and Jane Popham declare roundly: "Scott hated India. He never understood it and felt it alien to his personality." (Janis Tedesco and Jane Popham: *Introduction to "The Raj Quartet"*. Lanham MD 1985, p.ix.) Tedesco and Popham are following a tradition of sorts here, as the charge of hating India - like that of not understanding her - is routinely levelled at everyone in the West who has ever written about the country; it would also appear to be part of this tradition that such charges need not be backed up with concrete evidence. Tedesco and Popham certainly seem content to dispense with such tedious formalities. There is, quite apart from considerations of fairness,

There were also, at first, serious health-problems - he promptly went down with jaundice - which can hardly have endeared the country to him. Yet, during those difficult wartime years, India nevertheless cast a spell on him.

Scott was not immediately aware of it. It was only after he had left the country, having been transferred to Malaya in the final days of the War, that he noticed his feelings about India had changed: he found that there, in the tropical pleasance that was Malaya, his thoughts kept going back to a more austere, a starker beauty: "It was at this point that I realized . . . I had fallen in love with India." [3]

It was the beginning of a lifelong passion, which led him first to forego the comparative ease and luxury of military life in Singapore - by contriving to have himself posted to Calcutta - and later, back in England after his demobilization in 1946, to acquire and read his way through a small library of books on Indian topics; but above all, it produced, over the years, a flood of articles and reviews, of introductions and essays, and, not least, a handsome pile of novels. Of these none is more eloquent than *The Raj Quartet* in expressing what Scott himself called his ". . . affection and exasperation, admiration and nostalgia, and . . . [his] overriding belief in . . . [India's] ability to plough the furrows we never ploughed and plough them straight, in the way (at our best) we imagined them." [4]

'Why India?'

Literature, it is commonly agreed, is not created in a vacuum. The writer always draws in some measure on personal experience and observations made of those around him; their actions, foibles, preoccupations, and prejudices, all combine to act both as wellspring of his creative imagination and as material for it to work upon. While some

---

something peculiarly ironic about such 'black-and-white' criticsm directed against a novelist who had always sought to challenge simplistic assumptions.
[3] Ringold, p.29.
[4] Paul Scott, "An Idealist in Action". Review of "Indira Gandhi" by Zareer Masani. *Country Life* 19 June 1975, p.1643.

writers try their hand at a whole range of themes, others - and among them the not least successful ones - content themselves with working small but fertile patches. Many of the 19th century giants referred to by Anthony Burgess are cases in point. Dickens, for instance, we admire for the unrivalled descriptions of Victorian low-life which he produced in book after book (and feel perhaps less sure about his gallant foray into Revolutionary France). Similarly, we find it hard to imagine Jane Austen writing on anything other than polite society in the English shires and the 'tremendous trifles' that thrill and agitate it. Dickens, and Jane Austen are, of course, writers of genius; but genius apart, the success of their writing stems, at least in part, from its firm rooting in personal experience and observable contemporary reality.

Why then should we wonder that Scott chose to write about India? After all, here was something of which he had firsthand knowledge, which had left a powerful and lasting impression on his mind, and conjured up for him a thousand memories of faces, landscapes and incidents that made one reach for the pen; something, moreover, close enough to his heart to prevent its telling from degenerating into a mere exercise in exotic colour. And was it too much to hope that this strength of feeling would infuse his writing and create a sense of urgency and immediacy that might transcend both the geographical distance and the gulf of the years, separating the world of the Raj from that of his readers?

Looked at from this perspective, it may indeed seem almost inevitable that Scott should have written about British India. Most of his readers and critics certainly appear to have thought so, once the initial surprise had worn off. If a puzzled 'Why India?' had widely greeted the publication of *The Jewel in the Crown*, that question soon ceased to be asked; the very success of the *Quartet*, growing with each successive volume, seemed to answer it. Here was somebody who was evidently writing about 'his theme', elaborating on it and refining it in book after book; a lone survivor of the Raj presumably, who had chosen the vehicle of fiction to commit his memories, good and bad, to paper. Besides, there had been, as some of the critics dimly recollected, earlier novels with an Eastern setting, published long before the *Quartet*. It was perhaps not altogether surprising therefore that people occasionally jumped to conclusions and thought that Scott must have been born in India. [5]

In reality, things were somewhat less clear-cut. Scott had, for a start, spent little more than three years on the subcontinent, as indeed he was always the first to admit, "Until I went back to India in 1964 [when work on *Jewel* started], my personal contact with the country had been no more than that enjoyed - or not enjoyed - by thousands of other men who spent three years or so out there . . . during the last war." [6] The general belief that Scott had exclusively spun Eastern yarns was equally incorrect: reflecting on his oeuvre in 1968, in a lecture to the Royal Society of Literature, Scott could claim that only six of the ten novels he had then written (that number included the first two of the *Quartet*) had "mainly . . . Indian backgrounds"; [7] ". . . of the six", he goes on to say, "two use the background simply as a setting . . . . Of the remaining four I would admit three as being about Anglo-India."[8] He could therefore conclude - and with some justification - that "far from having consistently written about the Indian subject, I've only recently got round to it . . . ." [9] Which brings us back to the question heading this chapter.

Now, to ask 'Why India?' is not a futile exercise. For one thing, knowledge of a novelist's purpose in writing a particular novel may in itself provide a useful yardstick against which to measure its successes and shortcomings. If, for instance, Anita Desai claims that none of the portraits of the Indian characters in the *Quartet* show the kind of understanding Scott felt for his English protagonists, [10] or if Salman Rushdie complains, a trifle petulantly perhaps, that Indian characters

---

[5] Paul Scott, "India: A Post-Forsterian View". *Essays by Divers Hands: Being the Transactions of the Royal Society of Literature.* New Series 36 1970, p.116. (Reprinted in: Paul Scott, *My Appointment with the Muse: Essays 1961-1975.* London 1986) Scott claimed he felt "only marginally flattered" when asked if he had been, " . . . because the answer is that, as the writer I became, I probably was." (Ibid.)

[6] Ibid., p.115.

He adds, though, that those " . . . three years was - I was once relieved to discover - about the same length of time Forster spent, in two long visits, . . . , before publishing *Passage.*"

[7] Ibid., p.119.

[8] Ibid.

[9] Ibid.

[10] Desai, op.cit., p.27.

only get "... walk-ons, ... , remaining bit-players in their own history", their charges cannot be answered unless Scott's purpose is established.[11] True or not, they may be said to be beside the point, provided it can be shown that Scott's main concern did not in fact lie with the portrayal of the Indians and their disenchantment with British Rule. Should the *Quartet*, however, have been intended as an accurate mirror-image of the last years of the Indian Empire then those same charges would strike home.

There is yet another side to it: that of the anticipated public reception of a novel. While a novelist is, of course, free to write on any subject he chooses (this, at any rate, is a fundamental tenet of Western society and one to which, one would think, Mr Rushdie of all people might wish to subscribe) he must nevertheless expect his choice of subject occasionally to cause surprise and indeed comment; not because one should necessarily want to question his motives - though Rushdie has done precisely that in the case of the *Quartet* - but because some subjects are, by their nature, either so unlikely or so fraught with controversy - be it political or otherwise - as to guarantee more than just a few raised eye-brows. Writing about the British Raj a quarter of a century or so after its demise was bound to do so.

It was not, after all, as though there had been a shortage of reasons why a novelist might have been reluctant to take on that particular subject: apart from possibly giving offence overseas - a thought which weighed lightly in those happier days - there was the infinitely greater likelihood of a cold reception at home. A country busily forgetting its imperial past might not care to be reminded. It was a danger Scott was aware of, as he confided to his audience at the Royal Society of Literature: "There are moments when I, even, ask what on earth I'm up to, writing about the declining days of the now dead British Raj. One can hardly expect to create thereby a climate of instant enthusiasm."[12] There was yet another consideration weighing against it, and weighing heavily against it, too. The 'Indian subject' was not exactly virgin terrain; not only had it been traversed by a good many in its day, some of those earlier explorers had staked more permanent claims on it. Two names, in

---

[11] Rushdie, op.cit., p.128.
[12] "India: A Post-Forsterian View", op. cit., p.115.

particular, those of Kipling and E.M. Forster came to mind, and it was against their achievement that his own efforts would inevitably be measured.

Now, some writers achieve an exceptionally strong impact on the popular imagination, leaving lasting, almost indelible impressions on the minds of their readers; so much so, in fact, that not only do we automatically link their names with a particular time and place, we even get into the habit of equating that time and place with the writer's vision of it. Many of us, today, for instance (and to revert to our earlier example), conceive of Victorian London in purely Dickensian terms, or recreate in our minds an image of country life before the coming of the railways that owes everything to Jane Austen. This effect is necessarily more marked the farther the novel's setting is removed from the reader's actual realm of experience, both in terms of linear time and of geographical distance. British India had consequently always been peculiarly susceptible to it, and as actual memories of the Raj were rapidly fading, the visions and images of Kipling and Forster would, if anything, strengthen their hold on the collective imagination in Britain: merging or, in some cases, competing with each other. The entire Anglo-Indian experience, in fact, seemed, in the words of one critic, "... forever immortalized somewhere between Kipling and Forster." [13] Under these circumstances - one could be forgiven for thinking - only a very ambitious or a very foolhardy novelist would be eager to take on the subject.

Anybody who has so much as glanced at *The Raj Quartet*, with its highly intricate narrative structure, its enormous cast and its monumental length of two thousand pages or so, will agree that Scott was certainly nothing if not ambitious. Yet he never underestimated the extent to which the shadow of his literary predecessors hung over his chosen field. Kipling, it was true, had been somewhat overtaken and discredited by the course of events, but Forster's was still a commanding presence, and one Scott repeatedly acknowledged: "... I recognize that the ground I need to tread if writing about Anglo-India bears a certain person's footprints and to plant your own there is to invite comparison." [14]

---

[13] Moorhead, op.cit.
[14] "A Post-Forsterian View", p.113. cf. also Scott: "How Well Have They Worn?: 'A Passage to India' ". *The Times* 6 January 1966.

If the comparison was inevitable, it was, however, also actively sought. Indeed, a wish to contrast his perceptions of the declining years of the Raj with those reflected in *A Passage to India* was one of the reasons why Scott wrote the *Quartet*. It was not for nothing, after all, that he set out his views on the subject in a lecture, which he entitled "India: A Post-Forsterian View". This lecture to the Royal Society of Literature is almost a manifesto, laying down Scott's views on India, on his writing and on contemporary life in general, and doing so by relating them to those of Forster's as expressed in *Passage*. When he calls himself post-Forsterian, therefore, he does so entirely without flippancy.

Scott described himself as being post-Forsterian on three counts: in simple terms of generation, in terms of the time and nature of his own Indian experience and, lastly, of his perception of events there. The first point is self-evident, and so, surely, is the second: *A Passage to India* reflects, in the concensus of critics and contemporary Anglo-Indian readers alike, the impressions of Forster's first visit to that country. The India of *Passage* is, for all the well-documented allusions to the Amritsar Incident, and irrespective of its publication date of 1924, essentially a prewar, pre-Great War India: an India still basking in plenty of Edwardian sunlight. The novel, then, was, in some respects, an anachronism even when it first appeared. "Marabar was", in Scott's words, "a terminus, but not for Anglo-Indian history. The Anglo-India I took my own passage to was not quite the same as the one Forster knew ... The differences were marginal, but they existed." [15] And Scott is not talking here of mere trappings, of the inevitable but superficial change brought about by wartime conditions, but of change in the outlook and the attitudes of the Britons living in India: "The rate of history's flow is pretty slow, but in twenty years it can advance a yard or two, and did, even in Anglo-India." [16]

What weighed heavier in Scott's mind than these "marginal differences" were the misgivings he had about how the British in India had been represented in *Passage*. These misgivings - hardly new in themselves - did not just amount to a feeling that the Anglo-Indians, who had

---

[15] "India: A Post-Forsterian View", p. 117.
[16] Scott: "The Raj". In: Frank Moraes and Edward Howe (eds.): *John Kenneth Galbraith Introduces India* . London 1974, p.78.

"always had a bad press", had been hard done by;[17] to an impression of " ... moral judgement entered against them, without evidence for the accused being admitted", and to a corresponding wish to be fair to them and see justice done through his own work; [18] nor were they due to an excessive preoccupation with historical accuracy. Scott concedes readily enough that it was " ... irrelevant to Forster's purpose whether or not he got the Turtons completely, sociologically right ... " and accepts that even if Forster did not, he never got them "wrong in terms of his book, an important distinction to make". [19] What Scott was concerned with, however, was the question of verisimilitude. And on that score, he felt, the Turtons and Burtons failed lamentably: as characters they were not just flat, they were caricatures, worthy of a cartoon. [20]

---

[17] Ibid.

[18] Ibid.
The notion of fairness in this context brings to mind a letter of Forster's to Edmund Candler, an enlightened and, in his day, influential Anglo-Indian novelist. Candler had suggested a similarity of outlook, which Forster good-humouredly rejected; "I must firmly if gaily indicate the gulf between us! We both amuse ourselves by trying to be fair, but there our resemblance ends, for you are in the Club trying to be fair to the poor Indians, and I am with the Indians trying to be fair to the Club. By bursting ourselves blue, we arrive at an external similarity, but that's all ..." . ("Letter to Edmund Candler" 28 June 1924. In: Mary Lago and P.N. Furbank, *Selected Letters of E.M. Forster* vol.2 London 1985, p.62)
It is tempting to speculate what Scott might have judged his own position to be in those terms. The perspective of much of the *Quartet* would suggest that Scott was writing from within the Club, as it were; however, it is perhaps worth remembering that Scott was writing after the outcome of the historical conflict had been decided: there was now no longer any need of *trying* to see the Indian point of view, since it had become the generally accepted one; but there was, now perhaps more than ever, a need to try to be fair to the Club.

[19] "A Post-Forsterian View", p.118.

[20] Scott offers his own version of such a cartoon image in an effort to get at the root of the problem: "In Anglo-India, surely, the Sahib was shaved while he still slept, then led, stupified to the gusl-khana, folded into his tintub, doused, dried, powdered, dressed; creakily mounted on a no less creaky, ... pony, and pointed in the direction of the daftar ... . Arrived there, ... , he would ... order four peasants out of his sight, three fined, two rigorously imprisoned, one to the District and Session for deportation; and then address himself to the task of writing a sharp minute to the Divisional Commissioner about the ... plan to drain the marsh at Burrapore for the scheme that would drive out the duck and ruin the shooting. Thus kindled for the day, he would return to the bungalow, riding his pony to a lather of terminal fever, kick the syce in the seat of his pants for not catching him as the loyal beast fell dead at the foot of the bungalow steps, then stump up the verandah, in full view of the whole retinue of servants , ... , clatter into the dark polished dining room ... where for a moment he would be puzzled by the prescence of a sour-looking woman .... Then, remembering it was memsahib, he would mutter 'Hullo, old thing,' and bury himself behind the pages

The trouble with the Anglo-Indians of Chandrapore is, Scott feels, that we never see them at work:

> In a curious way, they are not occupied except in establishing proof of an anti-Indian animus or pose .... To see them occupied is not necessary, but without the aura of occupation they lack what was their chief justification. I don't get the impression of Turtons and Burtons running the country, either well or badly, nor the impression even that they would be capable of doing so. [21]

Words reminiscent of the broadsides that Nirad Chaudhuri, perhaps the fiercest and most implacable of Forster's critics, has been directing at *Passage* for what must be close to half a lifetime. Chaudhuri has always maintained that the Raj would not have lasted a day had its officials been even remotely like Forster's characters. [22] Unlike Chaudhuri, though, Scott is not primarily concerned with insults, real or imaginary, either to the Anglo-Indians or, by implication, the Indians themselves (who had spent years to be rid of them); for him, the key-words in the above paragraph are 'occupation' and 'justification'; and it is particularly in the importance he attaches to the former that the main difference lies between his view of the Anglo-Indians and Forster's.

In Scott's view, the idea of 'a man's work' takes on particular significance in the context of the Raj. It was the work they were doing in India, and - they would add - for India, that was commonly cited as the justification for the British staying in that country (and for being there in the first place). In later years, when the imperial conviction was on the wane, work offered, if no longer genuine justification, at least some-

---

of the *Civil and Military Gazette*" (Ibid., p.123.) For Scott the important thing is that ... "even if that cartoon were the truth, you would say that man had a philosophy and was emboldened to act thus by the knowledge that others shared it . . . . The cartoon conveys that man's view of life, and the cartoonist's, who clearly holds a different one." (Ibid.) Forster contented himself with holding up his own philosophy and pitting it against that of the Turtons and Burtons; he felt no wish, or no need, to explore an attitude he found objectionable; Scott, on the other hand, does.

[21] Ibid., p.121.
[22] cf. Nirad Chaudhuri: "Passage to and from India". In: Andrew Rutherford (ed.): *Twentieth Century Interpretations of "A Passage to India"*. New York 1970, p.71.

thing to be said in extenuation before judgement could be passed on the sahiblog. There existed, in the eyes of the sahibs, a clear nexus between the value accorded to their work as individuals on the one hand and the general standing of the Raj on the other. In other words, work to the Anglo-Indians was not merely a way of earning a living, it was the basis of their own view of themselves, of the world, and of their role in it.

To ignore these aspects is to avoid probing deeper into the nature of the imperial relationship, is to refuse to look for (or perhaps to face up to) the root causes of the Raj's conundrum: the inherent contradictions that proved its undoing.

Forster's view is, therefore, inevitably circumscribed, and in *Passage* he contents himself with merely skimming the surface of the Indian problem. Characteristically, he dodges the question of justification. Fielding, who acts as Forster's voice for much of the novel, refuses to be drawn on the subject; when his Indian friends press him on the fairness or otherwise of doing a job some Indian might want to do, his reply is a laconic "I'm delighted to be here ... - that's my answer, there's my only excuse. I can't tell you anything about fairness." [23] And, in similarly breezy tones, he suggests that as for those who don't like it in India, the answer is to "chuck 'em out". [24] In other words, Forster, while implying that those who did go out to India may not have been the right kind of people to serve there, studiously avoids all thought on the nature of that service: whether or not it was useful, desirable, or even morally acceptable. Such tiresome 'political' questions do not interest him; in fact they seem irrelevant to him in a world where personal relations are all that matters. And when he does permit himself a remark on Imperial affairs it is only to reiterate this belief in the paramountcy of sentiment and emotion: "One touch of regret - not the canny substitute but the true regret from the heart - would have made ... the British Empire a different institution." [25] These are the sentiments of the liberal humanist: honourable, but, as events have shown, ultimately inadequate.

Yet Forster was, in Scott's view, right to describe the conflict in India as being one between old-fashioned autocratic paternalism on the

---

[23] E.M. Forster: *A Passage to India*. London 1978 (Abinger Edition 6), p.102.
[24] Ibid., p.103.
[25] Ibid., pp.44 - 5.

one hand and enlightened liberal humanism on the other; or, in the terms of *Passage,* between " . . . Turtons and Burtons on the one side, and, on the other, Fielding and Mrs Moore . . . ." [26] The Indians in the novel were cast in a passive role, and, while in real life they " . . . took on an increasingly commanding part", Scott is adamant that the crucial confrontation remained to the end one between what he calls 'Turtonism' and 'Fieldingism'. [27]

He himself, of course, was in India during the last stages of this conflict, some twenty years after Forster had first described it; and, intriguingly enough, things developed in an unexpected way: they became less clear-cut.

> Turtons became more cautious in the face of the gathering strength of the opposing forces - the English forces, not the forces of the Indian Nationalism. . . . The . . . white men who year by year came out to take up the white man's burden . . . looked and sounded less and less like Ronny Heaslop and more and more like . . . Fielding. The illusion of their permanence glowed less vividly, and so did their confidence of their job. The job was now done by old-fashioned Turtons under a growing suspicion of its final futility and sometimes, I daresay, of its morality. The shadow-line between liberal and reactionary thought . . . was . . . narrowing in Anglo-India - but in reverse. The liberal pressures were then the stronger. [28]

If the liberal ideas, so dear to Forster's heart, did triumph over 'Turtonism', the glory was short-lived; in fact, they did not even survive the withdrawal from India, which had been the inevitable consequence of their triumph. For Independence went hand in hand with Partition, and Partition reinforced existing sectarian fervour, to which, however, it added a new narrow-minded nationalism. The inevitable result was an

---

[26] "A Post-Forsterian View", p.124.
[27] Ibid.
[28] Ibid., pp.124 - 5.
Forster, if anything, would seem to hint at a different outcome: at the end of *Passage* Fielding becomes noticeably withdrawn and appears to have closed ranks with the Anglo-Indians.

orgy of bloodletting all over the subcontinent. These events, and, on a wider stage, the horrors of the Second World War, brought about a profound disillusionment with the values of a philosophy that had so signally failed to prevent the carnage. It was a disillusionment experienced by most of Scott's generation and it produced in him an outlook he calls 'post-Forsterian'.

In this 'post-Forsterian' view of the world, British India takes on a new significance: it becomes for Scott synonymous with

> . . . a period and a place in which the liberal philosophy - which does not now excite us - last excited us . . . , and a place which peculiarly and vividly offered an uncluttered platform for the drama of the clash, because it was acted out by exiles surrounded by a people whose future and well-being both sides would swear to have at heart. [29]

Scott's fascination with the Raj becomes more understandable if we bear in mind this image of the "uncluttered platform" or - another favourite image, which he owes to Michael Edwardes, the historian - of India the "laboratory for English social experiment". [30] It was there, on the subcontinent, that the dominating philosophies, ideas and theories of the British people were acted out and put to the test. To look at the history of the Indian Empire is to see unfold before one's eyes the development of British thought over the last three hundred years. In Scott's own lifetime, events in India mirrored Britain's gradual loss of conviction in her mission and, indeed, in herself. The Raj, then, is for Scott " . . . representative of what the English people were when they last believed in the value of their product and their own peculiar value", and it seems to him, that "the act of putting the Raj to sleep was no less indicative of that belief than the longer act of keeping it alive." [31]

From this 'post-Forsterian' vantage point of universal disillusionment and lack of conviction even aspects of 'Turtonism' itself take on, in retrospect, a nostalgic glow, an almost seductive quality. Its absence of

---

[29] Ibid., p.125.
[30] Ibid.
[31] "The Raj", op.cit., pp.74 - 5.

doubt and firm sense of purpose seem enviable to us, adrift as we are in the moral vacuum of our day, and so does, in spite of all the obvious caveats, the idea of personal responsibility, which was at the heart of the Anglo-Indian ethos. The present-day visitor to the subcontinent can, on occasion, still get an inkling of this attraction. After meeting an old villager, for instance, who might recall with the nostalgia of the old the days of the Raj, he may, Scott tells us, "feel an unfamiliar glow, the effect of something subtler than flattery: the tug of an old sense of responsibility, of the good done to one's soul by doing or trying to do well for other people." [32] It is a glow that cannot last, but it does, for a brief moment, warm the heart.

The *Quartet* radiates some of this glow, which has given rise to considerable misunderstanding. Scott is not so much consumed, as one critic would have it, by "a devouring passion for the male world of high adventure . . . " as by a longing for the sense of satisfaction work in India could, at times, provide. [33] Work for the Raj, and the circumstances of that work, after all, made for a "moral challenge . . . of a kind and scope nowadays without parallel." [34] It did also, one may add, root a man firmly in society and in an ordered universe. None of this is available today: and, in this respect, India becomes symbolic of our loss; or, in the memorable phrase that recurs in Scott's writings, it was in India " . . . that the British came to the end of themselves as they were." [35]

In *The Raj Quartet*, then, India acts at once as setting and as an extended metaphor for the world we live in now: a universe without God, where man is faced with the problem of trying to make sense of the world around him and of his own existence. The first intimation in an Anglo-Indian context of this stark new world occured in *A Passage to India*. In Scott's reading of the book, " . . . Mrs Moore came out of the Marabar Caves . . . aware of nothing so much as the fact that a new definition of human being was essential". [36] If the experience of Marabar

---

[32] Ibid., p.72.
[33] Kay Dick, "Shades of Kipling". *The Spectator* 22 July 1966, p.127.
[34] "The Raj", p.78.
    A boy magistrate of twenty-two certainly had to show moral fibre when he found himself put in charge of a district of two or three million people.
[35] "A Post-Forsterian View", p.125. cf. also "The Raj", p.75 and *DS*, p.3.
[36] "How Well Have They Worn", op.cit.

was so shattering that Mrs Moore never recovered from it, it had, according to Scott, no less effect on her novelist-creator; Marabar was " . . . the end of the road for the Forster who wrote novels", it " . . . stunned him into silence." [37]

This silence, "both honourable and eloquent", [38] suggests to Scott that *Passage*, though

> . . . certainly 'about' British-Indian relations - and human relations in general - . . . was also about something far more important; so important to Mr. Forster, . . . , that having explored it in this novel as far as he felt emotionally and intellectually capable of going on his personal adventure into the unknown, and not having changed his mind, he has chosen, as a novelist to say no more. [39]

We are surely justified to approach Scott's own 'magnum opus', *The Raj Quartet*, also as something which, though certainly 'about' British-Indian relations and human relations in general, is no less about something far more important; so important to Scott that he chose to devote more than a decade of his life to its exploration: it is not just a long look back, at times angry, at times nostalgic, to the sinking headland of a now vanished world, it is also a sustained, though necessarily inconclusive, attempt to chart the land we inhabit today: the land that lies beyond Marabar.

---

[37] "A Post-Forsterian View", p.113.
[38] Ibid., p.114.
[39] "How Well Have They Worn".

2. 'The Road from Dibrapur': An Introduction to the Theme

The Raj Quartet is set in the India of the last five years of British rule: the period, in other words, between the turbulent days of protest and repression that followed Gandhi's 'Quit India' Campaign of 1942 and the general breakdown of authority in the final weeks before Independence. [1] It mirrors the actual course of events of the time and, appropriately, both opens and ends with the image of a dead Indian, killed in the riots of 1942 and 1947 respectively. It is, however, anything but a straight-forward, linear account of those years, and this is as much due to a deliberate choice of technique as to the fact that the *Quartet* was not originally conceived as a tetralogy. [2] While reflecting factual history - all the major milestones on the road to the 15 August 1947 duly appear in the narrative - and reflecting it so accurately that several studies have concentrated purely on the historical aspect, the *Quartet* is concerned, above all, with fictional events; in fact, it might be described as a sustained attempt to get to the truth of incidents first related in *The Jewel in the Crown*. All the protagonists involved in that affair - however minor their role at the time - are interviewed at one stage or another (either by the narrator, as in *Jewel*, or in the later books, by various other characters who find themselves somehow caught up in the aftereffects of the affair); and it is through their recollections, their significant omissions, their intentional or unconscious distortions that the truth gradually emerges. These investigations into past events and the unexpected light they throw on the workings of the Raj combine with the

---

[1] In August 1942, after the British débâcle in Malaya, the fall of Singapore and the beginning of the Japanese advance through Burma, the All-India Congress adopted a resolution calling on Britain to 'quit India', and to leave it, in Gandhi's memorable words, 'to God or to anarchy'. When it followed this up, with a campaign of civil disobedience, threatening to make India both ungovernable and undefendable, the Government of India, on orders from the Viceroy, responded by locking up all known Congress activists. There ensued several days of rioting and bloodshed, which, in effect, represented the last all-out confrontation between Nationalists and the Raj.

[2] cf. John F. Baker, "Interview with Paul Scott". *Publisher's Weekly* 208 (11) 15 September 1975, p.7.
   "It was really never designed as this grandiose four-part structure. . . . I felt that when I finished the first book it could stand on its own - but then there was always so much more to say. And as I went on I always hoped the next would be the last one." (Ibid.)

picture of the unfolding lives of the 'investigators' to form a collossal canvas of Anglo-India on the eve of Independence; and as the various strands of the story unite, Scott brings us right up to the end of the Raj, the moment of the demission of power.

Inevitably, this makes for an extremely convoluted story line; which is, in the words of Tedesco and Popham, "cyclical" rather than "linear" in pattern. [3] But we are not here concerned with questions of structure and narrative technique; this is just intended as a cautionary remark to stress that any synopsis of the *Quartet* is a very great simplification; also, it inevitably misses the point somewhat, in that it will only give an idea of the events in the *Quartet*, but little of how they are reported - something which is central to Scott's purpose. If this important proviso is borne in mind the following outline of the *Quartet* may be of some help.

The opening novel of the *Raj Quartet, The Jewel in the Crown*, is set in the fictional town of Mayapore and the surrounding district of that name. The first section of the book acquaints us with the story of the life of Edwina Crane, an elderly spinster and superintendent of missionary schools in the Mayapore district. We are told of how she first came out to India (as a governess), fell in love with the country and joined a mission - a decision which owed less to the strength of her religious conviction than to her determination to stay on when her employers prepared to return home - and we learn of her standing within the Anglo-Indian community, which hinges on her one claim to fame: as a young schoolmarm she had defied a group of rioters, preventing by this demonstration of English 'sang-froid' an attack on the mission buildings. In August 1942, at the moment of the opening of the *Quartet*, we find her setting out on a tour of inspection, oblivious to warnings about her safety. Once on the road, the car she is travelling in is indeed ambushed, both she and her Indian

---

[3] Tedesco, p.41.
  For questions relating to structure and technique, which largely fall outside our province here, see K. Bhaskara Rao, *Paul Scott*. Boston 1980 (Twayne English Authors Series), pp.124-134., David Rubin, *After the Raj: British Novels of India since 1947*. Hanover NH 1986, p.146., Margret Scanlan, "The Disappearance of History: Paul Scott's 'Raj Quartet'." In: *Clio: A Journal of Literature, History and the Philosophy of History* 15 (2) Winter 1986, p.162, Patrick Swinden, *Paul Scott: Images of India*. London 1980, p.398 and pp.95-98., Tedesco and Popham, op.cit., pp.38-41.

assistant are dragged from it, the young man is killed by the mob, Miss Crane herself beaten unconscious and left for dead.

This, however, is not the only outrage of that day. In Mayapore itself a young girl, fresh from England, has been brutally assaulted and raped. The culprits are quickly apprehended, thanks to the prompt action of the Superintendent of Police, one Ronald Merrick. But all is not as it seems. For one thing, the men cannot be brought to justice because the victim, Daphne Manners, flatly refuses to cooperate with the authorities, and even threatens to exonerate them publicly, should a case be brought against them.

This mysterious behaviour - clear to the reader, but not, till considerably later, to most other characters in the *Quartet* - is readily explained by the fact that Daphne was friendly with one of her alleged assailants, a young Indian with a public school background by the name of Hari Kumar. Indeed, it was during a tryst that the lovers were set upon, and the young man, bound and gagged, was forced to watch the rape, powerless to prevent it. His subsequent arrest, within the hour of the assault even, owes much to the fact that he had previously incurred Merrick's displeasure. A displeasure further compounded by the rejection Merrick had suffered at the hands of Daphne, when she had turned down his earlier proposal of marriage.

Unable to bring a rape charge, Merrick contrives to keep Kumar in detention without trial under the emergency provisions of the "Defence of India Rules". This ruse effectively prevents Daphne, and her influential pukka Anglo-Indian aunt, Lady Manners, from securing Hari's release. Daphne becomes pregnant, refuses to have an abortion, and dies in childbirth. At the end of the book, we get a glimpse of her (and Hari's) daughter, growing up in the house of Lady Chatterjee, Daphne's erstwhile host in Mayapore.

The second volume, *The Day of the Scorpion*, sees the action move to Pankot, a fictional hill station, where we are introduced to the Laytons, pillars of Anglo-Indian society with a distinguished record of service in both 'the Civil' and 'the Military'. The head of the family, Col. Layton, is away in Europe, prisoner of the Germans. Meanwhile, his wife Mildred, their daughters Sarah and Susan, and old Mabel Layton, the Colonel's stepmother, hold the fort.

It is only sometime into the book that links with the events in Mayapore become apparent. There is, for instance, the embarrassing moment when the Laytons, on holiday in Kashmir, discover that their houseboat is moored next to that of Lady Manners, a social outcast ever since she gave sanctuary to her disgraced niece and that girl's halfcast child. Only Sarah breaks family ranks and pays Lady Manners the customary courtesy call. A more important link is forged on the day of Susan Layton's marriage, in the native state of Mirat, where her husband-to-be, a captain in a pukka regiment, is on leave: a stone is thrown at the car in which the groom and his best man are travelling. Later that day, the wedding guests are caught up in an embarrassing scene at the station, when an Indian widow falls at the feet of the best man, apparently in supplication. Only the wily Count Bronowsky, a White-Russian emigré and wazir to the Nawab of Mirat, realizes that the best-man, one Lt. Merrick, is none other than the Merrick of the 'Mayapore case', and that the earlier unpleasantness must be connected with that affair.

Within months of her wedding, Susan is widowed - as her husband is killed in an ambush on the Assamese front. Merrick, with him at the time, suffers crippling injuries, while trying to rescue him. News of this disaster brings on a nervous breakdown in Susan, which reaches its climax when she tries to kill her baby boy.

If all these seem Pankot affairs, there is also news of Hari Kumar in *Scorpion*: Lady Manners has at last pulled enough strings to set in motion a review of the Mayapore case; while this does not result in an immediate release for Hari, the investigation does reveal the full extent of Merrick's misconduct, the sheer enormity of which leaves the authorities in a dilemma of what to do about it.

The third novel, *The Towers of Silence*, provides a new angle to the story of the Laytons. The book centres on another elderly missionary, Barbie Batchelor, a paying guest in 'Rose Cottage', old Mabel Layton's home. It is through Barbie's eyes this time that we see much of the ground already covered in *Scorpion*. And, inevitably, we see it in a somewhat different light. But as a character, Barbie serves more purposes than one: she is closer than anyone else to Mabel Layton, the doyenne of Pankot society, and it is through her that we hear of Mabel's growing unease about the morality of the Raj. It is Barbie also who provides a vital link between Pankot and Mayapore: firstly through what amounts to an obsession with the fate of Edwina Crane (whom she had met through her mission) and, more importantly still, by virtue of a face-to-face encounter with Ronald Merrick. This meeting is of crucial importance because Barbie, without prior knowledge of Merrick's guilt in the Kumar case, intuitively sees through him, and, in a shattering religious vision, recognizes in him a personification of the devil. It is an experience which leaves her bereft of her sense and, literally, speechless. At the end of this the most overtly metaphorical book of the *Quartet* we see her, wrapped in silence and patiently waiting for her death, staring out of the window of her cell at the distant 'Towers of Silence' where the Parsees leave their dead for the vultures to pick the bones clean.

The concluding novel, *A Division of the Spoils*, introduces a new character: Guy Perron, a total stranger to both Mayapore and Pankot, though not to India; an historian by training, and of aristocratic background, he has refused a commission out of eccentricity, preferring instead to serve as an N.C.O. in field intelligence. We meet him first in the Bombay of mid-1945, one of the thousands of men, waiting for new marching orders, as the war moves into its final phase.

Inevitably, his path soon crosses that of Merrick, by now a major in intelligence, who loses no time to have Perron attached to his unit. Perron, who has taken an immediate and healthy dislike to Merrick, is forced to watch both his superior's questionable methods of interrogation and his attempts to ingratiate himself with the Laytons, with whom he has stayed in contact ever since the ill-fated wedding in Mirat. It is Merrick's evident aim to become accepted as a pukka sahib, by being seen to associate with them. He appears to realize this amibition, when the widowed Susan accepts his proposal of marriage. Both Perron and Sarah Layton, who know (or suspect) the truth about Merrick, are aghast but unable to prevent the match. For Perron, at least, the days with Merrick are quickly over, as he contrives to have himself demobbed early.

The last act of the gathering tragedy opens two years later, in 1947, again in Bombay, and again with the arrival on the scene of Guy Perron. By now an established academic, he is back in India to observe the process of the demission of power. His first destination is Mirat, which he finds under curfew after intercommunal rioting. His attention is, however, soon arrested by an entirely different matter: a report in the local paper on the funeral of one Lt.-Col. Merrick. During the following days it becomes evident that Merrick has in fact been murdered - his murder being only the culmination of the long-running campaign of revenge, first described in *Scorpion*. But Merrick's murder is soon overshadowed by killings on a greater scale. As the British prepare to leave, Mirat - and indeed all of India - erupts into violence and indulges in an orgy of bloodletting.

For the European protagonists it is the nadir of their lives and careers in India: Count Bronowsky watches helplessly as the work of a lifetime is undone when Mirat goes up in flames; Sarah and Perron are unable to prevent the murder of Ahmed Kasim when the train they are travelling on is held up by rioting Hindus. When the train eventually moves on, it leaves behind it an embankment strewn with the mutilated bodies of butchered Muslims. If the *Quartet* began with the image of a dead Indian, it ends with nothing less than that of a massacre, faced with which the departing British are either reduced to mute despair or resolutely turn their heads from a scene they refuse to feel responsible for.

Though the four books of the *Quartet* can be read as separate novels - and it is in no small way a tribute to Scott's technical skills that they can be - they form an obvious unity, and will be treated here as such. The individual chapters will therefore discuss aspects of the entire tetralogy and their titles are not intended to reflect the structure of the *Quartet*; with the exception, that is, of chapters two and three, which, as their titles indicate, are devoted almost exclusively to a reading of *The Jewel in the Crown*. There is, it seems to me, good reason for such an approach. Unlike the other three novels, *Jewel* was intended to stand alone; as such, it offers a complete microcosm in a way that the subsequent books do not, and this, surely, merits extra attention.

The novel gets off to a slow start; in fact, if such a thing were possible, there is almost something of an anti-climax about the opening section. For, having been told in the third paragraph of the book that "this is the story of a rape, of the events that led up to it and followed it, and of the place in which it happened", the reader will find that nothing further is heard of it for seventy pages or so, not all that much about the place in which it happened, and though the events related do lead up to it, he may well doubt, at times, if they ever will. (*JC*, p.1) From the start, then, the pace of the *Quartet* is stately, imperial even, so to speak. But it is not just a question of pace. Scott does not merely take his time, he bides his time; he deliberately holds back, breaking off just when he has created interest. This is partly due, of course, to the exigencies of his chosen narrative technique, with its extensive use of flashback and foreshadowing, which allows him to paint in minute detail, as it were, without risk of loosing sight of the overall composition of the canvas. But there is another, perhaps more compelling reason.

Characterizing in a few words the individual novels that make up *The Raj Quartet*, Scott once described *Jewel* as "a statement of the theme".[4] 'The theme', therefore, whatever it may be, is presumably of paramount importance in *Jewel*, and considerations regarding 'the theme' it must have been that dictated the abrupt change of direction in the narrative. Scott may well have felt there was a danger that his readers would focus their attention too closely on 'the story', at the expense of the underlying 'theme'. So instead of treating us to the promised gory tale, he invites us to spend seventy pages in the altogether more wholesome company of Miss Crane, a somewhat desiccated elderly spinster working in the missions.

The story of her life it is then, related in great detail, which is intended to introduce us to 'the theme'. It is, in the words of M.M. Mahood, "... a kind of narthex in which, like medieval catechumens, we are put wise before we are admitted to the cathedral itself." [5] By looking more closely at the account of this life, we may, therefore, hope to find some clues as to the nature and meaning of the elusive 'theme'; clues, moreover, which will be relevant not just to our reading of *Jewel* but to that of the entire *Quartet*.

The first thing that strikes the reader about the opening section - admittedly, only in retrospect - is the fact that Scott's choice of character there, his decision to send in the unprepossessing Edwina Crane to open the bowling, is nothing less than a master-stroke. There is, for a start, the

---

[4] Barker, p.7.
[5] M.M. Mahood, "Paul Scott's Guardians". *The Yearbook of English Studies* 13 1983, p.244.

novelty of it. Missionaries have not, on the whole, loomed large in Anglo-Indian novels; and that, one suspects, has as much to do with the nature of a missionary's work as with the nature of colonial literature. Missionaries, though excellent in their way, are not widely perceived by the adepts of the genre as the stuff heroes are made of. Or heroines, for that matter. And heroes, preferably larger than life, and always with a capital H, is what colonial tales have been about ever since they first became popular in Victorian days. These yarns owed their success, after all, to the fact that they took the reader, as Susanne Howe puts it in her classic study of the genre,

> ... out of mean streets, hospitals and prisons into good English fresh air again. (Even if it was tropical air it was chiefly English-owned.) They took him out of the long, level, semidetached chronicles of drab lives ... , to places where people could frankly take sides again and sportsmanship was valued.
> The tales were nothing to be ashamed of; ... They were stories of high adventure, to be sure, but of work and effort also ... . They told of personal idealism and heroism for a great cause but were innocent of social reproach. [6]

They were innocent of all reproach, one might add, until Forster came along and ruined the 'high-brow' end of the market for good. After *A Passage to India* no serious novel could hope to present the sahibs as heroic and idealistic, and as for being able to take sides, the less said the better. Yet a degree of heroism and idealism (and a good deal of taking sides) had been part of the real-life Anglo-Indian equation, and this, Scott felt, would have to be reflected in any honest recreation of the time and the place. But would the modern, post-imperial reader accept that? What was needed, then, was a different, a new, or at any rate, unfamiliar type of Anglo-Indian: someone representing the acceptable face of colonialism, so to speak. Enter Edwina Crane.

Everything about her is calculated to inspire confidence in the 1960s reader: of reassuringly humble stock - not quite working-class, it is true, but the next-best thing: impoverished lower middle -, educated

---

[6] Susanne Howe, *Novels of Empire*. New York 1949, pp.6-9.

and suitably penniless, she is the victim of intense social snobbery, which, on the whole, she takes in her stride; exhibits a healthy liking for the uneducated working-class - embodied in the young English soldiers whom she regularly treats to tea (her easy and unaffected contribution to the war effort) - and, to cap it all, she enjoys the reputation of being something of an eccentric for her admiration of Gandhi (whose picture adorns her sitting-room wall) and her outspoken support for Congress and the Nationalist cause; and, lest the modern reader be disquietened by the missionary angle of her character, we are quickly informed that she has only taken up that kind of work because she likes India and the Indians, and joining the mission had seemed the only way of staying on. Besides, she does not actually go out and convert people: she labours in a different vineyard, spreading the alphabet rather than the Word. Moreover, though an unfailing churchgoer, she is "not a truly religious woman" and invariably falls asleep during the sermon. (*JC*, p.11) Nothing to worry about, then.

I am being unfair, of course. Scott's characterization of Edwina Crane is much more subtle than I am making out. And though hers is essentially a prefabricated character (following the finest tradition of the Anglo-Indian novel in this respect) it is well fleshed-out and never creakily stagey in the manner of Kiplingesque heroes, or, for that matter, Forster's Turtons and Callendars. But most important of all, it serves Scott's purpose admirably: by falling for this plucky little memsahib - and we fall for her lock, stock and barrel - we put aside all our initial misgivings and reservations about the role of the British in India. Forster's dreary little world is at last put into perspective; once again we breathe in freely good English fresh air, and, having glimpsed idealism and courage, we are ready for the heroic part of the tale: so that when the tragic moment comes, the moment of confrontation between the selfless Englishwoman and the ungrateful natives, as come it must, we know which side we shall be on.

If *Jewel* were to carry on in this vein, the story of Edwina Crane, with its reversal of sympathies and inversion of values, would be little more than the novelist's equivalent of a well-rehearsed sleight of hand. Clever, but ultimately annoying. But Scott never confuses means and ends. If he felt it necessary to his purpose to lay the ghost of Forster, he had no intention of resurrecting that of Kipling in its stead. He exorcises that unlovely spectre by providing the tale of Edwina Crane with a particularly neat twist. Throughout the story of her life and times in India, as it unfolds before us, and right up to her climatic encounter with the rioters, we hear, as M.M. Mahood has pointed out, a "low-pitched authorial murmur of 'Well done' ".[7] Or so we think. It is only after the event - in every sense of the phrase - that we discover how much we have been misled: for, to quote Mahood again, "the approbation we at first fancied to come from the author . . . reveals itself as emanating from the character".[8]

At a stroke, then, we have to revise our perceptions of everything we have read so far. The very ground on which we have pitched our tent, alongside those of the Anglo-Indians, has suddenly given way underneath us and we share something of the bewilderment and uncertainty which the upholders of the Raj experienced half a century ago.

In the light of this unexpected authorial revelation - and it has in its suddeness all the force of a revelation -, Edwina's experience on the road from Dibrapur takes on a different complexion. It is not a case of the White Man reaping his old reward, as Kipling would have it, and for which we, too, as readers, were prepared to see it; and by recognizing that it is not, by recognizing instead the enormity of her own and her countrymen's presumption - "Oh God, forgive me. Oh God, forgive us all" - Edwina explodes the myth of 'The White Man's Burden', revealing it to be nothing but arrogance, cant and self-delusion that will end in a bloodbath. (*JC*, p.57)

This moment of truth, stark and brutal, sets the tone for all of the *Quartet*; and it is a truth to which the readers, too, must face up before Scott allows them to enter 'the cathedral', to use Mahood's image.

Edwina Crane's story serves more purposes than one, though. It is on one level a warning by the author not to be too gullible and not to take too much at face-value; on another, it is a superbly effective way of characterizing a type of Anglo-Indian, and of presenting some of the problems and peculiarities of life in British India; lastly, it is - or rather the manner in which it is told is - an elaborate device to involve the readers.

---

[7] Mahood, op.cit., p.244.
[8] Ibid., p.245.

This it aims to do in two ways: by providing initially a vehicle to harness, or, as it turns out, to hijack, our feelings (thereby breaking down the barriers of historical and geographical distance from the world of the Raj) and by subsequently forcing us to reconsider these feelings. In the process we lose our snug sense of moral superiority: the facile belief that we would never have been capable of Anglo-India's follies and crimes which novels like *A Passage to India*, with their simplistic black-and-white view of the Raj, only encourage. Scott tricks us into committing ourselves, the better to expose us as being party, in a manner of speaking, to the events in India of decades ago. We find out as readers - and are found out - to have shared the proconsular ideal of the Raj, an ideal which Edwina Crane personifies, and which, like her, we recognize as a dangerous illusion only when it is too late. In that sense, "... we share," as Mahood puts it, "... her belated grasp of the truth as our own truth." [9]

The manipulation of the reader necessary to achieve this, or, in Mahood's words, the " ... playing upon the stock responses and prejudices that cause the readers to close their own ranks" is - at once means and end - in itself an illustration of the kind of psychological mechanism that was at work in India with such disastrous consequences. [10] To demonstrate it so drastically is, however, as Mahood rightly suggests, not entirely without danger. For, " ... the reader who is too clever by half may decide that this mixture of incipient violence and a prefabricated character is altogether too reminiscent of John Masters ... and drop out." [11]

"Prefabrication, however," as Mahood goes on to say, "is the point Scott is making." [12] And as with the sense of approbation discussed earlier, it is the character rather than the author who is at the origin of it. This is a prefabrication which owes everything to the peculiar, and peculiarly artificial, not to say unnatural position of the English in India. Edwina is only the first of a long gallery of characters in the *Quartet* who respond to the stresses of life as part of the Raj by 're-inventing' themselves, or, as Mahood calls it, by "moulding a persona" for themselves. [13]

---

[9] Ibid.
[10] Ibid., p.244.
[11] Ibid., pp.244-5.
[12] Ibid., p.245.
[13] Ibid.

One may choose any number of terms to describe such behaviour and call it 'play-acting, hiding behind a mask', or one may prefer the Jungian term of the 'persona' but its purpose can admit of no doubt: it acts as a defensive mechanism to counter a deep sense of personal insecurity and acute alienation. Almost invariably, this results in a good deal of over-compensation, and timid little creatures like Edwina Crane undergo strange metamorphoses to emerge as fully-fledged memsahibs: sure of themselves and of their place in the world, formidable and abrasive, English mems, in a word, who will not be stopped by silly talk of rioting.

Scott is probably the first writer on the Anglo-Indian scene to be fully alive to the psychological implications of colonial life and to recognize them as an important factor contributing to the failure of the Raj. [14] This awareness informs the *Quartet*, to such an extent that it has been described as being, amongst other things, "a journey into the mind". [15]

What makes Edwina interesting from a psychological point of view is that she is not, of course, an archetypal Anglo-Indian, either by birth, temperament, or outlook. Nor does her conduct correspond to the received idea of what a pukka memsahib should or should not do. In fact, she disapproves of pukka memsahibs and all their works, and, in conscious opposition to them, sees herself to be striving in both her private and official capacities towards a greater understanding between the races. It is with this lofty aim in mind that she places Mr Gandhi's portrait on her sitting-room wall and organizes tea-parties for Indian ladies.

Yet the very fact that all the station regard the famous picture and the teas not as dangerous sedition but as manifestations of a harmless eccentricity would suggest that they are never in doubt on whose side

---

[14] For a detailed analysis of the forces involved see Octave Mannoni's classic study of colonial Madagascar, the English translation of which appeared as *Prospero and Caliban: The Psychology of Colonization*. New York 1964. In the introduction to the English edition Philip Mason, the Anglo-Indian historian and former member of the Indian Civil Service, specifically endorses Mannoni's findings for India.

[15] Francine Schneider Weinbaum, "Aspiration and Betrayal in Paul Scott's 'Raj Quartet'". Doctoral thesis. University of Illinois at Urbana-Champaign 1976, p.2.
    cf. also: Weinbaum, "Psychological Defenses and Thwarted Union in 'The Raj Quartet'". *Literature and Psychology* 31 (2) 1981, pp.75-87.

she really stands. (Nor are the Indians, for that matter. When the political climate becomes more charged, they simply stop turning up for tea.) If Edwina joins the ranks of the sahiblog therefore, she does so unawares and very much in spite of herself. As such, she is a new addition to the time-honoured 'cast' of the Anglo-Indian novel: representing, to coin a phrase, the 'Reluctant Memsahib'.

Exploring a character like Edwina Crane, who exists, if not exactly midway between the two communities, at least very much on the fringes of her own, allows for a deeper and more immediate insight into the fundamental problem of contact between rulers and ruled than any 'mainstream' character, English or Indian, would. Besides, describing the niceties of Edwina's position in the Anglo-Indian cosmos and uncovering the contradictions inherent in it, provides Scott with ample scope for irony.

There is, for instance, the comic dilemma of her first employers, the Nesbitt-Smiths, of how to treat her in a country where all the servants are black:

> Her employers felt a duty to accord her a recognition they would have withheld from the highest-born Indian, at the same time a compulsion to place her on one of the lowest rungs of the ladder to their own self-contained society - lower outside the household than in, where, of course, she stood in a position far superior to that of any native servant.
>
> (*JC*, p.6)

If Edwina shows herself to be aware of all these niceties, she does so without a hint of self-pity; indeed, she proves to be unblinkingly rational in her assessment of the Anglo-Indian universe, and her own place in it, as the following reflection, made during a visit to the cantonment church, bears out:

> The god in this church ... was very much the god of a community, not the dark-skinned community that struggled for life under the weight of the Punjabi sky but of the privileged pale-faced community of which she was a marginal member. She wondered whether

she would be Crane to Him, or Miss Crane, or Edwina.
(JC, p.10)

Seen in this light, her resolve to strike out her own and work in the missions rather than seek employment with another English family amounts to a conscious decision to leave that " . . . charmed circle of privilege on whose periphery she spent her days". *(JC,* p.7) She does so not out of pique about the treatment she has received at the hands of the Nesbitt-Smiths and their ilk but out of love for India and the Indians: undefined and somewhat undirected, but love all the same; and in the hope of finding her love requited, of finding the affection she craves, which Anglo-India appears unwilling or unable to offer her. For this she is prepared to trade the sense of community and belonging which the sahiblog could and did provide, even for someone like her, and even when - as individuals - they would keep her at a distance and firmly in her place:

> That sense sprang, . . . , from the seldom-voiced but always insistent, even when mute, clan-gathering call to solidarity that was part of the social pattern she had noted early on and disapproved of. She still disapproved of it but was honest enough to recognize it as having always been a bleak but real enough source of comfort and protection. There was a lot to fear in India, and it was good to feel safe . . .
> *(JC,* p.7)

To reject such protection and sense of belonging is to go further than a Fielding ever was prepared to go, who had wanted to stay in with both Indians and the English, and who, as a result perhaps, had ended up firmly in the Anglo-Indian camp. Edwina, on the other hand, is fully aware that by going to work for a mission, which - in the nature of things - involves advocating universal brotherhood of man irrespective of colour of skin, she is more or less putting herself beyond the pale as far as the pukka sahibs and their mems are concerned; something which Mrs Nesbitt-Smith tries to impress on her when she exclaims, "'Good heavens, Crane! What on earth has possessed you?' And then added, with what looked like genuine concern, . . . , 'You'd be with blacks and half-casts, cut off from your own kind.'" *(JC,* p.12)

The irony is, of course, - and it is a bitter irony for Edwina - that while she does succeed in cutting herself off from 'her own kind' (about which she has few regrets), she never quite manages to cast off the mantle of the memsahib herself. For all her earnestness of purpose and the undoubted sincerity of her effort, she fails to achieve the kind of acceptance among the Indians she had sought. That she does not, is due both to her own personal limitations and to overwhelming forces outside her control. It is this combination of personal failing and untoward circumstances that makes Edwina Crane a tragic figure in the classical mould; it is a combination, moreover, that sets the tone for the entire *Quartet*, for it evidently seemed to Scott to sum up the essence of Britain's dealings with India.

Where Edwina fails is in her personal relations; and here, as elsewhere, she is clearly intended to stand for all of Anglo-India. The inability to form and to sustain normal personal relations runs through the *Quartet* like a leitmotiv and, as many critics have noted, represents at once an analysis of and a methaphor for the failure of the Raj. [16] It was the absence of love, Scott suggests, that doomed the British enterprise in India. "By love", as Allen Boyer says, "Scott represents the positive values that could have made imperialism successful: trust, acceptance, and love among individual Britons and Indians ... ." [17] And it is the absence of such love, or rather her curious inability to direct it at individuals, that dooms Edwina's own efforts from the start.

Her singular inadequacy in this field stems from the fact that she is, as Lili Chatterjee says of her in *Jewel*,

> ... an old-style English liberal in the sense that I grew to understand the term, someone who as likely as not had no gift for broad friendship. In Miss Crane's

---

[16] cf. Richard M. Johnson, " 'Sayed's Trial' in Paul Scott's 'A Division of the Spoils': The Interplay of History, Theme, and Purpose". *Library Chronicle of the University of Texas* 37 1986, p.91.
   He writes , "'Every man is an island', Scott wrote; and that theme underlines the action throughout the *Raj Quartet*. His [Scott's] characters meet but do not merge; they collide but do not cohere; they lust but do not love."
   cf. also Francine Weinbaum, who speaks of "thwarted union" as the main theme of the *Quartet* ("Psychological Defenses", op.cit., pp.75-87.)
[17] Allan Boyer, "Love, Sex and History in the 'Raj Quartet'". *Modern Language Quartely* 46 (1) 1985, p.65.

> case ... it went further than this. I think she had no gift for friendship of any kind. She loved India and all Indians but no particular Indian. ... she made friendships in her head...and not in her heart.
> (JC, p.104)

This squares fully with Edwina's own belated recognition that she had tended to regard the tea parties she had organized for Indian ladies "not as friendly but as meaningful gatherings". (*JC*, p.34) She had never felt any empathy for these women, nor had they even interested her particularly; the reason why she had invited them regardless - indeed the only reason why she had invited them at all - was to demonstrate to them that polite social intercourse between the races was possible; that the English and the Indians could sink their differences and get on with their common task: that of making India a better country to live in.

Never does it seem more imperative to do so - to the British at least - than in the summer of 1942, when the Japanese are at the country's gates. Yet Gandhi, whom she has so much admired, appears to be playing the enemy's game, and the ladies stop coming to tea. Edwina's reaction to this is revealing: she puts the blame for it firmly on the Indian camp. It does not occur to her for a moment that it might be seen as final proof of her countrymen's failure in their professed mission; that the Raj and its concept of 'man-bap' - of the British being mother and father to the Indians - must have failed if their wards appear to prefer Japanese domination to continued British guardianship. For Edwina it is all undisguised treachery, and, given her earnest efforts over the years to promote the cause of Nationalism, it amounts to a particularly bitter personal blow: "She felt, in fact, let down." (*JC*, p.2) And while she remains dedicated to the ideal of interracial understanding, regardless of these disappointments, she cannot help wondering

> ... whether her life might not have been better spent among her own people, persuading them to appreciate the qualities of the Indians, instead of among the Indians, attempting to prove that at least one Englishwoman admired and respected them.
> (*JC*, p.3)

Accordingly, she redirects her efforts, or at least changes her priorities; so that when she revives the institution of the tea parties, it is British soldiers whom she entertains: young men, who have come out to defend India even while Gandhi and Congress, her erstwhile heroes, are plotting treason. (And as for the likeness for Mr Gandhi on her sitting-room wall, it disappears in a trice, with nothing but a dark patch left to indicate its former place.)

This change of priorities comes a shade too readily, one feels; indeed, Edwina is more than a little uneasy about it herself. The symbolism of the teas is not lost on her, and, scrupulously honest to the last, she repeatedly questions her own motives: "Sometimes she wondered to what extent her decision to entertain the soldiers had been due to an instinct finally to find refuge in that old privileged circle that surrounded and protected the white community." (*JC*, p.34)

Edwina's failure to achieve any real rapport with the Indians is, however, only partly due to temperament and instinct, important factors though they are. The fundamental obstacle in her path is one for which she carries no blame: it is the nature of the Raj itself. Try how she may, she remains, in the eyes of the Indians, a member of the ruling race. This immediately puts distance between her and the people she is trying to reach. It thwarts most of her efforts from the start, and undermines her work even when she tries hardest. An incident at the beginning of her career provides graphic illustration of this effect. When she first applies for a job in the mission school, she finds to her mortification that her visit, " . . . on which she had set out in the role of supplicant was looked upon . . . as the visit of an inquisitive memsahib", for whom a special programme of entertainment, complete with songs and welcoming speech must be laid on, and who must be thanked profusely afterwards for honouring the school with her presence. (*JC*, p.13)

This kind of reception, and the almost unbridgeable gap it instantly creates, bedevil her efforts to the very last day of her working life: as she sets out on the fateful journey back from Dibrapur, an entire village turns out to see her and presses a meal on her, which she has to consume before a crowd of onlookers; "I hate it, she thought, . . . , this being watched like something in the zoo . . . ." (*JC*, p.50) Scott is clearly sympathetic to Edwina's plight. He had experienced similar occasions himself and knew that they were " . . . the quickest way of being made to feel like Sanders of the River . . . ." [18] He also knew (and had experienced) the consequences, which were even more disconcerting: "And after a while I started giving orders, and when crossed, raised my voice. Upon my Fielding face I felt, superimposing itself, my Sahib's face." [19]

It is this alarming effect of the pressures of colonial life on the European psyche (and, therefore, on the behaviour of the expatriates) which interests Scott, and which he explores through the character of Edwina Crane. Scott is, in the terms of Forster's novel, less concerned with hardened Turtons and Fieldings 'sans peur et sans reproche' (the existence of either of which in real life he doubts somewhat) than with the embryonic Turton who, he suspects, lurks within each Fielding. "Turtonism", as he says elsewhere, "is an instinct, not a faith." [20] And it was the discovery of a "thick layer of Turtonism" in himself, a discovery which utterly appalled him, that may have shaped, in no small measure, tone and message of the *Quartet.* [21]

For Scott, then, the experience of India was, if one allowed oneself to be cut off from the safety of the cantonment - "Edwina Crane's charmed circle" - frequently disturbing. Climate, ill-health, overall conditions, the strange country, the alien culture, and, perhaps most important of all, the complete lack of privacy - the sea of brown faces watching the Westerner's every move - combine to demoralize the expatriate; under these pressures, Scott suggests, even the most determined Fielding may turn into a sahib.

One is reminded here of the tortured Orwell of *Burmese Days* and "Shooting an Elephant", who, having danced the "'danse du pukka sahib' for the edification of the lower races" himself, had arrived at a similar conclusion. [22] Forster, on the other hand, seems to have known none of this; he appears to have taken in his stride even the most bizarre experiences at the court of Dewas. But then, it was all so very amusing. The tone of his recollections in *The Hill of Devi*, certainly, is one of unwavering amusement; yet it somehow does not always ring true: the hilarity

---

[18] "A Post-Forsterian View", pp.142-159.
[19] Ibid.
[20] Ibid., p.130.
[21] Ibid.
[22] George Orwell, *Burmese Days.* London 1961, p.51.

seems, at times, a trifle forced, and India (and some of the Indians) may have been, as more than one critic has suggested, rather more disturbing than Forster was prepared to admit. [23] Besides, his stance of relentless amusement is itself a little disturbing: both *A Passage to India* and his recollections in *The Hill of Devi* are pervaded by a faint, but persistent whiff of condescension.

If Scott is free of such condescension, he is so because he has faced up to the disagreeable truth: he is not afraid to suggest that, in the colonial context, the question of race itself can be an alarmingly efficient barrier; that misunderstanding, incomprehension, mutual distrust, and fear are ever ready to interpose and so impede normal commerce between White and Brown. He is not afraid to let Edwina Crane mention " . . . this little matter of the colour of skin, which gets in our way of seeing through each other's failings and seeing into each other's heart." (*JC*, p.61)

Predictably, such frankness has earned Scott little love from those inclined to suspect the motives of any Englishman writing about the British Empire. But it was left to Salman Rushdie, the self-appointed arbiter in matters imperial, to accuse Scott of playing on "white society's fears of the darkie . . . ." [24] Yet Rushdie himself accepts implicitly that such fears exist, and what Scott is trying to show in the *Quartet* is surely that these irrational fears - while no excuse for European behaviour in the East - were nevertheless one of its root causes. In *Jewel*, Scott explores several aspects of this phenomenon, including the horrific violence it can and did lead to.

In Edwina Crane's case these psychological forces are never allowed to get out of hand. She is, after all, a liberal in the Fielding mould: out to be pleasant to the Indians. But she is not immune to such forces. No one is; which is, of course, Scott's point.

Faced with a crowd of onlookers or any other tricky or unpleasant situation, Edwina steels her nerves and assumes all the outward signs of the pukka mem, just as Scott himself had felt the hard-set lines of the Sahib's face stealing over his Fielding front.

---

[23] cf. Richard Cronin, "'The Hill of Devi' and 'Heat and Dust'". *Essays in Criticism* 36 (2), pp.142-159.
[24] Salman Rushdie, "Outside the Whale". *Granta* 11, p.127.

> And in my voice, she said to herself, there - always there - the note of authority, the special note of *us* talking to *them*, which perhaps passes unnoticed when what we talk about is the small charge of everyday routine but at times of stress always sounds like taking charge. (*JC*, p.47)

Edwina's transformation from a timid little creature into a true pillar of the British Raj is now almost complete; all it needs is a little mental adjustment to her new role: "But then, she thought, we are, we are in charge. Because we have an obligation and a responsibility." (*JC*, p.47)

Fielding, it is worth remembering, had arrived at a similar conclusion, at the end of *A Passage to India*.[25] And if Forster refused to take us further, because doing so would have meant showing Fielding and Aziz in opposing camps, and so instead had to call on the horses, the earth and the sky no less to join efforts in thwarting their friendship, Scott, writing after the collapse of the Raj, could no longer afford to dodge the issue, however artfully; which is why we see an obstinate Edwina Crane ignoring her assistant's pleas as she sets out in pursuance of what she regards as her obligation and her responsibility; and we see her also witnessing that man's death: a death she is not only powerless to prevent but has, unwittingly, helped to bring about.

The various stages of Edwina's personal development are reflected, and often first hinted at, by her changing attitudes to another picture on her sitting-room wall: a Victorian allegory, entitled "The Jewel in Her Crown"; its very title, echoing as it does that of the novel, an indication of its importance. (The picture also re-surfaces at crucial moments in the later books, suggesting links between apparently unrelated characters and incidents.) It shows an aged Queen Victoria on a canopied throne under blue, tropical skies, surrounded by "representatives of her Indian Empire: princes, landowners, merchants, ... , sepoys, ... , servants, ... , and remarkably clean and tidy beggars." (*JC*, p.18) Statesmen, soldiers, and angels attend the Queen, while a native prince presents her with an

---

[25] cf. E.M. Forster, *A Passage to Inda*. London 1978 (Abinger Edition 6), p.311: "Fielding had 'no further use for politeness', he said, meaning the British Empire really can't be abolished because it's rude."

impressive-looking gem; a gem, which - as Edwina explains, when she first comes across the picture in the schoolroom of her first posting - "was simply representative of tribute, . . . the jewel of the title [being] . . . India herself . . . ." (*JC*, p.18)

In the absence of all teaching aids, Edwina makes use of the picture as a starting point for language classes: "This is the Queen. That is her crown. The sky there is blue." (*JC*, p.18) Inevitably, this is misinterpreted by her superiors, who take it for a sign of the firmness of her imperial convictions: "'Ah, the picture again, Miss Crane, . . . , admirable, admirable . . . . To teach English and at the same time love of the English.'" (*JC*, p.19) Not surprisingly therefore, it is a copy of "The Jewel in Her Crown" that is chosen as a suitable gift for her in recognition of her courage after she has seen off a rioting mob. The choice of gift is somewhat ironic, however, because, privately, Edwina has entertained doubts about its message and meaning all along: she is perfectly aware that "the India in the picture had never existed outside its gilt frame, and the emotions . . . [it] was meant to conjure up were not much more than smugly pious." (*JC*, p.21) Yet, over the years, her attitude to it changes; and, while her reservations about it do not disappear completely, it does nevertheless acquire " . . . a faint power to move her with the sense . . . of glory departed . . . " and she begins to detect in it " . . . a feeling . . . of shadowy dignity." (*JC*, p.21)

Scott uses the picture, then, to chart Edwina's changing personal aspirations, the gradual shift in her sympathies away from the Nationalists and her eventual espousal of (and subsequent disillusion with) the imperial ethos. We therefore see Edwina turning to the picture as an increasing source of comfort: a point of reference, an inspiration, an ideal to emulate, which imparts to her own life a sense of purpose. Accordingly, she begins to look on the picture as a comment on her own existence, as the following passage demonstrates:

> There was, for Miss Crane, in the attitude of the old Queen on her thone something ironically reminiscent of the way she herself had sat years ago on a dais, . . . , and the message she was always trying to read into this stylized representation of tribute and matriachal care was one that conveyed the spirit of dignity without pomp, such as a mother, her own mother had

> conveyed to her as a child, and the importance of courageously accepted duties and obligations, not for self-aggrandizement, but in self-denial, in order to promote a wider happiness and well-being, in order to rid the world of the very evils the picture took no account of: poverty, disease, misery, ignorance and injustice. (JC, p.21)

Scott carries this use of the picture one step further even. For just as Edwina increasingly identifies with it, and the values it stands for, so she herself is increasingly associated with it by the world around her: her schoolchildren begin to confuse her with the Queen, and in *The Towers of Silence* the sight of the picture conjures up for Barbie Batchelor the scene of Edwina sitting by the side of her murdered assistant, which, ironically enough, she misinterprets completely: "The attitude of the . . . Queen inclining her body, was then suddenly an image of Edwina . . . holding her hands protectively above the body of the Indian." (TS, p.67)

At this stage, before the encounter with the rioters that is, Edwina does indeed embody, as David Rubin says of her, "the highest ideals of the British mission"; yet, as he also notes, she cannot fulfill them. [26] That she cannot, is due to the fact that these ideals are based on illusions and racial arrogance - a home truth she eventually has to face up to. But even while she tries to defend the Imperial ideal - not least against what she sees as its corruption by power politics - she realizes that the tide is against her and her kind. For just as she cannot quite bring herself to believe in the allegory of "The Jewel in Her Crown" so, on a wider stage, do her countrymen now lack that certainty of the divine nature of their mission which had sustained them in earlier generations. One of the young soldiers she entertains to tea does, in fact, spell this out while admiring the picture:

> 'Things were different those days, . . . simpler, sort of cut and dried.' He felt, however unconsciously, the burden of the freedom to think, to act, worship or not worship, according to his beliefs; the *weight* left on the world by each act of liberation; and if in his relative innocence he read a religious instead of a

---

[26] David Rubin, *After the Raj: Novels of India since 1947*. Hanover N.H. 1986, p.140.

social message into the picture... , well, ... , it came to the same thing in the end. God, after all, was no more than a symbol, the supreme symbol of authority here on earth; and Clancy was beginning to understand that the existence of authority was not an easy business, especially if those who exercised it no longer felt they had heaven on their side.
(*JC*, p.24. Scott's italics)

Yet without a God to sanction their enterprise, the very morality of the British Raj becomes doubtful, as Kipling had noted half a century earlier. [27] For, if it is not by Heaven's command that the British are exercising their stewardship of India, if they are not doing so in pursuance of a sacred duty imposed upon them by the hand of the Almighty, if they are not, in fact, divinely-appointed guardians of the natives, responsible for their happiness and wellbeing, then the loftiest ideals of the Raj are a sham: at best, illusion or self-delusion; at worst, nothing but a smoke screen to hide the ugly spectacle of a nation jostling for power and financial gain.

It takes Edwina a long time to face up to the truth and its implications for her own life; a life, which had been "... essentially a political statement", as Tedesco and Popham remark, "a sacred duty, a liberal cause." [28] To discredit the imperial ethos, therefore, is to rob her life of all meaning. And here Edwina clearly does not just share this predicament with all the other upholders of the Raj, she becomes a powerful image of the Raj itself: a missionary who has lost her faith but has plodded on regardless; someone who inspite of all the evidence of failure has yet, subconsciously, clung to the discredited values (or illusions) of an earlier generation. Edwina, like the Raj, is an anachronism: not fit to

---

[27] cf. Rudyard Kipling, "The Conversion of Aurelian McGoggin" in: *Plain Tales from the Hills*. London 1900, pp.108-9.

"Life, in India , is not long enough to waste in proving that there is no one in particular at the head of affairs. For this reason. The Deputy is above the Assistant, the Commissioner above the Deputy, the Lieutenant-Governor above the Commissioner, and the Viceroy above all four, under orders of the Secretary of State, who is responsible to the Empress. If the Empress be not responsible to her Maker - if there is no Maker to be responsible to - the entire system of our administration must be wrong." Kipling could still add, "which is manifestly impossible".

[28] Tedesco and Popham, p.28.

survive in the harsh world of the twentieth century. If the Raj is duly put to sleep with its declared business unfinished - and put to sleep with such desperate haste that what little has been achieved promptly comes undone -, this is reflected, or rather foreshadowed, by Edwina's own end: faced with the truth about her life in India, she collapses and commits suicide.

What one might call Edwina Crane's spiritual disintegration, the rapid ebbing of her will to continue her work or even just to go on living, is brought on by feelings of guilt, of personal culpability for the death of her assistant. She had realized too late, as Weinbaum points out, that "in her ... desire to be courageous and face responsibilities, ... she might be endangering the lives of [others] ... as well as her own." [29] And if, as we have shown earlier, Scott intends the character of Edwina Crane to stand for the Raj, then this death of an Indian on the road from Dibrapur must be seen as the first, oblique, comment in the *Quartet* on the manner of the British withdrawal from India: when, again in a desire to face responsibilities (albeit this time in a conspicuous absence of courage), the lives of so many are sacrificed. In both cases solemn promises are broken: Edwina had given her word that she would stop her car under no circumstances; when she does so all the same (admittedly for fear of running over the rioters blocking the road), she seals her assistant's fate; not surprisingly, his dying words haunt her ever after, "Do you only keep promises you make to your own kind?" (*JC*, p.56) In 1947 it is again their closest allies that the British betray, when they leave the Princes at the mercy of their sworn enemies in Congress; and again, the little matter of a promise is not allowed to stand in the way of accomplishing greater things. [30]

Added to her sense of guilt is that of regret, of despair even, that the murdered Mr Chaudhuri had been another Indian she had tried to reach out to, and had yet failed to reach; even though she had, in his case, come closer to success than ever before. For a brief, magic moment, till the rioters broke the spell, there had been between them "an unexpected mutual confidence" (*JC*, p.53); " ... [the] respect and the kind of affection

---

[29] Weinbaum, "Aspiration", p.67.
[30] The fate of the Princes, and the morality, or otherwise, of Partition, are discussed at length in *Spoils*.

that came from the confidence one human being could feel in another, however little had been felt before." (*JC*, p.54)

It is the hurtful lack of such respect, affection and confidence in her own house during the first tea after the assault that precipitates the final crisis in Edwina. When her soldier guests pointedly ignore her old Indian servant they prove as unable or unwilling to distinguish between individuals as her assailants had been (who had only seen Edwina's white skin). They also remind Edwina through their behaviour that she has never really left the 'charmed circle' of the Raj. In the atmosphere of privilege that had surrounded her all along her efforts to reach out to the Indians had been little more than empty gestures. Edwina is of sufficient moral fibre, however, to face up to the truth: she has " . . . the courage to see how all her good works and noble thoughts had been going on in a vacuum", to see that she " . . . had never dirtied her hands, never got grubby for the sake of the cause she'd always believed she held dear . . ." (*JC*, p.104) It had taken an ambush and a murder for her to reach out with genuine feeling for the hand of an Indian.

Indeed, that moment on the road from Dibrapur had been the only time she had broken free from Anglo-India. Squatting in the mud and mourning the death of an Indian had been something no true memsahib would have done; by guarding the corpse of Mr Chaudhuri she had at last shown genuine human emotions, had committed herself, had finally 'dirtied her hands'. And it is significant that most British characters in the *Quartet* fail to understand the meaning of that gesture. While some regard it as the first sign of a madness which led her to take her own life, others see it as Edwina's (and the Raj's) "apotheosis": to them it seemed to "sum up the meaning of her life in India", a gesture worthy of the woman who had once before confronted rioters - Indian rioters - to save Indian lives. (*TS*, p.65) It is only later, when some of them equal Edwina's courage and face up to the truth themselves - a truth which is as much their own as Edwina's - that they see the incident for what it really was: "For me that image is like an old picture of the kind that were popular in the last century, which told stories and pointed moral lessons. I see the caption, 'Too late '." (*TS*, p.200)

There remains only one thing for Edwina to do, if she is to salvage anything from the wreckage of a lifetime's endeavour: she must find the courage of her convictions and give her life in defence of the values she had held dear; if there is to be a bonfire of illusions, she herself must not escape the flames; which is why she mounts the funeral pyre, clad in the white sari of mourning (the first time that she wears the dress of her adopted country), to perform what faithful Hindu widows used to regard as the purest act of love: that of becoming 'suttee'. Edwina's gruesome suicide is an act which, born of despair, has yet about it something approaching defiance: a refusal to acquiesce and live passively in a world that has become intolerable. The significance of it does not go unnoticed: Ronald Merrick himself, the villain of the piece and the living embodiment of everything Edwina had opposed, cannot help feeling a secret admiration for it. It is he also who first makes the connection between Edwina's 'suttee', the picture of the old Queen, and the concept of 'man-bap' that underlies both. More significantly still, he compares Edwina's death to that of Lieutenant Bingham, also by fire - though in his case as a result of an enemy ambush. Bingham, as will be remembered, had gone to try to convince a group of former soldiers of his own regiment, who had turned coat and were now fighting for the Japanese, to give themselves up. For Bingham, too, the world had collapsed around him in a moment and all his personal efforts were shown to have been in vain, when 'his' soldiers, his 'sons', had proved untrue to the salt. Bingham, in short, went to his death in circumstances which, like those of Edwina's, seem to the coolly rational Western mind those of madness; yet choosing death (or risking it, as Bingham did) was the only way open to them, if they wanted to remain true to their convictions. And such is the power of the message of those deaths, that even the cynical Merrick is fleetingly attracted to the old values of the Raj:

> ... for a moment ... I really fell for it, the whole thing, the idea that there really was this possibility. Devotion.Sacrifice. Self-denial. A cause, an obligation. A code of conduct, a sort of final moral definition, I mean of us, what we're here for - people living among each other, in an environment some sort of God created. The whole impossible nonsensical dream.
> (*DS*, p.397)

And surely these are also Scott's feelings; this is what fascinated him about the Raj; what fascinated him enough to have written a monumental elegy on its passing and its inevitable failure, and to have devoted a decade of his life to that purpose.

To sum up then, the Raj in the twentieth century had been an anachronism: its ideals, its moral justification even, those of an earlier age. In its final decades it was sustained by people like Edwina Crane, who tried to live according to its values, even if they could no longer believe in its religious and philosophical foundations. If there can be no doubt in Scott's mind about what the verdict on the actual record of the British Raj must be - and there is, even in the opening section of the *Quartet*, the body of a dead Indian as evidence for the prosecution - he nevertheless cannot help feeling a nostalgic longing for the "impossible dream" and the certainties it offered to those who believed in it. Besides, there are, as Edwina's life demonstrates, the individual efforts to be taken into account; and the fact that they appear to have been futile, counter-productive even, does not, in Scott's view, devalue them totally. One is reminded of Eliot, an acknowledged influence, and the passage from "East Coker" Scott quotes at the end of his lecture to the Royal Society; particularly of the lines, "For us, there is only the trying. The rest is not our business." [31]

In this way, the story of Edwina Crane - her aspirations, her ideals, her shortcomings, her failure, her guilt, but also her good intentions, and her courage - are a complete introduction to the theme of *The Raj Quartet*: the passing of the old view of the world as an ordered universe, where man had duties and obligations and could look forward to reward or punishment, and its replacement by an altogether bleaker vision, a vision we are all familiar with, for it is a mirror-image of the world in which we live now.

---

[31] cf. "A Post-Forsterian View", p. 132.

3. 'Mayapore' - the End of Liberal Humanism

Edwina Crane, as could be seen in the previous chapter, serves as an ideal introduction to the theme of the *Quartet* for in her - in her temperament as much as in her aims - are reflected the two dominant strands of English thought of the period: enlightened liberal humanism and opposing it, fighting it, at times though almost merging with it, and ultimately failing like it, conservative paternalism. While Scott could hardly avoid devoting some of his attention to that struggle, if this portrayal of the last years of the British Raj was to be in any way true to the actual historical events, his main interest did not lie in that direction: the outcome of that clash - the inevitable defeat of a philosophy which had already lost out in England long before - was probably too predictable to excite him greatly. The disillusion with liberal humanism, however, which followed that of its rival hard on the heels, fascinated Scott, since it confounded all expectations and since there did not, and still does not, exist any philosophy to take its place. *Jewel* then was intended to explore the reasons and some of the consequences of that unforeseen failure, and the central characters of the novel are all in one way or another illustrations of it.

As such, *Jewel* is an inevitable target for comparison with *A Passage to India*, and scarcely any critic has felt able to resist pointing out a few rather obvious, if superficial, similarities in plot and characterization. Yet there is a case for such comparisons: not because they might reveal the influence of one novelist on another (there is on the whole little evidence for Scott borrowing from Forster), nor even because they point to different approaches, techniques, and, dare one say it, different degrees of success (there does appear to be a wide critical consensus that the *Quartet* fares rather well in any direct comparison with Forster's vision of Anglo-India), but because a comparison of *Jewel* and *Passage* shows the full extent of the general loss of confidence which the West had experienced in the forty odd years between the publication of the two novels.[1] Seen in this light, the *Quartet* emerges as a clear refutation of Forster; a refutation not so much of his values as of the confident old humanist beliefs in man's essential goodness and reasonableness. These,

---

[1] The one dissenting voice being that of Salman Rushdie.

already severely dented by the carnage of the Great War, simply did not survive the Second World War and its revelation of hitherto unsuspected depths of human cruelty and depravity. Both in plot and characterization the *Quartet* is informed with this tragic knowledge.

Daphne Manners, for instance, the heroine of *Jewel*, seems specifically designed to highlight the breakdown of liberalism and the shortcomings of its exponents. She appears, when we first hear of her, to be a character straight out of the Forsterian mould: convinced of the paramountcy of personal relations and their power to overcome any difficulty, innocent of all prejudice, an all-round good egg in fact, rather like the Adela Quested of the first chapters of *Passage*. (Even Daphne's gawkiness and lack of physical appeal are reminiscent of Adela). The similarity is almost too obvious to be explained away as a coincidence. And discounting both a somewhat gauche homage to Forster and a teasing reference to *Passage* as out of character - and as not tallying with Scott's self-confessed unhappiness about the incessant comparisons of his novel and Forster's - , there remains only one likely explanation: Adela Quested must have been lurking at the back of Scott's mind, suggesting herself mutely but insistently as an earlier example of the failure he was describing.[2] And the similarities serve, after all, to highlight the differences.

For, contrary to first appearances, Daphne Manners is no Adela Quested; she is not simply "another of those English girls ... with bees in their bonnets about the rotten way we treat the Indians", as Ronald Merrick realizes, having initially underestimated her like everyone else in Mayapore. (*DS,* p.214) There is more to her in every sense; she is, for one thing, made of sterner stuff than most visiting English roses, and so perhaps is her novelist-creator who shows himself ready to go where Forster feared to tread. For if Daphne - like Adela before her - is

---

[2] cf. "A Post-Forsterian View", p.113.
   Scott speaks of experiencing ". . . a mood of childish irritation brought on by yet another comparison of the novels I write about India with this one Forster wrote . . . ".
   Hilary Spurling suggests in her biography of Paul Scott that Daphne Manners may owe a lot to Caroline Davies, an Australian girl, whom Scott met in India in 1964. Miss Davies was the girlfriend of Neil Ghosh, the story of whose life, it seems, provided the inspiration for the character of Hari Kumar. (cf. Hilary Spurling, *Paul Scott: A Life.* London 1990, p.293)

attracted to the Indians, and to one Indian in particular, that attraction is nevertheless of a different order from the one Adela experienced with Aziz; or rather, the nature of the attraction is, of course, identical, but Daphne is prepared to acknowledge it for what it really is, and, once the initial hesitation is overcome, to act in accordance with what she recognizes to be her true feelings. Not so Adela or, for that matter, Forster himself. Not only do they refuse to examine the disturbingly suggestive nature of her hallucination, they quickly seek refuge from such uncomfortable thoughts: Adela in the warm embrace of an Anglo-India outraged on her behalf, the novelist in the wider mysteries of the Caves and a reassuringly imponderable universe.

"The most conspicuous difference between Adela Quested and Daphne Manners", writes Gomathi Narayanan, "is that neither Daphne's love nor her rape is platonic. . . . her love is real; so is her rape." [3] Daphne is altogether more 'real', one might add, which is not just proof of Scott's hand for characterization but, more fundamentally, the result of the way Daphne and Adela function as characters within the two novels. Adela seems at times less a character (let alone a person of flesh and blood) than a narrative necessity: an agent whose sole purpose it is to show up the Anglo-Indians as the callous and bigoted brutes of Forster's imagination. She is of importance only because she unleashes through her alarming experience in the Caves the storm in the Anglo-Indian tea-cup necessary to Forster's purpose. Beyond that, Forster was profoundly uninterested in her and what she might have stood for. (The motif of love transcending racial barriers he reserved instead for Fielding and Aziz, which, in the nature of things, rather limited his scope for exploring it.) Daphne Manners, on the other hand, is a fully-rounded character, which, as a genuine protagonist, she needs to be. What she thinks, feels and does, and what others think she feels and does, is at least as important as her actual experiences in connection with the rape. Like Forster, Scott uses the motif of rape to create a situation that peculiarly highlights all that is fundamentally wrong in the relationship between Britons and Indians. Whereas Adela Quested's hallucinations, however, are purely means to an end so that the sahiblog can rush to her defence, hot with

---

[3] Gomathi Narayanan, "Paul Scott's Indian 'Quartet': 'The Story of a Rape'. *The Literary Criterion* 13 (4), p.45.

indignation and a sense of vicarious injury, and reveal in the process their objectionable selves, Daphne's rape is as much the *result* of as the spark to an explosion of prejudice.

Inevitably, this greater realism in the characterization of Daphne (to say nothing of the greater cogency of the plot) results in a comparably higher degree of realism in the reactions her perceived conduct produces. While Forster's sahibs come across as distinctly ludicrous, pompous old fools - an impression which detracts unhappily from the sheer scandal of their behaviour (and consequently blunts Forster's condemnation), Daphne Manners's experiences serve to reveal her compatriots in a genuinely new and chilling light: laying open behind their affable fronts distinctly unpleasant natures; or rather, they reveal a disturbing side to perfectly ordinary good-natured and even well-intentioned people, which somehow carries a greater force of conviction. Scott's Anglo-Indians are not the extravagantly theatrical, puffing and panting would-be villains of Forster's novel but everyday people, who are evil in an incidental way. Most of them are not even that though. They are just unthinking, unimaginative, insensitive or even afraid. And that rings truer, of course. As does the fact that Daphne herself is not entirely free from the very qualities she sees and objects to all around her. Unlike most Anglo-Indians of Mayapore though, she tries to fight these less admirable sides of her personality.

The greater realism in this respect begins to show in Daphne's attitude to India, something which all Anglo-Indian novelists seem to regard as a litmus for a character's moral trustworthiness. One must love India, of course, love it unquestioningly and uncomprehendingly; those who do not are deeply suspect; depending on the novelist's outlook, they show either a lack of moral fibre, or unimaginable insensitivity and callousness. But bereft of the secure moorings of an Anglo-Indian childhood or a betrothal to an upholder of the Raj, and lacking that education of the heart which regular playing of Beethoven and repeated exposure to the Italian countryside will effect in the young, Daphne can feel no immediate empathy for the country; indeed, she finds it, if anything, rather unsettling. The unfamiliarity with everything around her, the overwhelming strangeness of India, becomes, after a while, a distinct strain; it threatens her initially detached hold of the situation, and results in a phase of acute revulsion for everything Indian:

> I hated everything . . . because I was afraid of it. It was so alien. I could hardly bear to leave the bungalow. I started to have awful dreams, not *about* anything, just dreams of faces. . . . I suppose I was obsessed with the idea of being surrounded by strangers.
> (*JC,* p.101. Scott's italics)

While this feeling of being surrounded by strangers extends to her fellow-expatriates (and even to her aunt), it is not hard to see how it might, given time, have become directed exclusively at the alien race and resulted in a desperate, and fundamentally unhealthy desire to seek refuge among one's own kind. If it had not been for the silent example of the enlightened Lady Manners, whose whole mode of existence refutes such a false sense of security, Daphne might well have succumbed to it and have been ". . . assimilated into that inbred little cultural circle of Englishwomen - men, too, but particularly women - abroad in a colony." (*JC,* p.101)

There is here a first intimation of complications in the commerce between the races that go beyond the boorishness of the English sahibs and the obnoxiousness of their mems. Daphne feels quite early on what Forster only half-allows Adela to experience in the Caves, namely racial fear (with an unconscious attraction on the other side of the coin, as it were). Daphne experiences both throughout her relationship with Hari Kumar and recognizes that they are indeed inextricably linked; manifestations both of the same principle: the longing common to all men to break out of one's own constricted little world and reach out to the next man, coupled with dim fears for one's safety. Daphne, and surely she speaks for Scott here, is soon enough convinced that ". . . this longing for peace and security is wrong and that we should . . . put ourselves out on a limb, [and] dare other people to saw the limb off, whoever they are, black or white." (*JC,* pp.101-2) She is under no illusions, however, about the difficulties involved in trying to live by such maxims, and under no illusions either about her own personal limitations. Indeed, the memory of an occasion when she herself had snatched a blouse of hers from the hands of a native servant because she could not bear the sight of the man "*touching it with his black fingers*" is one she has to live with, and one which inevitably makes her less critical of her fellow-expatriates. (*JC*, p.101. Scott's italics) She still disapproves, but, shamed by an acute awareness of such instances of her own fears and prejudices, she feels less able to judge. Again, this must be the voice of Scott himself, the voice of a man who had been appalled to discover in himself a thick layer of what he calls 'Turtonism'; and again, the contrast to the world of *Passage* is striking. Though the values, the aims, and the dislikes are largely identical, the innocent and perhaps always somewhat facile assumption of one's own moral superiority are gone for good.

From the start, then, things are never as uncomplicated in the *Quartet* as they were in *Passage*, and never as clear-cut. This is also immediately obvious in Daphne's feelings about the club - that other traditional litmus. Again, her attitude is equivocal: balanced against an awareness of the club being "both self-conscious about its exclusiveness and yet so vulgar", is the honest recognition that there are compensations to be found in the company of one's fellow-countrymen, however uninspiring. (*JC*, p.102) For one thing, conversation becomes less of an effort. There is, after all, as Daphne puts it, "a kind of shorthand in conversation" used by people of similar backgrounds, where much that is being said is actually left to gestures and inflexions of the voice, secure in the knowledge that the message will be understood. Such assurance does not extend to outsiders, however good their command of the language. Conversation therefore becomes more of an effort, and in India " . . . anything that needs effort is physically and mentally tiring, and you get short-tempered, then tireder and more short-tempered from trying not to let the temper show." (*JC*, p.102) Daphne has experienced the creeping element of doubt which can so easily subvert conversations with foreigners; doubt as to whether one is being understood rightly and, equally, whether one has understood rightly oneself. Such doubts even occur initially in her exchanges with Lady Chatterjee whose whole mode of speech is so genuinely and unmistakeably English:

> Those dry amusing things she sometimes comes out with. If she were English you'd laugh at once, but because she's not, . . . you think . . . What is she

getting at? What's behind that remark? How am I supposed to . . . react without giving offence or appearing to have taken offence?

(*JC*, p.93)

Contrast this with *A Passage to India* where misunderstandings occur exclusively when Indians somehow manage to get the wrong end of the stick and are promptly beset by wild suspicions, which, we are to understand, and are indeed specifically told, is a character defect peculiar to the Oriental. Daphne Manners, on the other hand, does experience doubt and suspicion, and she is honest enough also to admit to a sense of " . . . *relief* . . . *simply to be among my own kind* ." (*JC*, p.102. Scott's italics) And in a country where Daphne, as a distinctly self-conscious member of the ruling race, feels under a constant obligation to be on her best behaviour towards the Indians, she enjoys at the club "the luxury, the ease, of being utterly natural. Giving as good as you got if someone was edgy or bitchy. Being edgy or bitchy yourself. Letting it rip, like a safety valve." (*JC*, p.359)

This, of course, is peculiar to life in a colony, where relations between individuals always were less than entirely natural. Why, then, choose something as unlikely, as uncharacteristic as India to demonstrate the failure of the liberal philosophy?

Scott, like Forster before him, realized that the two main obstacles in human commerce - class and race - provide the acid test for the effectiveness or otherwise of the liberal values. Forster knew that if his cherished Cambridge beliefs survived the glare of the Indian sun they would survive anywhere. Scott, knowing that they did not, because they could not, felt that in the peculiar circumstances of British India one would see magnified, as it were, a failure which was universal and certainly not limited to the world of the Raj.

The narrative core of *Jewel* centres on what for want of a better word one might describe as a triangular relationship between Daphne Manners, Hari Kumar and Ronald Merrick. This triangle includes both a race and a class motif which interact: Merrick is not really Daphne's social equal (nor even, in some ways, Kumar's) but in the context of the Raj, it is Kumar who must doff his cap and touch his forelock. It differs from a classical triangular relationship, however, in that there is for the most part no real romantic aspect to it; and leaving aside, for the moment, the more obviously complicated part played in it by Merrick, this is also true - initially at least - of Hari's and Daphne's side of the triangle. This, of course, is intentional and indeed crucial to Scott's purpose.

Daphne's 'association' with Hari - the term is Merrick's, but is later also used by Daphne herself since it covers best the many aspects of their relationship - her association, then, begins in strictly Forsterian terms: mutual sympathy, which should mature into friendship, but not necessarily more than that. In Scott's Mayapore, however, things are not that simple. The empathy is real enough, but a friendship between two individuals does not, after all, develop in a vacuum; both Hari and Daphne are, whether they like it or not, caught up in their own social worlds. Since this is British India these are kept strictly apart. (In Mayapore the European cantonment is even separated by a river from the old native town.) The stock material for a tragic love story, in other words. Yet *Jewel*, though a story about love, is never a love story: for one thing, Daphne is a somewhat unlikely Juliet, and Hari is not originally interested - not in a romantic relationship, that is. Neither, perhaps, was Scott. What Scott wanted to demonstrate was that even an ordinary friendship, of the kind dear to Forster's heart, would be doomed to fail in conditions such as those obtaining in British India.

It all starts promisingly enough in a near-perfect Forsterian world: not only does a young English girl visiting India decide to stay with an Indian woman, her host is conceived in scarcely less ideal terms; deeply rooted in Indian civilization, yet unmistakeably and endearingly English in habit, speech, and mannerisms, she represents the very model of a marriage of East and West. What is more, she has succeeded in a town where mistrust between the races has a long tradition, to make her house a place of ". . . trust, compromise, [of] something fundamentaly exploratory and noncommital, as if the people in it were trying to *learn*, instead of teach - and so forgive rather than accuse." (*JC*, p.434. Scott's italics) And this new atmosphere in the MacGregor House is all the more significant, as there is much to forgive. For the house itself - Daphne's home in Mayapore - and the Bibighar Gardens, directly opposite it on the other bank of the river - the scene of Daphne's rape - are linked with, and through, the history of earlier injustices and earlier unsuccessful attempts to bridge the gap between natives and conquering invaders. Between the two places, "the place of the white and the place of the black", ". . . there have flown the dark currents of a human conflict . . . [across which] no bridge was ever thrown . . . and stood." (*JC*, p.136) Thus the shadowy bulk of the MacGregor House, with its memories of unhappy love begetting violent hatred, itself subverts the mood of Forsterian optimism and suggests from the outset that the love between Daphne and Hari is merely another enactment of an endlessly repeating spectacle, the tragic outcome of which is a forgone conclusion. Indeed the reader is never allowed to entertain the slightest hopes that the young lovers' fate might prove an exception to the general pattern. The opening page of *Jewel* already conjures up the image of a vast darkness, refers to ". . . a girl running in the . . . shadows cast by the wall of the Bibighar gardens . . . ", and the same page identifies the novel as "the story of a rape". (*JC*, p.1) This, as Tedesco and Popham note, is characteristic of the narrative technique in the entire *Quartet*: Scott recounts the events of the past as though they were happening now before the reader's very eyes, ". . . giving the illusion that the result is still to be determined", but combines this with ". . . casual one-line references to outcomes before they occur"; the resulting superimposition of the future on the present making in its uncompromising abruptness for "an overwhelming sense of destiny." [4]

Even while Scott salutes the efforts of someone like Lili Chatterjee then - and salutes them generously as a very creditable effort - he casts doubt on the effect such efforts can achieve. How much trust can there be in a house, like the MacGregor, haunted as it is by the ghosts of the past?- It is, we are told, in fact literally haunted by a ghost of the past: that of a young Englishwoman killed by mutinous sepoys, and may since have become haunted by Daphne Manners herself, as the narrator on his visit to the house playfully suggests: "so how account for the occasional sound of stoutly shod feet mounting the stairs or crossing the tiled floor of the main hall except by admitting Miss Manners's continued presence?" (*JC*, p.71) How can those honest and well-intentioned Britons and Indians mixing in it not be affected by the shadows of history, and how can they succeed in shutting out the hostile world outside the MacGregor House?

---

[4] Tedesco, p.38.

The answer to either question is, of course, that they cannot. "The mixing," as Daphne observes in retrospect, "was as self-conscious as the segregation. At the club you stood on *loud*, committed ground. At the MacGregor House it was silent and determinedly neutral." (*JC*, p.379. Scott's italics)

What was needed, then, was a friendship that would not be silent, neutral, and tentative, but loud and committed. And this could best be done in terms of 'boy meets girl'. Such an association would go straight to the heart of the problem, testing Forster's values for what they are really worth. It would also confront head-on what Forster had recognized but funked treating directly: namely the nexus that seems to exist between sex and race. For, as Patrick Swinden puts it, " . . . the ultimate test of the colour bar was the willingness or otherwise of men and women, . . . , to transgress it in the cultivation of sexual relationships." [5] Or, one might add, the willingness even just to countenance the spectacle of men and women behaving as though they might be prepared to transgress it. And here the reactions of the by-standers, so to speak, are just as interesting - and revealing - as the feelings of those more immediately involved.

These reactions range from the ill-disguised hostility of Daphne's peers at the club (who already hold it against her that she should be staying in an Indian house) to an anxious and, in its way, well-intended warning from Ronald Merrick on the one side, and the subtly-modulated response of Lady Chatterjee's on the other. Merrick and Lady Chatterjee are in fact the only actors in the Bibighar drama who are struck from the beginning by the potentiality of the situation; the rest of Mayapore are so hopelessly caught up in the mentality and conventions of the Raj that they do not even guess Daphne's true feelings; indeed, as far as they are concerned, the whole idea is simply unthinkable, and they refuse to believe it even when, given Daphne's behaviour after the rape, the truth is staring them in the face. Similarly, the good people of Pankot in *The Towers of Silence*, while being eager to discover the truth about the 'Mayapore case', find themselves unable to accept it when they are confronted with it. To a succession of visitors from Mayapore - all of them British, but not Anglo-Indian, and therefore unblinkered - the case may be obvious: Daphne and Hari must have been in love; to the sahibs such

---

[5] Swinden, op.cit., p.76.

talk seems "peculiarly unacceptable." (*TS*, p.82) What makes it so peculiarly unacceptable is not the idea of love and physical connection between White and Black as such, as the fact that it is the *girl* who is white. This is something that even the most confirmed liberals of Mayapore find "terrifying" - ". . . because even they could not face with equanimity the breaking of the most fundamental law of all - that although a white man could make love to a black girl, the black man and white girl association was still taboo." (*JC*, p.355)

And, as so often in the *Quartet*, it is Merrick, the eternal outsider, who puts the thing most succinctly, (and provides in the process a memorable illustration of the way racial and sexual prejudice feed on each other). A white man living with a native woman, he declares in ringing tones, would not feel "diminished" by such an association because he would enjoy ". . . the dominant role, whatever the colour of his partner's skin"; and since Indian culture has traditionally shared this belief in the superiority of people of paler skin, it follows for Merrick that "a dark-skinned man touching a white-skinned woman will always be conscious of the fact that he is - diminishing her. She would be conscious of it too." (*DS*, p.217)

Merrick, of course, is an extreme case; he dares to say what others merely think. But by the same token, nothing he says has not been secretly thought and felt at one time or another by the more restrained Anglo-Indians, even by the most confirmed liberals among them.

For the failure of the liberal 'by-standers', of those not originally hostile to Daphne (nor to Hari) to prevent the gathering tragedy stems not only from a lack of nerve but, crucially, from a lack of imagination. Though they may abhor Merrick, they share his inability to recognize a common humanity beyond all divisions. As Daphne remarks in retrospect, none of her friends actually tried to discourage her from seeing Hari; they simply preferred to ignore what was happening. Daphne remembers them, as being united in an ultimately fatal conspiracy of silence,

> . . . almost as if holding their breath, perhaps wanting me to like Hari, for himself, simply as a man, but scared of the consequences and also of the other thing, that I was attracted to the idea of doing something unconventional for the hell of it, which of course

would have hurt him more than me.

(*JC*, p.355)

Even the most well-intentioned of the Europeans in Mayapore, then, cannot quite bring themselves to believe that they are witnessing a developing love affair. Merrick - definitely not well-intentioned, though not originally hostile to Daphne - can do so even less. He immediately intuits that Daphne might be prepared to cross the colour bar; that she is, in fact, someone who does not "... see why a line had to be drawn." (*DS*, p.214) But since he considers physical connection purely in terms of dominance and submission (voluntary or otherwise), and given his views on the 'natural' superiority of the pale-skinned races, he cannot conceive of love entering into it. And so, inevitably almost, the idea of rape is introduced: the black boy trying to "diminish", to score off, to insult, to debase the white girl. Love and rape become indistinguishable. As such, they must be met with the same unvarying severity of the law. What ensues is a travesty of justice, which no one, not even Daphne as victim and only witness of the Night of the Bibighar, is able to prevent. In the light of what follows the whole concept of an impartial administration of justice, the pride and joy of a century and more of enlightened liberal rule in India, becomes unsustainable. It was, Scott suggests, never more than wishful thinking on the part of the rulers. The reality of "a blundering judicial robot" highlights perhaps more than anything else the fundamental flaw in the nature of the Raj. (*JC*, p.425) For it is, as Daphne puts it, "a white robot", unable to

> ... distinguish between love and rape. It only understands physical connexion and only understands it as a crime because it only exists to punish crime. It would have punished Hari for this, and if physical connexion between races is a crime he's been punished justly.
>
> (*JC*, p.425)

Merrick, representing as ever the undiluted, or perhaps the concentrated, essence of Anglo-Indian feelings, proves this point in his own unforgettable terms. Kumar must accept his responsibility for the rape, irrespective of whether or not he took part in it personally: "If you were a hundred miles away you'd still be responsible." (*DS*, p.298) And - what is even more revealing - Merrick tells him to "... forget the girl" because "what... happened to her ... [is] unimportant." (*DS*, p.298)

This striking sentence provides, I would suggest, the key to the correct understanding of Daphne's rape as the central incident in the plot of the *Quartet*. When we speak of it as the central incident, however, we must not forget Daphne's own italicised remark that " ... *there has been more than one rape.*" (*JC,* p.434) This, we may feel, refers to what is habitually called 'the rape of India', a motif underlying the entire *Quartet.* (As an image it is so much part of the common coinage of post-Independence thought and speech that Scott evidently preferred to allude to it only indirectly.) [6] But there are - less metaphorically - at least two further instances of rape or near-rape that come to mind: namely the horrific experiences of Edwina Crane and of Hari Kumar, and the latter's especially. For, whereas in Miss Crane's case the abuse remains verbal, Hari suffers at the hands of Merrick an altogether more serious and comprehensive assault; what happens to him in the secrecy of a subterranean 'interrogation room' may just stop short of actual rape, but it surely merits that term in view of the nature and ferocity of the physical and psychological abuse to which he is subjected. Once we accept Hari's ordeal as a case of rape, and as a not all that metaphorical rape either, everything falls into place. We see Daphne and Hari suffer similar fates, in each case as a direct consequence of their manifest disregard of the colour bar and all it stands for; both have crossed Merrick's 'line'; both have, more generally, overstepped the mark; and both are promptly punished for it by those (on either side) who will not tolerate such blatant breaking of ranks. In the Bibighar Gardens, it is the spectacle of the consummation of a love between Black and White on the very night of an all-out confrontation between the Indians and their rulers which drives the hidden onlookers to violence.

Since this central incident of *Jewel* has attracted possibly more critical attention than any other aspect of the entire *Raj Quartet,* and given the sheer fury of some of the objections vented in various learned

---

[6] The anonymous reviewer of *Jewel* in the *TLS* seems not to have been plagued by such scruples, or perhaps his professional instincts got the better of him and he decided that here was a heading a journalist could not afford to reject: " The Rape of India". *The Times Literary Supplement* 21 July 1966, p.629.

and not so learned journals, this point is worth repeating and deserves, perhaps, to be italicised: the attack in the Bibighar Gardens is not directed against a white woman *as such*, but against a white woman *and* a black man; what matters to their attackers is not their individual colour of skin but their common refusal to be bound by the demands and conventions of what can only be called tribal solidarity. [7] Christopher Hitchins has tried to make much the same point when he says that Scott "... uses his rape and its aftermath as a metaphor of divide and rule". [8] (Hari, after all, is beaten up by his fellow-Indians with the same gusto with which White Mayapore later devotes itself to the hounding of 'that Manners girl'). Similarly, Hari is punished by Merrick not so much for a suspected rape - which is just the ostensible reason for arresting him - but for having overstepped the line in more general terms: for having behaved as though there were no rulers and ruled. It is only when we bear this in mind that Merrick's extraordinary words to Hari make any sense: "... forget the girl. What ... happened to her ... [is] unimportant." (*DS*, p.298)

---

[7] It seems necessary to lay such heavy emphasis on this point in view of Salman Rushdie's notorious outburst in *Granta*. In an article long on strong feeling and general pronouncements but short on reasoned argument and detailed textual analysis, he finds Scott guilty of - amongst other things - calumny: "the calumny, to which the use of rape plots lends credence, that frail English roses were in constant danger from lust-crazed wogs ... ". (p.138)

Perhaps the most disquietening thing about the *Granta* article is the nonchalance with which these accusations - and they are grave accusations - have been made; Rushdie never once deigns to illustrate his point with a quotation from the *Quartet*. This and the fact that he is so glaringly and consistently wide of the mark must ultimately arouse suspicions about the extent of his familiarity with the actual *text* of the novels; could it be that the fit of rage to which the article evidently owes its existence was induced by certain images flickering across the screen in the Rushdie sitting room? One cannot help wondering whether the opening sentence of his broadside - "Anyone who has switched on the television set ... or entered a bookshop in the last few months ... " - does not actually give the game away? (p.125) One may feel hot under the collar, one's fingers may itch to reach for the type writer, and a copy of the *Quartet* may not be at hand. But surely Mr Rushdie would not be so unprofessional as to judge a novel by its television adaptation? Or would he?

[8] Christopher Hitchins, "A Sense of Mission: 'The Raj Quartet'". *Grand Street* Winter 1985 4 (2), p.197.

Hitchins adds, in answer to Rushdie's article, "The Hindu boys who are flogged, fondled and framed by the British are also given beef disguised as mutton by their Muslim warders. The ramifications of this blasphemy ... would not be attempted by an author who sought merely to counterfeit Forster."

What is important in Merrick's eyes is Kumar's presumption, which to him - and not only to him either - seems simply staggering: for a member of a lesser breed to have possessed a white girl, to have vied for her attention even, is a crime of such monstrous proportions that it calls for the severest punishment. The nature of this 'punishment', that which merits it the term 'rape', owes everything of course to Merrick's own proclivities and private compulsions; but to suggest, as it has been suggested, that these are the main or even the sole reasons for his treatment of Kumar is, in the light of what he himself tells Kumar, not so much an oversimplification as a genuine misinterpretation. [9] Daphne's rape in the Bibighar Gardens and Hari's subterranean experiences in the police jail form a unity, their common fate a powerful symbol of the failure of liberal values. [10]

Rape as the ultimate expression of contempt for another person, that person's feelings and value as a human being will require no further comment; and as a symbol of force being substituted for love it seems particularly apt in the *Quartet*, given Scott's vision of the relationship between Britain and India as an "imperial embrace". But rape, in the colonial context, seems to carry other, additional meaning. It may be instructive, therefore, to pause and look more closely at a motif which sent the usually unflappable Mr Rushdie scuttling to his typewriter in such a near-apoplectic state.

Gomathi Narayanan speaks in his illuminating essay on this subject of the "powerful" and apparently enduring "... appeal that the theme of sexual assault has on the white imagination in an interracial context", and he draws our attention to the "reverberations, amplifications or muted versions of the theme of an Indian attack on an Engish woman ..." ringing through the entire body of Anglo-Indian fiction. [11] If "serious, conscientious artists" like Scott, or Forster before him, use such sensationalist themes in their work, it must be, Narayanan suggests, "because of the presence of an archetypal pattern in it, which appeals to

---

[9] In fairness, it must be said, however, that the reviewer in the *TLS* who suggested as much had only seen *Jewel* at the time. cf. "The Rape of India".
[10] The fact that they do form a unity is also very obvious in terms of the structure of the *Quartet*: Hari's fate at the hands of Merrick fulfills the same function in the later books that Daphne's rape performs in *Jewel*: they are the two centres of the plot, the twin anchors of the storyline, as it were.
[11] Narayanan, op.cit., p.45.

them as containing the essence of a situation."[12] Narayanan identifies this archetype as the 'Prospero Complex', as described by Octave Mannoni. Mannoni, who was perhaps the first to look at the mind of the colonial with the eyes of the professional psychologist, felt he had discovered in Shakespeare's *Tempest* a strikingly accurate description of the forces of the subconscious, such as he himself had had occasion to observe in his countrymen in French Madagascar: "The 'Prospero Complex'", he writes,

> ... which draws from the inside, as it were, a picture of the paternalist colonial, with his pride, his neurotic impatience, his desire to dominate, at the same time portrays the racialist whose daughter has suffered an attempted rape at the hands of an inferior being.[13]

Shakespeare, who, Mannoni reminds us, had never set foot outside his native land, must have drawn from common European archetypes his inspiration for much of the incidents, thoughts and suspicions that flesh out his tale of the enchanted isle. Prospero's belief that Caliban had attempted to rape his daughter is only one such example of an archetype, but one of obvious interest in a discussion of *Jewel*; (one, moreover, worthy of our especial attention since it serves as Prospero's excuse for exploiting Caliban). Mannoni cites as further evidence for his theory that Prospero's suspicions are indeed manifestations of a powerful archetype the apparently widespread belief in eighteenth-century Europe "... that apes would carry women off to rape them."[14]

On closer examination, then, Mannoni's 'Prospero Complex' reveals itself as a projection of the unconscious, or, to put it another way, as the result of a heady cocktail of emotions: there is, to start with, the fear of the unfamiliar (reflected in *Jewel* in Daphne's early experiences on the subcontinent); to this dim primeval fear, common to all mankind, is added a different kind of fear in the colonizer: "... a guilt-engendered fear, the ruler's fear of persecution by the ruled, which is the con-

---

[12] Ibid.
[13] Mannoni, op.cit., p.110.
[14] Ibid.

sequence of his ... [living] in the midst of the dispossessed."[15] The resulting dislike of the 'native', which can reach the pitch of violent irrational hatred, is something, as Francis Hutchins suggests, the normally level-headed European feels he needs to justify to himself; he does so "... by the perception of an imagined threat ...".[16]

All this may seem far removed from the Decline of Liberalism, which we set out to chart in this chapter, and finding ourselves suddenly in such uncomfortably opaque psychological waters, we may be forgiven for wondering whether, in trusting Narayanan's lead, we have not perhaps allowed ourselves to be blown off course somewhat. Indeed, we may be anxiously craning our necks for the safe, but apparently receding, shoreline of more conventional literary criticism. But such worries are unfounded. Scott, as we have seen before, was acutely aware of the forces at work in the subconscious of the people he was engaged in describing, and the *Quartet* reflects this awareness throughout. (The repeated insertion of the dreams of the protagonists into the main narrative might suffice in itself to allay our fears on that count.) And with his next sentence Narayanan dispels what doubts remain and leads us back into more familiar seas :

> Once the presence of this closely related triad of guilt, fear and hate in the colonial ruler's mind is granted, it is easy to see how the theme of rape can serve as an objective correlative in literature for the same phenomenon.[17]

---

[15] Narayanan, p.48.

Mannoni likens the Westerner's initial response to a black face to that of a child glimpsing the face of a stranger: the child may decide - and for no apparent reason - to see in the stranger a 'friend', in which case he will smile; or, again without apparent reason, he may take fright and start to cry. In much the same way, Mannoni writes, " . . . the black man rouses in us at first this anxious hesitation, and makes us doubt ourselves. We do not want it said that, like children, we are frightened of the face we have made ourselves terrifying, so we prefer to maintain that this unpleasant thing stirring to life in ourselves is due to something evil in the black man before us or inherent in his race . . . . Naturally, once we begin to doubt ourselves when confronted with a human being of a type so different from our own, all kinds of things become possible." (Mannoni, p.199.)

[16] Francis Hutchins, *The Illusion of Permanence*. Princeton 1967, p.71.

[17] Narayanan, p.48.

Having thus reassured ourselves that Scott's use of the rape plot is 'legitimate' and owes nothing to prurience or sensationalism, (let alone to racial prejudice, as Mr Rushdie would have us believe), there yet remains to be answered the unspoken question of how a rape plot in the *Quartet* should come to symbolize - or illustrate - the decline of the liberal philosophy when it had served in *Passage* to expose the opposite: the unacceptable side of paternalism.

The answer is that while in Forster's novel Fielding, as the exponent of Good, remains unaffected by the universal paranoia, Scott, in accordance with his more sombre and perhaps more realistic vision, allows none of his characters to stay untouched and untainted. Even the most confirmed liberals in Mayapore fall prey to what, quoting Mannoni, we may call the 'Prospero Complex', and become incapable of realistic, dispassionate judgement. One by one they troop to Daphne's sickbed to commiserate and vow to bring the assailants to book. But to a man the same honest and decent people find that they simply cannot believe her protestations of Hari's innocence; the more charitable of them assume that Kumar must still exercise some unbreakable hold over the poor girl, while others soon join those voices which had always considered Daphne 'unsound'. The thought that Kumar may indeed be innocent does not occur to any of them. Truth thus becomes impossible to tell, since no one would believe it. Connie White, enlightened wife of an enlightened District Commissioner, comes within inches of guessing the truth, when she says to Daphne, " . . . you know if Hari had been an Englishman I could have understood his silence better, although even then it would have had to be the silence imposed on him by a woman." (*JC*, p.439) Yet even then and even to Connie White it seems impossible to speak out, as Daphne later writes in her account of the affair:

> . . . there really was nothing I could do . . . . My legs bare from the knee down - were an anachronism . . . . To play the scene with anything like *style* I needed a long dress of white muslin, and a little straw boater on my head. I needed to be conscious of the dignity of the occasion. Indeed to be able to say, 'But Harry is an Englishman', and then to rise, put up my parasol and detach myself from Constance White's company, so that she would *know* but say nothing because this was

> a world where men died in the open and women wept in private, and the Queen sat like a wise old lady on her throne and succeeded in that difficult feat of proving that there was a world where corruption also died for lack of stinking air.
>
> (*JC*, p.439. Scott's italics)

It is no coincidence that Scott should here be conjuring up a vision of a Victorian world: of Victorian conduct, Victorian sense of honour, Victorian integrity and rectitude. These find their purest expression in the uncorruptible Queen herself, who had combined a passionate belief in her country's imperial mission with a genuine and well-documented love of what she habitually referred to as "my poor Indians". And as in the case of Edwina Crane and the allegorical picture on her sitting room wall, this evocation of an earlier and seemingly happier age is used to highlight the shortcomings of our own; The "lack of stinking air" around the old Queen only heightens our awareness of the stench of corruption behind the respectable façade of the Raj, epitomized by Ronald Merrick. In Mayapore this still goes largely undetected; in the later books, it gradually infects the whole edifice with its contagion, so that in the end this miasma itself is felt to be the truest expression of the Raj.

Even discounting Merrick, however, as an extreme and not altogether typical Anglo-Indian, the sahiblog emerge in a distinctly unflattering light when viewed against the image of the benign and wise old lady on her throne. For, faced with a twin assault on Anglo-Saxon womanhood, white Mayapore quite simply loses its head, and not even the staunchest liberal escapes the general hysteria. Indeed, the District Commissioner himself, habitué of parties at the MacGregor House though he is, is momentarily forsaken by his usual cool and dispassionate judgement; he allows himself to be manoeuvered into abdicating overall authority in the district to the Military, who quickly move to 'restore order' - albeit at the price of a minor bloodbath, with distinct echoes of Amritsar.[18] The spectacle of British troops firing indiscriminately into the crowd represents a nadir in the history of the British enterprise in India; what

---

[18] There too the authorities had panicked after an assault on an Englishwoman. That Amritsar, as a turning point in Imperial history, should be of obvious interest to Scott need hardly be stressed.

more, it signals, as D.C. White is only too keenly aware, the complete moral bankruptcy of liberals like himself, and of liberalism altogether. While Scott, the meticulous chronicler of the declining years of the Indian Empire, records and analyses these manifestations of failure in a long section entitled "Civil and Military", the creative writer in him thinks up a basic plot containing the essence of that failure. And it is the skillful juxtaposition of the two - the fates of people like Daphne and Hari, acted out against the vast and vividly-drawn historical backdrop - that make the *Quartet* so rewarding for reader and critic alike.

Francine Weinbaum, who has drawn attention to the theme of "thwarted union" underlying the *Quartet*, traces what she calls "microscopic-macroscopic correspondencies" throughout the tetralogy.[19] One such - indeed one of the two principle ones - is the thwarted union of Daphne and Hari, which, she explains, corresponds to that of England and India.[20] She suggests that the character of Hari Kumar symbolizes nothing less than the entire history of the British-Indian relationship: ". . . a man", she writes, "created and destroyed by the British can represent not only what the British have done to India but the abandoned hopes and diminished possibilities they feel themselves."[21] This takes us back once more to the relationship of Daphne and Hari, back to the very core of the plot of *Jewel*, in other words.

One of the most striking things about this relationship is the way Scott presents it: the time and space he devotes to developing it gradually, and the care he takes throughout to counter the effect of the traditional clichés of the genre, of all the usual trappings of what George Grella calls "Indian Gothic".[22] Thus Hari's and Daphne's love affair gets off to a decidedly slow start. Theirs is never a tempestuous affair, no 'coup de foudre' which might - at least momentarily - sweep aside in the whirl-

---

[19] Weinbaum, *Aspiration*, op.cit., p.166.
[20] cf. ibid., p. 67.
[21] Ibid.
[22] George Grella, Preface to Brijen K. Gupta, *India in English Fiction: An Annotated Bibliography*. Metuchen N.J. 1973, p.xi.
This concern is understandable since Hari's and Daphne's love affair - and its ramifications - are, in the words of Count Bronowsky, ". . . interesting . . . but in a rather cliché-ridden way." (*DVS*, p.169) David Rubin echoes these sentiments when he says, "Scott takes all the stock material of the Anglo-Indian novel . . . and transforms it into highly original fiction. (Rubin, op.cit., p.151)

wind of passion beloved of the popular novelist all obstacles in the lovers' path; nor is it the scarcely less well-rehearsed case of a powerful and mysterious Oriental casting a spell on a guileless English maiden: Scott presents two English expatriates of similar age, background and interests, thrown together in alien surroundings; except that one of them happens to be brown. And there's the rub, of course.

Hari, then, is hardly very Indian, and his rather unusual background was in fact the object of critical comment when *Jewel* first appeared. The reviewer for the *TLS*, for instance, remarked that " . . . the scales appear to have been heavily weighted" and suggested they might have been rightened " . . . if Daphne had fallen in love with an ardent Indian nationalist rather than an anglicized Indian." [23]

The man is right of course. The scales are weighted. But quite apart from the fact that a love affair between the niece of a high government official and some would-be insurrectionist is the kind of cliché Scott was wise to leave to lesser novelists, (and quite apart also from the fact that Scott had met a real-life Kumar who was defintely no political radical), this highly anglicized background serves a definite purpose: Scott has his heroine fall in love with someone who is to all intents and purposes English and then shows the sahiblog's reaction to this love. In this way, he cuts right through the Kiplingesque cant of "East is East" "and never the twain" to expose the naked racialism which underlay it all along; or, in the terms of *Jewel*, there emerges what Lady Manners calls "the real animus" with a starkness no other plot would have allowed. (*JC*, p.447) [24]

For there can be no talk here of incompatibility due to differing customs, religious beliefs or levels of education. Hari and Daphne speak the same language (in every sense of the phrase), use the same slang expressions even, listen to the same records of the same London crooners, and he knows no more about India than she does. He is, in a word, the perfect product of British rule, a living specimen of Macaulay's 'brown Englishmen'; the kind of man the Raj aimed to produce, or said, at least, it aimed to produce, and to whom it said it would eventually hand over the

---

[23] "The Rape of India", op.cit.
[24] For a detailed description of Scott's meeting with the man who provided the inspiration for the character of Hari Kumar see Spurling, op.cit., pp.293-303.

reins of government. The fact that the sight of such a brown Englishman sauntering off into the garden of the MacGregor House at the side of a genuine, that is to say, white English girl should fill the assembled liberal élite of Mayapore with unease is, therefore, utterly damning; and, in a sense, the subsequent persecution of that brown Englishman by the man Merrick, who breaks every rule in the book and gets away with it because the same set of Fieldings cannot bring themselves to believe that a countryman of theirs could be capable of such misconduct, is almost irrelevant in that it adds little to the original outrage. (Which is why Scott is content to provide no more than mere hints of it in *Jewel* and only reveals the actual details in the subsequent books.)

It is damning enough that there should be nowhere in Mayapore for Daphne and Hari to meet - not as lovers, simply as friends; it is damning enough that there is so little social intercourse between Britons and Indians. The usual places for white Mayapore's social outings - the club, the restaurants, the European cinema etc. - are all closed to non-whites and the Indian venues, while theoretically open to both, are hardly very attractive, not least because of the minor sensation which the sight of a white face there invariably produces.

On the few occasions when Hari and Daphne can meet in public, they do not meet as social equals. At the 'War Week Exhibition' on the maidan, for instance, Daphne can slip away for some refreshment into the tea tent, but Hari cannot follow her there, since the marquee is reserved "for 'Officers and Guests'", which, she later explains, " . . . was really only a polite way of saying 'Europeans' because there were plenty of civilians there . . . too, but only white civilians." (*JC*, p.361)

Inevitably, all this has repercussions on their relationship. On the maidan, for instance, Hari, still unsure of her motives, tries to find some outlet for his impotent rage, and decides to punish Daphne by acting the part circumstances would force him to play: Daphne finds she ends up " . . . feeling more and more like the squire's daughter condescending to the son of one of her father's tenants, because that's how he seemed to *want* to make me feel." (*JC*, p.363. Scott's italics) She herself though does not treat him entirely like her equal either, for all her genuine delight to have met someone of her own age with similar memories of 'home': "I was conscious at the 'maidan' of doing a good deed. The thought revolts me now." (*JC*, p.368) And when Daphne finally decides to take matters into her own hands and invites him round to the MacGregor House, it becomes evident that even there, away from all disapproving glances and hostile comment, they " . . . were having to work at a basis for ordinary human exchange . . . ". (*JC*, p.370) "A friendship", as Daphne says in retrospect, " . . . can't be limited in this way . . . . You can't not be affected by the fact that it's a friendship you're both having to work hard at." (*JC*, p.368)

The truth of the matter is that there can be no friendship between them: faced with such overwhelming odds it cannot survive. Daphne's belated recognition of the comparative impotence of the individual in the face of a hostile crowd is Scott's answer to the sunny optimism of *Passage*. He exposes quite mercilessly the fundamental fallacy, or, to put it more kindly, the fundamental self-delusion necessary to sustain the Forsterian belief in "only connect": the refusal to accept that there is inevitably a factor X in any equation involving two human beings, with X standing for class, or race, or creed, or whatever defines and preoccupies a group of people. Ultimately, Scott suspects, the pressures of a hostile society will prove stronger than the aspirations and the goodwill of the individual. For Daphne and Hari, therefore, there is no hope in Forsterian terms. They " . . . could be enemies, or strangers, to each other, or lovers, but never friends because such a friendship was put to the test too often to survive." (*JC*, p.399)

Yet their love, too, is constantly put to the test; not only because of the pressures and the disapproval from outside but also because of the intrinsic uncertainties of their relationship: the recurring doubts both of them have about each other's motives and as to whether the other fully understands the difficulties and dangers they might face:

> . . . it was never uncomplicated. . . . on his side the complication of realising that the possession of a white girl could be a way of bolstering his ego, on mine the complication of the curious almost titillating *fear* of his colour. How else to account for the fact that in dancing . . . we stared (I think fixedly) over each other's shoulders, as if afraid to look directly into each other's eyes.. . . . neither of us could be certain that the other fully saw the danger or understood the part that

might be played by the *attraction to danger* in what we felt for each other.

(*JC*, p.372. Scott's italics)

Again one notes the sombreness of tone, the depth of pessimism, which characterize Scott's vision. How different from Forster's sunny little world where the Fieldings and Azizes (or perhaps only the Fieldings) suspected nothing of such abysses!

If Scott is more realistic than Forster was in assessing the relative strength, or weakness, of the liberal values, he is also more convincing in his description of the forces ranged against those values. Daphne's response to the attraction she feels towards Hari, and the reaction this produces in Mayapore, allows him to expose more clearly than Forster could in his determinedly sanitized plot the crude racialism which had always lurked behind the respectable face of the Raj. "Even from her protected background", she realizes, as Christopher Hitchins notes, "that the sex thing and the race thing have a kind of sickly connection." [25] She also quickly becomes aware that the resulting awkwardness works both ways, affecting black *and* white, and that the effects of it seem to be more pronounced and more insidious in women than in men. This, she reflects, is because

> ... a white man in India can feel physically superior without unsexing himself. But what happens to a woman if she tells herself that ninety-nine per cent of the men she sees are not men at all, but creatures of an inferior species whose colour is their main distinguishing mark? What happens when you unsex a nation, treat it like a nation of eunuchs? Because that's what we've done, isn't it?
>
> (*JC*, p.400)

Daphne is different. She refuses to "unsex" and to be "unsexed". She reacts to Hari as she would to a white man whom she might find attractive. In this the most human respect, then, she is utterly natural: acting in a way Forster might have wanted his characters to act, while not daring to suggest as much in *Passage*. For the attraction Daphne feels is,

---

[25] Hitchins, op.cit., p.193.

at first, purely physical. This, as Sister Ludmila, a clear-eyed and reliable observer, remarks, is not all that unusual: other white women in Mayapore had also been aware of his looks, but they had always "... found it easy enough to resist temptation because they saw him as if he stood on the wrong side of the water in which even to dabble their fingers would have filled them with horror." (*JC*, p.136) Daphne, however, refuses to succumb to this convenient self-delusion: she fights and overcomes the horror "... because she knew it to be contradictory of what she first felt when she saw him." (*JC*, p.136) By rejecting such a "notion of horror", she gives Hari back his humanity and reasserts her own at the same time, both as a woman and, more generally, as an individual. She had realized "... that it was no good waiting for a bridge to be built, but a question of entering the flood, and meeting *there*, letting the current take them both." (*JC*, p.136. Scott's italics) Her feelings for Hari, then, lead Daphne, to reconsider not only the sense, if any, of her own existence in Mayapore but of life itself. And she concludes, as Sister Ludmila goes on to say, that

> '... life is not just a business of standing on dry land and occasionally getting your feet wet. It is merely an illusion that some of us stand on one bank and some on the opposite. So long as we are standing like that we are not living at all, but dreaming. So jump, jump in, and let the shock wake us up. Even if we drown, at least for a moment or two before we die we shall be awake and alive.'
>
> (*JC*, pp.136-7)

In the light of such reflections, Daphne's love for Hari takes on a wider meaning. It is much more than love fighting against overwhelming odds, much more even than the logical end (in both senses of the word) of the British enterprise in India; it is an attempt to "... break out of ... [the] separate little groups and learn how to live together." (*JC*, p.355) As such, Daphne's actions transcend the world of the Raj and touch at the fundamental constraints of the human condition. For we who never knew the Raj, who perhaps have never even set foot outside our own little worlds, have nonetheless all felt at one time or another "... that old primitive savage instinct to attack and destroy what we ... [don't] understand because it ... [looks] different ...". (*JC*, p.401) And we, too, are caught up in the meshes of our own tribal instincts, which are no less constraining, no less absurd, and no less destructive than those of the sahibs in the vanished world of British India; and like them, we are guilty of the worst sin of our century, that of thinking collectively rather than individually: of seeing an apparently uniform mass rather than a group of individuals, each distinctive and unique.

Jill Bonheim has argued persuasively in her study *Paul Scott: Humanismus und Individualismus in seinem Werk* that the theme of the value of the individual, recurrent in his 'œuvre', reflects a preoccupation with this quintessential liberal value reminiscent of Forster, but that his actual concept of individuality differs sigificantly from his literary predecessor's. For Scott, she suggests, the value of the individual depends on his or her ability to achieve what Sister Ludmila calls a 'wholeness': that is to say a harmony of thought, feeling and action. [26] And, she writes, Scott assumes implicitly that the natural feelings of the individual do not correspond to the demands of society. Individuality for Scott, then, is not merely being different, and rejoicing in the private knowledge of being different, as it is for Forster, but springs from the recognition that social norms tend to contravene the most elementary natural feelings of the individual; therefore, as Bonheim goes on to say, true individuality cannot, in Scott's view of things, remain a private affair: it must declare itself publicly and translate itself into action. [27] Individuality that remains limited to the realm of the theoretical or the subjective, (as in the case of Edwina Crane) is no true individuality worthy of the name, but an existence lacking in 'wholeness'. This, indeed, is the main difference between Daphne and Edwina: whereas Edwina is possessed of a love for *the* Indians, Daphne loves *one* Indian; where Edwina would merely have seen a young Indian, Daphne sees an individual; and while Edwina would have earnestly tried to develop a friendship born of her mind, Daphne's relationship with Hari arises from her feelings for him as a woman and not as an unemotional emissary of her nation. Daphne's thoughts and feelings towards Hari are in complete, natural, harmony with each other, but at the same time in diametrical opposition to the

---

[26] cf. Jill Bonheim, *Paul Scott: Humanismus und Individualismus in seinem Werk.* (Neue Studien zur Anglistik und Amerikanistik 23) Frankfurt/Main 1982, p.65.
[27] Ibid., p.67.

demands of Mayapore society. She must, therefore, act if she is to realize her own new-found individuality. Her defiance of Anglo-India, then, has as its aim purely personal objectives, and is free from all crusading zeal. "When there is wholeness", as Sister Ludmila observes, "there are no causes. Only . . . living. The contribution of the whole of one's life, the whole of one's resources, to the world at large." (*JC*, p.137)

And this is surely the voice of Scott himself. Now that both the autocratic paternalism of old and the nineteenth century liberalism are discredited, and no obligations discernable for countries to fulfill, and none for individual men, now that God is either dead or content to remain an idle spectator of the affairs of men, there are, indeed, no causes left. There is only living. And if such living is to be successful, or at any rate no outright failure, then the whole of one's resources must be employed. Those - like Daphne - who have the courage and the strength to do so can hope to withstand the vicissitudes of twentieth century life and instil a measure of meaning into it.

For Daphne - in the context of the Raj - it means that a now less compartmentalized Mayapore has suddenly grown: by striking out into the world beyond the white station and the no man's land which is the MacGregor House, she discovers that Mayapore now " . . . extended to the other side of the river [i.e. the native town] and, because of that, in all directions . . . ". (*JC*, p.378) If Mayapore had got bigger, Daphne herself feels smaller. This is the result of her rejection of the fake glory that surrounded the sahibs; that sense of proconsular dignity had always been an "irrelevance to the business of being in India", as a character in a later book puts it. (*TS*, p.210) To accept reality, then, is to recognize one's own comparative unimportance in an India that is infinitely more than the small, absurdly self-important world of the Anglo-Indians. But if Daphne feels smaller that is also the result of gauging realistically for the first time the extent and force of the general hostility against Hari and herself. Her

> . . . association with Hari - the one thing that was beginning to make me feel like a person again - was hedged about, restricted, pressed in on until only by making yourself tiny could you squeeze into it and stand, imprisoned but free, diminished by everything

        that loomed outside, *but not diminished from the inside* . . . .
                                            (*JC*, p.379. Scott's italics)

    This, as we shall see time and again in the discussion of the *Quartet*, is the greatest measure of success Scott's characters can hope for; to bear the shackles lightly, unbowed and therefore undiminished, is the closest anyone gets in Scott's universe to happiness and fulfillment.

    The notion of feeling 'diminished' is a key-idea in Scott's perception of life in our century; it recurs throughout the *Quartet* and also in his other writing. In "A Post-Forsterian View", for instance, he says that the experience of events during and since the war had resulted in a definite "feeling of having diminished"; [28] a feeling not so much due to the relative decline of Britain, but " . . . to a realization that in most cases the opposite of what had been worked for had been achieved, and in other cases, where a hope had been fulfilled, to a suspicion that the fulfillment revealed flaws in favour of it." [29]

    In Daphne's case, too, actions seem to lead to the opposite of what had been worked for. Hari, whom she had wished to help even before she fell in love with him, she leaves imprisoned; and in trying to save him from the wrath of the sahibs, she effectively abandons him to the judicial robot. For Daphne this is the moment of truth: of the shattering recognition of her own and man's inability in general to contend with hostile fate. Yet if she is to remain 'undiminished', she must stand up and be counted. And she is not found wanting: it takes courage, after all, to refuse to cooperate with the powers of the Raj, and even greater courage to defy them openly. When she publicly exonerates the men accused of assaulting her, adding, for good measure, that for all she knows the real culprits might have been " . . . British soldiers with their faces blackened" (*JC*, p.152), she has finally given up her stance of half-way house, "holding one hand out, groping, and the other out backwards, linked to the security of what was known and expected". (*JC*, p.383) She has decided to 'jump' rather than conform since there is, as she says, " . . .

---

[28] "A Post-Forsterian View", p.121.
[29] Ibid.

nothing to conform with, except an idea, a charade played around a phrase: white superiority". (*JC,* p.399)

And yet for all that, there is failure, palpable failure on several counts. There is, for instance, the disturbing moment in the hours after the rape, when she flinches at the mere sight of Lady Chatterjee's old servant. Though she forces herself to call him back to apologize to him, she had nevertheless experienced again the half-forgotten fears of her first months in India; which proves, as she well realizes, that even her love for Hari had not completely banished that unlovely spectre. She had simply made "an exception" of Hari and his blackness, which was indeed "inseparable from his physical attraction", investing it "with a special significance" and taking it "out of its natural context instead of identifying ... with it *in* its context." (*JC,* pp.411-2. Scott's italics)

The most disastrous failure, however, occurs immediately after the assault, when she panics and *orders* Hari to leave her alone and let her return unaccompanied to the MacGregor House. In these crucial moments she never gives him a chance to argue that the truth alone might save him; on the contrary, she swears him to silence and demands that he should leave her to deal with everything. She does so, as she says later, because "... even in my panic there was this assumption of superiority, of privilege, of believing I knew what was best for both of us, because the colour of my skin automatically put me on the side of those who never told a lie." (*JC,* p.425)

The same fatal arrogance, in other words, that Edwine Crane had been guilty of on the road to Dibrapur; there it had resulted in the death of, here in the torture and imprisonment of an Indian. And it is significant that these are the actions not of die-hard white supremacists, not of crusty old sahibs or arrogant mems, but of enlightened people who under normal circumstances would ridicule the idea of one race being superior to another. This, of course, is Scott's point, and it makes the *Quartet* much bleaker reading than *A Passage to India*: there are no Fieldings in the real world, or rather scratch a Fielding and you will find a Turton lurking inside.

Yet for all that, Daphne Manners, the gawky awkward girl, is the undoubted heroine of *Jewel,* someone whom Scott clearly holds up as an example whose courage and determination we can only hope to equal.

And again, as with Edwina Crane, actual success in her endeavours, or lack of it, is almost irrelevant. It is her determination and her courage to *try* that make hers a successful life, and it is in this sense that we can only hope to equal her achievement. Lady Chatterjee feels some of this when she says with undisguised admiration, "She had to make her own marvellous mistakes. I say marvellous." (*JC*, p.104) For, unlike Edwina Crane, for instance, Daphne never shrunk " . . . from getting grubby. She flung herself into everything with zest. The more afraid she was of something the more determined she was not to shrink from experiencing it." (*JC*, pp.104-5) These are the qualities which earn her the affections of her novelist-creator, who makes her, as Weinbaum, points out, "one of the two *central* female figures," even " . . . though she only appears in the first volume of the *Quartet* . . . ". [30]

She is, moreover, successful - distinctly and unreservedly successful - on three counts: if she cannot actually save Hari from wrongful imprisonment (and in a sense no one can), she nevertheless helps to thwart his conviction on the rape charge and publicly exonerates him and his fellow-detainees; secondly, she is courageous enough to go through with her pregnancy in the face of universal outrage, so that her and Hari's child becomes, after her own death, a living reminder of their defiant love. (This mood is splendidly echoed by the no less uncompromising Lady Manners, who has the birth of the offending child announced in *The Times of India* and chooses the unapologetically Indian name of Parvati for the little girl.) Thirdly, and perhaps most importantly of all, Daphne is successful on a personal level with an Indian man: through her love she gives Hari back his humanity and, as Mahood points out, his identity, which White Mayapore had earlier taken from him by regarding him as 'yet another black face'. [31] For, as Mahood goes on to say, "Daphne's 'good' end not only brings to life Parvati; on its own that would have been an altogether facile image of regeneration. More importantly, she leaves Hari remade, a man who has cast a shadow." [32] And in Scott's terminology 'casting a shadow' is the most a man can hope for in a meaningless world: to have left a sign of one's existence, to have

---

[30] Weinbaum, "Aspiration", p.69. (Weinbaum's italics).
[31] cf. Mahood, p.256.
[32] Ibid.

made an impact on human affairs, however minor, however transitory. In these terms, Daphne is successful, and her lasting reputation in Mayapore is proof of it. It survives the sahiblog's determined efforts to destroy it, for it is a reputation rooted firmly in the native town: for,

> ... when tempers had cooled and the English had forgotten ... the affair ..., the Indians still remembered it. They did not understand it. ... But out of it, out of all its mysteries, to them there seemed to be at least one thing that emerged, perhaps not clearly, but insistently, like an ache in an old wound that had healed itself. That Daphne had loved them. And had not betrayed them, even when it seemed that they had betrayed her. ... And so, after the event, honoured her for the things she was reported to have said which [had] shocked them ... as much as they [had] shocked the English.
>
> (*JC*, p.152)

In other words, Daphne, too, has cast a shadow, and her achievement seems considerably more solid (and more deserved) than the one Forster accords his heroine, when he has an uncomprehending crowd chant "Esmiss Esmoor." This, as much as anything else, illustrates the difference between Forster's celebration of liberal values and Scott's mournful reappraisal of them forty years later. For Scott there can be no easy successes, but there can be something one might call a triumph in defeat; it may not seem very much, but it is enough for life not to have been in vain. Daphne had devoted all her energies to a cause: she had *lived* her life; and in the light of this achievement, the actual success or failure of her efforts become unimportant. They still matter, of course, but they are not, as Eliot has taught us, a useful yardstick with which to measure human endeavour. Indeed, in a sense the whole of Daphne's life seems designed to illustrate Eliot's point in "Dry Salvages": it is only by trying, and trying again, that we can hope to overcome the obstacles which time and history put in our path; or in the words of the poet, "And right action is freedom / From past and future also. / For most of us this is the aim / Never here to be realized; / Who are only undefeated / Because we have gone on trying".

If Daphne Manners is an illustration of the inevitable failure of the individual liberal in spite of his most earnest efforts, Hari Kumar is symbolic of nothing less than the failure of the entire liberal system: the beliefs and values that underlay the British enterprise in India, in theory if not always in practice. And like Edwina Crane, or Daphne Manners, Hari's character, though entirely convincing, seems specifically designed to highlight this failure.

He is, after all, a true child of Empire. His father, possessed of an ardent love for England takes his baby boy to Britain, sends him to a distinguished public school and tries to make sure that young Hari grows up in a purely English environment - to the point of forcing himself not to see his own son too often, lest the boy pick up an Indian accent. The object of all this is, of course, to make a perfect Englishman out of Hari; someone indistinguishable from his British contemporaries: a *brown* Englishman, in fact. Kumar's father had read his Macaulay; indeed, as we know from an oblique remark in *Jewel*, had read him with avidity. His own son, then, would become a brown Englishman and, as such, a wielder of power, as Macaulay had promised. This touching innocence of the older Kumar, who took the textbook passages his British teachers set him for gospel truth, is yet another instance of 'weighted scales', but is surely legitimate: how else to measure the worth of a philosophy but by taking its exponents at their word?

Initially, though, everything does go according to plan, and Hari grows up in England, in the liberal atmosphere of Chillingborough (a thinly-disguised Haileybury - the traditional forging house of Imperial administrators). But then the money runs out; Hari's father, only too keenly aware that this spells the end for his son's prospects, commits suicide, and the young man himself is sent to India to a rude awakening.

The India Hari "goes out to" - and it seems appropriate to use that phrase since England was and would remain "Home" to him - is every bit as alien to him as it is to any other English boy sent out East; but it is not the India an English, that is to say a white, boy would come to.

> 'Our paths began to diverge in the region of the Suez Canal. In the Red Sea my skin turned brown. In Bombay my white friends noticed it. In Mayapore I

had no white friends because I had become invisible to them.'

(*JC*, p.241)

Hari, with his impeccable English, his public school education (and the accent to go with it) provides the acid test for the Raj's willingness to turn theory into practice and live up to the ideals by which it claimed to live: for in terms of the Raj's official aims - namely, elevating the poor, ignorant natives, so that one day they might be able to look after themselves and thus relieve the White Man of his Burden -, in terms of these professed aims, Hari is a signal success. All the doors in British India should be wide open to him; which, of course, they are not. On the contrary, they are shut to him more firmly than to any locally educated young Indian; for Hari, by virtue of his upbringing, demands to be treated as an equal: even if he does not say so in so many words, his accent asserts that claim in itself.

His very existence, therefore, is a challenge to the sahibs of Mayapore. Inevitably perhaps, they react with great determination to what they perceive to be the most glaring example of native impudence yet. By taking the Raj at its word, Hari not only succeeds in bringing out the worst in the Turtons of Mayapore, he also manages to offend the Fieldings of the station to a man. (Even Lady Chatterjee, whose education and background make her something of a 'brown Fielding', promptly takes offence when Hari does not show himself sufficiently grateful for her help during his first encounter with Merrick.) His unspoken demand to be treated as an equal highlights the difference between theory and practice, even liberal practice; or, in the terms of the *Quartet*, it focuses our attention on the "unmapped area of dangerous fallibility between a policy and its pursuit." (*JC*, p.183) [33]

---

[33] Francine Weinbaum is not alone to be reminded here of lines from Eliot's "The Hollow Men": "Between the idea / And the reality / Between the motion / And the act / Falls the Shadow. / Between the concept / And the creation / Between the emotion / And he response / Falls the Shadow." (cf. Weinbaum, "Aspiration", p.4)

Although several critics have remarked on Eliot's influence on Scott - notably Mahood, who writes that ". . . Eliot helped Scott to view India , which calls for the largest vision, through the eyes of the seers." Mahood, op.cit., p.258) - there has been, to my knowledge, no comprehensive study of this subject to date; such an undertaking would be immensely rewarding since it might reveal the remarkable extent to which a novelist can be indebted to a poet, and might throw some light in the process on the workings of the creative imagination, which transformed in

What Scott tries to show in much of the *Quartet* is precisely this crucial difference between a high-minded policy formulated in the dispassionate drawing rooms of the Home Counties and utopian college rooms at Cambridge as much as in the actual corridors of Whitehall, and the manner in which these were carried out on the spot by rather less high-minded, dispassionate and utopian Anglo-Indians. The picture that emerges is of a host of dyed-in-the-wool sahibs "irrevocably violating" these policies by their "personal passions and prejudices", as an Indian observer, the Congress politician Srinivasan, puts it in *Jewel*. (*JC*, p.183) And these people are crucial for they are, in Srinivasan's words - and he clearly echoes Scott's own convictions here - "the quantity left out of the official equation". (*JC*, p.183)

Thus far, Forster might have agreed with Scott's analysis of the imperial condundrum. He, too, saw Anglo-India riddled with prejudice, and he would have been happy to agree that the memsahibs who ignore Hari, ignore him not because of his manners, his sense of dress, or for fear of imbroglios, but quite simply because he is Indian - just another dark face in a sea of dark faces: invisible, in a word. Where Scott differs from Forster, however, is, as we have seen, in his belief that every Westerner in India can, and to some extent, will turn into a sahib. The story of Hari's English friend Colin provides further illustration of this point. Forster could never have conceived anything like it. He would have baulked at the idea of a friendship flourishing in one country and shrivelling in another. In a Forsterian novel Colin would have appeared, if at all, as the villain of the piece. Scott, however, describes Colin as a thoroughly decent chap, whose friendship with Hari in England was genuine; but in the strictly segregated society of British India the strains on their friendship are too great for it to survive. Where, after all, can an English officer and a native reporter meet socially? Colin just does not possess the necessary energy to overcome these obstacles, or is perhaps not courageous enough to face the inevitable raised eyebrows of his brother-officers for being seen to be chummy with a 'wog'. If Scott seems more charitable than Forster in this respect, he is by the same token also more pessimistic. He describes Colin as deeply unhappy in Mayapore and

---

this instance the poet's images and turned them into scenes and entire subplots in a novel.

has him apply for a transfer after a few months. But not before he and Hari had actually come face to face with each other. And here, in what might have been a quintessentially Forsterian situation where emotion and personal empathy would sweep aside all obstacles, the full extent of the difference between the two novelists' vision of human affairs becomes evident: for Colin fails to recognize Hari. He does not ignore him, he does not have to ignore him even; he genuinely does not see Hari: he only sees an Indian, a faceless creature who, like most Indians present on that occasion, is probably a servant.

And here again, Scott stresses the importance of that other quantity left out in Forster's wishfully simplistic equation: that of class. Hari and Colin had been social equals in England - and their friendship probably only developed because they were. But in India where one of them suddenly belongs to the ruling caste and the other to the subject race their friendship promptly withers. It is one thing, Scott implies, for someone like Lady Chatterjee - a Rajput princess and the wife of a baronet of the British Empire to boot - and the District Commissioner to be on amiable terms, quite another for a British officer and a two-anna bazaar correspondent. (And it is yet another thing if the bazaar boy walks into an Englishman's office and demands to be treated as an equal; especially if the Englishman enjoys a position in India he would never have enjoyed in England, and if his only claim to it rests precisely in the pinkness of his skin.) These are ramifications of the 'Indian question' which Forster never attempted; and a character like Hari Kumar, who seemed to the disapproving eye of the reviewer such a very special case, can therefore highlight these perhaps unfamiliar, but nonetheless fundamental, aspects of the Raj.

Someone like Kumar - and Kumar alone - can illustrate the manner in which the basic issue of rulers versus ruled was, in fact, further complicated by the background of so many of the lesser sahibs: English class consciousness in other words, impinging on the already charged relationship between White and Black. The engineer at the Mayapore factory for instance, whom Hari sees for a job interview, immediately recognizes the genuineness of Hari's public school accent and relishes the opportunity to get back at the 'toffs' - a satisfaction denied him in encounters with his own countrymen.

Similar emotions play a significant role in Merrick's attitude to Kumar. Merrick's manic persecution of Kumar springs not least from a sense of having suffered an injustice in England and the realization of being finally presented with an opportunity for revenge on someone who had been privileged: " . . . what Merrick is beating and humiliating in Kumar is", in the words of Patrick Swinden, "not only the envious Indian for whom he feels contempt, but the contemptuous English public schoolboy for whose class, accent and perfect manners he feels the deepest, though unself-acknowledged [sic] envy." [34] This is further compounded by the fact that Merrick feels threatened by Hari's demand to be treated as an equal; for to do so would be to accept that people like himself are not needed in India, and would thus compel him to lead the kind of existence in England from which he had sought to escape by chosing a career in the colonies. This is why Hari must be made an example of. By destroying Kumar, Merrick hopes to restore what he regards, and must regard if he is to retain his position in India, as the natural order of things.

Merrick's actual persecution of Kumar, and the form it takes, is in a sense of secondary importance only, given Scott's concern in *Jewel* with the decline of liberalism. It is an aspect of the Raj, to be sure, and an important one too (and is as such treated in depth in the later volumes of the *Quartet* where Scott is engaged in nothing less than an all-round description of British rule), but it is extraneous to the 'liberal dilemma', and might only distract from it; which is why Scott confines himself to mere hints in *Jewel* as to what actually went on inside the police jail. The important thing for Scott in the first book of the *Quartet* was to drive home to his readers the essential hopelessness of Hari's position in Mayapore. In this way, Hari's very existence, as that of a product of British rule, is the most glaring indictment imaginable of the Raj. He is, as Nigel Rowan, who leads the secret Government inquiry into the Mayapore case, remarks, "a charge to our account" (*DVS*, p.189), or as Lady Manners puts it, using a different image, "he is . . . the loose end of our reign, the

---

[34] Swinden, p.89.
The same emotions come into play in Merrick's dealings with Guy Perron in *Spoils*.

kind of person we created - I suppose with the best intentions." (*JC*, p.446)

For Hari himself this means coming to terms with the shattering truth that " . . . his father had succeeded in making him nothing, nothing in the black town, nothing in the cantonment, nothing even in England because in England he was now no more than a memory . . . ". (*JC*, p.234) And Scott does not allow us to go on deluding ourselves that all might have been different if only there had been more Fieldings in Mayapore. One such Fielding, Nigel Rowan, who had breathed the same liberal air at school that Hari had, and had, in fact, met him at a school open day, cherishes such illusions almost to the bitter end. If only, he exclaims during the Bibighar inquiry, he had " . . . known years ago what . . . [Kumar] was having to face. There must have been several old Chillingburians out here who'd have been willing to help him" (*DS*, p.269) Significantly, it is Rowan's Indian assistant in the investigation, Judge Gopal, who dispels such illusions with brutal finality, "'Do you think so, Captain Rowan? Willing, perhaps. Able - no. He is an English boy with a dark brown skin. The combination is hopeless!" (*DS*, p.269)

A character like Hari Kumar, then, was of added interest for Scott because he saw him as symbolic of a kind of ongoing imperial responsibility - which did not end with Independence - towards those people whose lives had been shaped by the Raj; and, as Hari's fate would suggest, it is a responsibility Britain failed to face up to. But there is yet another aspect of the imperial relationship which the character of Hari Kumar allows Scott to investigate: the question of the extent of Indian identification with British values and ideals, and the rejection by the Raj of the very people who most identified with them. Hari is the most extreme case on both counts, but he is by no means the only one in the *Quartet*. There are at least two more characters who come to mind: Lady Chatterjee - scarcely less anglicizied than Hari but, unlike him, shielded from the worst excesses of the ruling race by her exalted social position - is one; Mohammed Ali Kasim, the Congress politician who plays a significant part in the three later volumes of the *Quartet* is another. He, too, started off with a keen admiration for the British, and the policies he pursues within the Congress movement are all, in their way, a tribute to British ideas and traditions, even though only few of the Anglo-Indians are prepared to recognize them as such. What is common to all three, then, is their attitude towards Britain, which is one of love and not of rejection. This is of relevance when one considers the wider issue of the British-Indian relationship, which Scott had characterized on the opening page of *Jewel* as

> ... the spectacle of two nations ..., ... locked in an imperial embrace of such long standing and subtlety it was no longer possible for them to know whether they hated or loved one another, or what it was that held them together and seemed to have confused the image of their separate destinies."
>
> (*JC*, p.1)

Hari, Lady Chatterjee, M.A. Kasim provide in effect an answer to the uncertainty of this sentence: the 'imperial embrace' was indeed not without love; and people like Edwina Crane, Daphne Manners, old Lady Manners, and, in the later books, Barbie Batchelor, Sarah Layton, and old Mabel Layton all return that love and try, with varying degrees of success, to express it; but for the most part such love remained unrequited and turned sour: the love "in this curious centuries-long association" having always been a "... love with hate on the obverse side, as on a coin." (*JC*, p.60)

Against the reality of this love, then, must be seen the myriad illusions which pervade Mayapore. Mayapore is quite literally 'the city of illusions', as David Rubin tells us: for that is what the name of 'Mayapore' apparently means in Hindi. [35] And all of these illusions, both on an individual and communal level, are shattered in *Jewel*: the idea of the impartiality of the administration of justice in British India, the pious hopes of the Raj furthering the interests of the natives, and, most importantly of all, the illusory belief in the power of liberal humanist ideals to transcend the divisions between East and West, Black and White, rulers and ruled. Eventually, these uncomfortable truths dawn upon all the major actors in the drama played out in Mayapore. Some of them, though, prefer to take no notice. And whilst one might expect to find any

---

[35] cf. David Rubin, *After the Raj: British Novels of India Since 1947*. Hanover NH. 1986, p.124.

number of thick-skinned sahibs amongst that group, it comes as some surprise to discover a few Indians among them too. Of the latter, Lady Chatterjee is a prime example.

Her background - she is of Rajput stock, her position in the Indian Empire as the widow of a man knighted for his services to the Crown, and her complete familarity with English customs and speech - the result of formative years spent at an English public school, all assure her of a position of privilege in Mayapore. There is nothing illusory about this privileged position either: in the turbulent days of August 1942, for instance, she is perhaps the only Indian in the province who need not fear arbitrary arrest; on the contrary, the District Commissioner himself telephones at the height of the disturbances to make sure that all is well with the old lady. They are, after all, on first name terms. But privilege has its limits; particularly in the world outside the congenial circles of Government House. There the same Lady Chatterjee is subject to all the petty discrimination of the colour bar. The D.C. may telephone, but he cannot offer to have her evacuated to the club - which serves as the general bolthole during the unrest - because he knows he would never get her past the doorman (indeed the Viceroy himself would have to admit defeat there, should he have been rash enough to make such a promise to an Indian friend). [36] Which is why Lady Chatterjee wisely prefers not to stray too far beyond parties at selected private houses, confining herself mostly to her own home, the MacGregor House. This she has turned into something of an enchanted spot: a liberal Shangri-La which Forster himself could not have capped for its congenial atmosphere. But as with all Shangri-Las it is advisable not to venture outside, for to do so would be to confront the real world. *Inside*, of course, make-believe becomes reality, thanks to the ready connivance of all the habitués, who wish to preserve, like their host, an illusion without which they feel they cannot live: for here, at the MacGregor House, at least, the enlightened sahibs can prove to themselves that race really makes no

---

[36] Scott relates in *DVS* the story of one unsuspecting Viceroy, Lord Willingdon, who on one famous occasion found that his personal guests - several of the grandest maharajahs - had been turned away at the door of the Bombay Club. When he tried to take the club secretary to task over it, he was politely informed that his viceregal powers did not extend beyond the door step of the Bombay or any other club in India.

difference whatsoever, and the Indians are happy for once to feel able to agree. As so often in the *Quartet*, it is the iconoclast Merrick who first cuts through such self-deception. What goes on at the MacGregor House, he observes is " . . . [the] top layer of Indian society . . . [mixing] with our own top layer, but that's not real intimacy. More like necessary mutual recognition of privilege and power". (*DS*, p.214)

Merrick, of course, cannot conceive of anyone actually wishing to do away with the colour bar - and to this extent he does the MacGregor House set an injustice - but otherwise he is not very wide of the mark. For whenever Europeans are unaware of who Lili Chatterjee is, or feel no need to be polite to her, things quickly turn unpleasant: to travel first class on the train is to invite unspeakable behaviour from white fellow passengers; to visit one of her English friends at the sickbed in the white hospital - where all the doctors are on first-name terms with her - is to risk being shown the door by some junior nurse. And just as Hari's public school accent only makes things worse for him with those Anglo-Indians who are not 'top drawer' themselves, it is her title that guarantees extra venom on such occasions :

> If I'd been just Mrs Chatterjee the whole thing would have been a joke to them . . . . But being Lady Chatterjee, the widow of a man knighted by their own King, that made it awfully serious, something they really had to take a stand over, quite apart from the personal jealousy they might feel not being Knights' ladies themselves.
>
> (*JC*, p.79)

Though she proves quite unperturbable in such situations, she understandably goes out of her way to try to avoid them. She may therefore sparkle in mixed company at the D.C.'s dinner table, knowing that she can rely on the gallantry of the men, but is decidely more reticent afterwards in the exclusively female atmosphere of the drawing room; Edwina Crane, who first met her under such circumstances, judges her to be " . . . although not afraid, . . . , certainly on her guard, as stuffy in her own way as the English women." (*JC*, p.32)

And it is this perceived need to be constantly on her guard which is responsible for her own share in the general failure to reach out to those who might need help or comforting; it is this and not natural aloofness, lack of interest or compassion. The consequences of her inaction, however, are no less devastating than that of her white fellow-liberals. She fails to help Hari and Daphne, when she alone in Mayapore might have been able to do so; and, above all, she fails to reach out to Edwina Crane, at a time when a gesture from an Indian might have saved her from the depths of a despair that would lead her to take her own life. She visits Edwina in hospital, to be sure, inquires politely after her health and senses all the time that something serious must be amiss; yet she cannot bring herself to ask a genuinely personal question, or express her own genuine concern for her, for fear of yet another 'unpleasant scene'.

It is the spectacle of this ever-cautious Lili Chatterjee, never entirely at ease outside her own home, yet driven by her education and upbringing to seek the company of those whose real equal she can never hope to become in British India, the spectacle of someone who is determined to ignore the reality of petty indignities and humiliations which leads Daphne to observe,

> There is that old, disreputable saying, isn't there? 'When rape is inevitable, lie back and enjoy it.' *Well, there has been more than one rape.* I can't say, . . . , that I lay back and enjoyed mine. But Lili was trying to lie back and enjoy what we've done to her country.
> (*JC*, p.434. Scott's italics)

And so, finally, we return again to the theme of rape as being central to plot and imagery of *Jewel*. And now, at last, the difference between Scott and Forster becomes fully apparent. A character like Lady Chatterjee, who would have symbolized to Forster a successful marriage of East and West, and the supreme triumph of liberal values, emerges in Scott's Mayapore as a doubtful heroine: the forbearance with which she greets the daily injustices seems eventually like weakness, rather than strength. In Scott's vision of the world it is people like Hari Kumar and Daphne Manners who are the real heroes; who risk all, and are ready to pay the inevitable price for it. In contrast to them, Lady Chatterjee, charming, upright, and well-intentioned, epitomizes the enlightened liberal who remains an impotent onlooker, admiring other people's courage. This is not to say that Scott is critical of her: he never presumes to judge; indeed he is full of sympathy for her, and those like her. Not the least affecting scene in *Jewel* is the glimpse we get of her showing the narrator around the Mayapore of 1964 - now at last able to go to the club, but otherwise still cutting a distinctly lonely figure; an absurdly westernized old lady living in a third world country that has put its colonial past - which had been her world - firmly behind it. Indeed, in 1964 she seems more isolated than ever: still trying to get on with the sahibs, a new breed of sahibs - the army of technical experts and their wives, who manage to combine the shortcomings of the old sahiblog with a lack of breeding uniquely their own. In her own way, and in a less dramatic sense than Hari Kumar, she is another 'loose end' of the British reign, another bit of 'unfinished business'.

She is, like the more active players in the tragic farce that was the British Raj, among " . . . the chance victims of the hazards of a colonial ambition", as the narrator in *Jewel* puts it. (*JC*,p.71) But while that goes for practically everyone caught up in the threads of the unravelling tapestry of the Indian Empire, she - and Hari Kumar - are more than that: they are the creatures - and the victims - of all the fond illusions of nineteenth century liberal optimism, of a philosophy whose crowning glory they were to have been, and whose pitiful inadequacies they revealed instead.

And so, inevitably, the tone of the concluding pages of *Jewel* is very different from that of Forster's novel: Forster ends on an upbeat note - Aziz and Fielding have put behind them all misunderstanding and the future still holds the promise of a wider, freer friendship for them and their countries. Scott, having witnessed the ignominous end of the Raj, and having met the new race of sahibs into the bargain, can allow us no such hope. The best he can do is to offer us a glimpse of Parvati, a true child of love (and a symbol of what the union between Britain and India might have been), growing up to be an Indian girl, with no chip on her shoulder. And it is by raising her as an Indian girl that Lili Chatterjee herself proves that she, too, has ultimately faced up to the truth and abandoned the liberal illusions of a lifetime.

4. Pankot: Twilight of Paternalism

If Mayapore in the vast and dusty plains of India was the setting for the failure of liberalism to be acted out, the decline and the collapse of the grand old-fashioned paternalism in which the Raj was steeped is observed, appropriately enough, in the rarified air of the hills: in Pankot, the hot weather capital of Scott's fictional province of Ranpur. No contrast could be more complete. For what emerges before the reader's eyes in the second volume of the *Quartet* is a scene far removed from the squalor, the tedium, and the underlying hostility which characterized life in the India of *Jewel*. Here, in the foothills of the Himalayas, the sahiblog are permitted to forget the every-day care and woe of a proconsular existence and enjoy an atmosphere of ease and comfort. Though scenery and setting are very grand, spectacular even, the station itself is not without a certain homeliness and reflects in this unlikely combination something of the nature of the Raj itself: of perfectly ordinary people who in answering the call of Empire had found themselves translated into the position of rulers, were conscious of the dignity that came with that position, conscious also of their duty to preserve this dignity hedging their office (and, by extension, their persons), and were yet happy to remain, they liked to think, perfectly ordinary people.[1]

The station itself, we hear, was fittingly dominated by the Governor's summer residence, so that the very sun ". . . setting behind the West Hill seemed to have to pause until the upper windows of the summer residence released its last reflection, and the Raj allowed night to fall." (*DVS*, p.334) Such grandeur was only appropriate, indeed indispensable, for all things connected with the serious business of administering India; but for the rest, Pankot was agreeably intimate: the Raj as it were letting its hair down, settling back in an easy chair, and putting its feet up by the fire. Here, indeed, one could have fires in the winter,

---

[1] "Greatness", as Scott reminds us elsewhere, "was a mystical, inward, knowledge and best supported by a deprecating outward modesty, an appearance of ease that amounted to languor, of being awfully ordinary, as greatness was when shared by an entire nation. Only abroad could an Englishman allow some consciousness of his superiority to show, and then showing it was a duty. Abroad the Englishman was an emissary charged with his country's trust but exposed to un-English influences and under a personal obligation to hint at the consequences of any insult to his nation through an act of incivility to his person." ("The Raj", pp.75-76.)

congenial wood replaced unwelcoming stone as the main building material, the architecture was an exuberant "Indo-Tyrolean" (*DS*, p.53) rather than the ubiquitous stiffly-formal "Anglo-Indian palladian" (*DS*, p.52), and Nature herself - normally so hostile to the ruling race - seemed to smile upon them here where " . . . mists gathered in the evening and the early morning" (*DS*, p.53), "the air was crisp", and winter rather "like an English spring". (*DS*, p.52) "It was [all] thoroughly English"; "a place," in a word, "to let off steam in." (*DS,* p.52)

The spate of quotations above is intended to give some idea of the elaborate care Scott devotes in the second volume of his tetralogy to setting the scene. Pankot and the surrounding hills are described in even greater and more graphic detail than Mayapore had been in *Jewel*. Scott, of course, is never a hurried, impetuous novelist content to create a sketch with a few deft strokes and then move on, or to concentrate on the centre of his composition and leave the rest to the reader's imagination: he delights in working the great canvas and believes in filling his space. But if, as in all great art, detail is never an end in itself, this painstaking description of Pankot must be more than just a splash of local colour, serving instead as an introduction to, perhaps even a first veiled explanation of, the tale that is about to be told. This seems all the more likely, since Scott is always particularly alive to what Patrick Swinden calls "the interpenetration of human activity and the surfaces upon which that activity takes place"; so that, as Swinden goes on to say, ". . . the topographical backdrop . . . against which it proceeds . . . becomes more than a [mere] backdrop . . . ." [2] The detailed description of Pankot with which he prefixes his account of the breakdown of the paternalist tradition of the Raj must therefore, it is safe for us to assume, contain vital clues as to " . . . where the fault had lain and why there could have been no other end . . . ." (*DS*, p.431)

Yet, at first sight, there seems to be precious little to support that view. Indeed, for all the unmistakable ironic undertone of his description of Pankot, Scott does not immediately play too much on the incongruity of the scene either. Instead, he tries to get across the very real, if somewhat autumnal, charm of the place, and to contrast it with the hot, dusty, filthy and ugly Mayapore of *Jewel*. And so the reader does feel trans-

---

[2] Swinden, p.8.

lated - albeit only briefly - into a happier world, where things are simpler and more straightforward than in the plains, and life itself seems ordered and blessed with meaning; a haven of peace: ideal for weary bodies and minds. Not surprisingly, Pankot was, as the narrator doubling up as our cicerone tells us, especially popular with older Anglo-Indians, who retired thither to live out

> ... their remaining years in a place that was peculiarly Indian but very much their own, ... where servants were cheap, and English flowers could be grown ..., and life take on the serenity of fulfillment, of duty done without the depression of going home wondering what it had been done for. (*DS*, p.54)

Pankot, in other words, is a happy remnant of a vanished Edwardian, or even Victorian, world, which in *Jewel* had been evoked only by Edwina Crane's allegorical painting of the Great White Queen.

It is an older, earlier British India then, in which the reader finds himself at the beginning of the second volume of the *Quartet*. An India apparently untroubled by the relentless March of History in the plains: something of an earthly Paradise. Although it is, as the narrator's comments indicate, a paradise with a question mark hanging over it; a paradise, moreover, which can even now be preserved only by banishing firmly all thought about the disquietening world outside. This, as Swinden demonstrates in his study on Scott, the most comprehensive and consistently well-informed to date, touches at a concern central to Scott's œuvre: for, Swinden writes, "from the beginning of his career as a novelist [Scott] ... has been preoccupied with Paradises that are already lost, and he has sought to bring his characters to terms with that loss." [3] In Pankot the characters do not just have to come to terms with the loss of their paradise, they must also accept that it had been a highly questionable one in the first place.

All but the most gullible readers will, of course, have suspected as much all along. For by the time we reach Pankot in the course of the narrative, we have not only seen Mayapore, but have witnessed at the beginning of *Scorpion* the indescriminate round-up and internment of

---

[3] Ibid., p.2.

Congress politicians in 1942. In the light of such knowledge the idyll in the hills had always seemed rather too good to be true. Scott confirms our suspicions quite subtly. Having prefixed the description of the station with a long aside on the history of the Pankot Rifles - the local regiment, which dominates the social and working lives of the station - our tour guide turns to point out the War Memorial; this, we are told, received annually for Remembrance Day " . . . a wreath of poppies, offerings of ghi, buttermilk and flowers." (*DS*, p.53) The very picture of racial harmony. But his next sentence shatters the illusion. For Pankot, he goes on to explain, was built on two hills in the shape of a V, with the War Memorial at the lower tip of the V; from it the ". . . left-hand fork led . . . to a lower area where rich Indians and minor princes owned chalet-style houses . . . " - " . . . an area", he adds, "the generality of the English had little knowledge of", since to them " . . . Pankot was properly reached by taking the right-hand fork." (*DS*, p.53) There is no further comment on the matter, and at this stage in the *Quartet* none is required.

Here then, on the high ground, in an India agreeably free from all Indians (except for those indispensable living props in uniform or servants' tunic who blend in so well with the furniture or the landscape) the Anglo-Indians live, watched by their native retainers

> . . . for clues to the trick . . . [they] were performing to sustain the illusion of . . . [their] ordinariness, the illusion that the Sahib-log too liked to eat and take a rest and did not live like birds of paradise, perpetually in flight, feeding on celestial dew.
>
> (*DVS*, p.363)

There is no mistaking the ironic tone here: a significant contrast to the generally more earnest voice in *Jewel*. (Though *Jewel* too, had not been without its moments - the "Edited Extracts from the unpublished memoirs of Brigadier A.V. Reid, DSO, MC: 'A Simple Life' " being an obvious case in point. In it the hapless brigadier had been allowed to unmask his own insensitivity and incomprehension of events through his hilarious 'I-am-just-a-simple-soldier' phraseology). Much the same goes for Pankot and the voices of its social scene. In both cases the "element of high irony" serves, in the words of George Woodcock, as " . . . a kind of litmus to test the moral chemistry of the declining Raj."[4] It is hardly surprising therefore that irony, for all the real drama and tragedy, is never very far from the surface in the two middle books, and all but dominates in the concluding volume of the tetralogy.

It is certainly much in evidence when Scott describes the life style and traditions of the pukka sahiblog with a mock-seriousness that mimicks the attitude of an ethnologist recording the strange customs of a primitive tribe, or that of a naturalist even, intrigued by the unexpectedly intricate social behaviour of a population of insects.[5] Take, for instance, the question of a girl's season (and the allied one of her marriage), an obvious target perhaps for this sort of treatment. We learn that the whole process lasted three years: during the first year a girl held "power over herds of - as it were - panting young men", "fired by climate and scarcity [of females]." (*DS*, p.123) "The second year was the year of engagements and marriages; the third year was devoted to maternity. With the first grandson or granddaughter one could sit back with a sigh of relief that one's duty had been properly done." (*DS*, p.123)

The tongue-in-cheek use of the word duty here - a key word in the vocabulary of the Raj, and one that was nowhere spelt with a bigger capital D than in British India - shows that Scott is not simply trying to get comic mileage out of the sahibs: tone and wording here amount to an authorial comment on their preoccupations, their scale of values, and their views on life, all of which are, as the ironic treatment shows, very different from the author's. Indeed it is obvious from the outset that

---

[4] George Woodcock, "The Sometime Sahibs: Two Post-Independence British Novelists of India". *Queen's Quarterly* 86, p.45.
 The irony is correspondingly mordant on occasion, as for instance in the scene when Reid inspects the building activities at a new airfield: watching the native women-labourers balancing basketsful of building stones on their heads, he finds that his "heart goes out to [them] " and he cannot but contrast the Mahatma's attitude - whose strike call, he feels sure, would have condemned such women to starvation - to the ministrations of two young memsahibs " . . . who were doing their best to attend single-handed to the screaming wants of Hindu and Muslim babies and to pregnant women who had collapsed under the weight of the baskets." (*JC*, p. 292)
[5] There is of course an implicit equation of men and insects underlying such an attitude. It is most noticeable in the eponymous scene of *The Day of the Scorpion*, though there it is not the narrator but the character, Susan Layton, who equates her fellow-Anglo Indians with helpless insects.

Scott cannot take the subject of the collapse of the paternalist world quite as seriously as he had taken the breakdown of the liberal values in *Jewel*.

The ironic mode also serves another obvious purpose though: that of distancing narrator - and reader - from the events recounted. From the start in what might be called 'the Pankot books' Scott uses it as a device to control the degree of identification of his readers with the Laytons and the Binghams: the central characters of the middle books. The reason for Scott's evident determination to keep a tight rein on his readers' emotions is not far to seek. Indeed, one need look no farther than the most obvious difference between the first and the subsequent volumes of the *Quartet*: that in setting. For to move the narrative centre of the novel from the fringes of Anglo-Indian society to its very heart, as Scott does in *Scorpion*, is to shift the angle from which his stills of British rule are taken. In the two middle books, then, (and to a lesser extent in the concluding volume) Scott is dealing with the Raj from *within* it, listening to the prattle of the mems or stealing upon the protagonists in their thoughts and dreams. This is in marked contrast to the technique used in *Jewel,* where we saw things nearly always through the eyes of outsiders (Daphne Manners, Lili Chatterjee, Sister Ludmila, Mr Srinivasan, etc.); or when we did not, as in the case of D.C. White's account of the 'Quit India' riots, we viewed them across the safe distance of the years. (And it is no coincidence that when for once an authentic Anglo-Indian voice of pre-Independence vintage was allowed to reach our ears - via the pages of Brigadier Reid's recollections - Scott promptly spiked the old soldier's guns with particularly crippling irony.) In Pankot, however, where we mix freely with the sahiblog - having morning coffee with them at the club or dropping in on them for a rubber - we naturally hear only one side of the argument and might run the risk of believing what we are told. Hence the narrator's great care to deflate the more self-important of the sahibs at every twist and turn, and to temper our enthusiasm for the more acceptable members of the ruling race through an occasional dose of gentle irony.Without this, the story of the Laytons and Binghams might easily have degenerated into an Anglo-Indian dynastic saga, where the fates of the protagonists would prove of such absorbing interest as to obscure the wider issues.

Scott's care to avoid such dangers shows clearly in the description of Teddie Bingham's arrival on the scene. Here is a hero in the traditional mould of the Anglo-Indian novel: a pedigree sahib with an impeccable background of service in pukka regiments going back several generations; a man full of integrity, courage, and devotion to 'The Cause'; handsome too, in a reassuringly conventional and unostentatious way: every inch, in fact, the 'Man-the-Empire-Needs'. Yet this impression is immediately undercut by the narrator's ironic two-sentence summing-up of Teddie's life to date:

> School, military academy, regiment, baptism of fire, staff-college: the next logical step was marriage so that the process could be repeated through a continuing male line. Arrived in Pankot Teddie metaphorically cleared his throat, put up his head and looked round for a girl with whom to take it.
>
> (*TS*, p.95)

This (and comments in a similar vein) is, however, more than just a device to establish or sustain a certain narrative tone. It can be a superbly effective means of characterization. In Teddie's case, for instance, the narrator's laconic two sentences really do sum up the essence of his being at the time of his arrival in Pankot. And if that makes him seem a rather one-dimensional character, well and good, for the real life Teddie Binghams were, Scott insists, distinctly one-dimensional too, at least for as long as they were solely concerned to project the conventional image of the pukha sahib. (Significantly, Scott swiftly wipes the wry smiles off our faces once Teddie discovers - through marriage - that there is more to life than just being a Muzzy Guide). In this way the ironic description of Pankot and its social scene does indeed contain the clues to the fatal errors of the Raj, or to quote again Sarah Layton's memorable phrase, to " ... where the fault had lain and why there could have been no other end." (*DS*, p.431)

It is characteristic of this rather oblique approach that the first real indication of change within this questionable hill-side idyll should come disguised and buried in yet another gossipy paragraph about marriages. For all, we hear, is no longer well on the lower reaches of the Himalayas. The war in Europe, distant enough from Pankot though it might seem, has nevertheless begun to reveal its disruptive character. This takes the form of an alarming decrease in the number of eligible girls, as so many of that precious human commodity have become discouraged from venturing East by the perils of long wartime sea voyages, while on the other hand the sudden burst of military activity on the subcontinent has meant that " . . . the supply of men had become a torrent of all sorts where once it had been a steady dependable flow mostly of one sort only - the right. . . . One felt, as it were, besieged." (*DS, p.*124)

"Besieged"! - the dramatic adjective with its echoes of the mock-heroic should not mislead us: its use here is just a means - and an extremely effective one too - of driving home a point without preaching or launching into a long and tiresome historical lecture. It should certainly not be taken to mean that Scott is anything less than serious. Indeed, this notion of Anglo-India feeling besieged, and something of a siege actually being laid against them by the sahibs' own countrymen, is central to Scott's reading of events in the India of the last years of the Raj. But it is introduced so casually - smuggled in almost - amid the amusing welter of the memsahibs' prejudices and snobberies that one may well fail at first to take in its full significance. But as one meets in the course of a narrative meandering in and out of Pankot more and more Englishmen who are in India through wartime necessity not inclination, who are, moreover, definitely no sahibs (even if they might otherwise qualify for the epithet 'pukka') - as one meets them and witnesses first their incredulous surprise, then their mounting anger, and finally their barely-controlled fury at what they see around them, it becomes evident that the siege is real enough. And since the besieged can only look to England for help, the very country whence the besieging masses are pouring from, the eventual fall of this beleaguered fortress is a foregone conclusion.

The isolation, then, is twofold. Not only is Pankot closed off against India and the Indians, it is no less cut off from an England which to the sahibs seems to have been taken over entirely by "vulgar money-grubbers" and desk-wallahs "trying to paint out the pink parts of the map". (*DS, p.*425) It is Scott's emphasis on the latter isolation that distinguishes the *Quartet* from most other novels about the Raj, including *Passage* (where the fact is noted but not investigated; or if it is, is attributed solely to 'underdeveloped hearts' as the inevitable result of a public school education). The other kind of isolation, that from all things Indian, comes as no surprise, it being something of a stock ingredient of Anglo-Indian literature. Yet in the Pankot scenes even this is carried to an extreme: save for the loyal old retainers, a few picturesquely roguish bazaar wallahs, the odd street urchin and an occasional nameless and faceless Pankot Rifleman, no Indian is allowed to intrude on the scene.

This has been the target of fierce criticism by Indian critics who have tended to agree with Gita Mehta that, all things being equal, the *Quartet* " . . . might as well have been set in Eastbourne, in boarding-houses for retired sahibs . . ." ;[6] or with Salman Rushdie's furious objection, already referred to earlier, that the part played by the Indians in the collapse of the Raj was not adequately reflected in Scott's version of events (which therefore amounted to a falsification of history).[7] Such criticism, which owes perhaps more to offended national sensibilities than to purely literary criteria, misses the point. And surely the point Scott is making (and one which neither Gita Mehta nor Salman Rushdie would presumably want to dispute) is that the sahiblog in the hill stations were living in an absurdly unreal world; that they might indeed have been living in Eastbourne for all they cared, so complete was their determination to create a corner in a foreign field that would remain forever England. It is a point emphasized in *Scorpion* through touchingly absurd comparisons with 'Home', such as the one likening the Pankot scenery to - of all things - "the Surrey hills near Caterham" - an impression that could, of course, only be sustained when the distant range of the Himalayas was shrouded in mist (which it obligingly remained for the greater part of the year). (*DS,* p.54) "But", the narrator adds significantly, "occasionally [it would be] revealed, like the word of God", thereby cutting everything down to size: Pankot, the sahibs and their

---

[6] Gita Mehta, "The Rage for the Raj". *New Republic* 25 November 1975 , p.27.
[7] cf. Rushdie, p.128.
Rushdie writes, "The *Quartet*'s form tells us in effect, that the history of the end of the Raj was largely composed of the doings of the officer class and its wife. . . . Once this form has been set, it scarcely matters that individual, fictional Brits get unsympathetic treatment from their author. The form insists that *they are the ones that matter*, and that is so much less than the whole truth that it must be called a falsehood."

presumptions, and by extension the whole British enterprise in India. (*DS*, p.52)

After all, it is precisely this reluctance to accept as it is the land in which they have put down roots and which they yet refuse to call 'home' that is at the heart of the tragedy of the sahibs. Their inability to come to terms with the real India eventually loosens their hold on reality itself: on the geographical, historical and political reality of the subcontinent; which is why the near-total absence of Indian characters in the Pankot scenes - which might worry the historian - should not alarm the literary critic. For it is surely sound literary practice to emphasize through exaggeration traits that have been recognized as characteristic, as containing the essence of a situation. In this way the exclusion of the Indians from so much of the narrative combines with the striking image of a Tunbridge Wells or Cheltenham perched precariously on the edge of the Himalayas to form a singularly eloquent comment on the British Raj and its upholders.

As for the other charge laid against the *Quartet*, that of failing to present in sufficient detail the activities of the Indian Nationalists, the answer to that is that it simply will not do to confuse the roles of the novelist and of the historiographer. The latter is expected to adhere closely to the sequence of historical events; the former is under no such obligation. Indeed, very few actual historical events are explicitly portrayed in the *Quartet*. Scott generally prefers to have them reported (by various characters, by the narrator, or even, as in *Spoils*, through the description of a series of political cartoons culled from an Indian newspaper). In this respect, as has been widely noted, sections of the *Quartet* are, at times, reminiscent of a play.[8] K. Bhaskara Rao, for in-

---

[8] cf. inter al. Mahood, pp. 248-9 who speaks of Scott's narrative techniques as being, ". . . like those of many great novelists, . . . always exploratory . . .", and K. Bhaskara Rao, *Paul Scott*. (Twayne English Authors Series) Boston, p.129 who regards what he calls Scott's "creative use of the techniques of the cinema and the stage" as ". . . a significant contribution to the novelist's art."
Scott himself emphasizes in an interview with Francine Ringold what he says are the essential similarities between the novelist's and the dramatists' craft: " . . . well it's the same thing. Because underneath every novel - though a good novel will not have all the trappings of the stage directions etc. - still, every page should be in a proscenium arch: well-lit, dressed, directed, spoken, filled with action." (Francine Ringold, "A Conversation with Paul Scott" *Nimrod* 21 (1) 1976, p.22.) And again in the same interview: "I'd like to instil the idea that a novel is not prose on a page. It is a form of shorthand for producing images of life, situations. It's a drama,

stance, is reminded of the Greek dramatists, with whom, he observes, Scott shares a preference for having the "... more violent actions offstage"; nor is this, he adds, the only similarity: for Scott "... even uses the memsahibs of Pankot, when they gather to play bridge, to perform the role of a chorus and comment on the action outside ... ."[9]

The use of this narrative device is no mere authorial whim or empty display of technical brilliance; it has its definite purpose: that of heightening still further the already potent sense of unreality which is the hallmark of the Pankot scenes. This ties in with Scott's own observations during the final years of British rule in India. Far from suggesting therefore, as Rushdie thinks it does, that only the memsahibs' stories matter, Scott says *through form alone* that the exact opposite is the case: nothing said or done in Pankot makes one jot of difference to the outcome of a historical conflict which had long since bypassed Anglo-India. The frantic chatter of his gaggle of mems only helps to underline their essential inertia, and the inability of the sahiblog in general to influence events, reducing their actions to mere gestures and adding further to the already pronounced 'as-it-were' atmosphere pervading British India. There is in no doubt in Scott's mind that the fate of the Raj was decided - and sealed - not in Pankot (and the real-life hill stations it stands for), nor in Simla or Delhi (the twin seats of the Government of India), nor in the rebellious towns and villages of the Indian plain (pace Salman Rushdie), nor even on the battleground in the jungles of Burma and Malaya, - though events in all of these contributed to hasten the outcome -, but by the groundswell of moral pressure against it in Oxbridge common rooms and Whitehall corridors.

In a sense then, Scott's chosen technique merely reflects the essential theatricality *of real life* during the last years of the Raj: the feeling of taking part in a charade which befell the more observant Anglo Indians at the time. (The word "charade" is in fact used by several characters in the later books of the *Quartet* to describe what they feel

---

but it happens to be done not with actors, and props, but only with words. (Ibid., p.31)

[9] Bhaskara Rao, p.129.

Bhaskara Rao cites as a further example of an echo from the theatre the narrator's "favourite phrase, 'Imagine if you will'" with its "Shakespearean ring". (Ibid.)

their actions amount to.) Nothing, Scott thinks, demonstrates this more clearly than the actual historical end of the Indian Empire: for in a sense, the curtain fell before the conflict on the subcontinent itself had been resolved; the ostensible protagonists in the tragic farce that was the British Raj - the Anglo-Indians on the one side and the Indian Nationalists on the other - both stood completely dumbfounded when in 1947 Mountbatten, a real-life deus ex machina, suddenly appeared on the scene to announce that the English audience had grown tired of the spectacle, was now more interested in putting on a new show called 'the Welfare State', and that consequently the stage lights would be switched off and the play must end.

It is the gulf between the attitudes of the English 'at home' and their cousins in India, which such events demonstrated, and had made possible in the first place, that Scott sets about exploring in the 'Pankot books'.[10] And as with the events in Mayapore, he is not primarily concerned with an historical process per se but with the effects of an historical process on individual lives. And in Scott's chosen period in the history of Empire this means, as Swinden observes, looking at ". . . the effect the loss of India had on the Anglo-Indian community."[11] Therein, as David Rubin has pointed out, lies the main difference between Scott and most other writers of the Indian scene: Scott looks beyond the superficial changes in the administration and the circumstances of everyday life during the final years of British rule to concentrate instead on "the more profound spiritual dislocation" which is the inevitable by-product of this particular process.[12] If we are to appreciate this "spiritual dislocation" in anything like its real magnitude, we must remind ourselves first of what India meant to the Anglo-Indians.

India, as Swinden has shown, represents nothing less than Paradise for Scott's sahibs.

> Or, if not Paradise, a setting for their lives which they feel can be replaced by nothing else. They have defined themselves, their duties, their professions,

---

[10] cf. "A Post-Forsterian View", p.124 where Scott speaks of the Anglo-Indians' "spiritual exile" from their own country, "where the real challenge came from".
[11] Swinden, p.73.
[12] Rubin, p.122.

their moral values, their habits of social behaviour and personal assessment, in relation to India. Scott shows that for the British who lived there India was an all-embracing experience. Their minds admitted only dim recollections of 'home' in England. [13]

Yet this India of the sahibs is not, as Forster's Adela Quested had rightly suspected, the 'real' India: that is to say the country in which the Indians live. And that word 'real' was well-chosen. For it implied that the India of the sahibs was always somewhat less than entirely real; that there was something not merely artificial but delusive, almost hallucinatory, about it; that it was, in fact, little more than the figment of a remarkably powerful collective imagination. The land in which the Anglo-Indians lived was not a land dominated by the pathetic struggle for every-day survival, by the banality of having to scratch a living, it was the romantic, half-mythical world of the British Raj: a world of selfless service and base ingratitude, of undying loyalty and fiendish treachery, of Khyber heroics and bazaar plots - *Boy's Own* stuff in a word. In a sense the sahibs must rank among the most successful creators of fiction of all time. For they were not content merely to dream up a fictional universe within their minds - a comforting world of make-belief, in which occasionally, in schoolboy fashion, to take refuge from the daunting world outside - they constructed their fictional universe all around them, and eventually came to regard it as the 'real' world. And in a sense, of course, it was real, in that it was inhabited by real-life people, who, at least on the Anglo-Indian side, conformed exactly to the idea everybody had of what life in India was like. [14]

"Indeed," as Swinden observes,

> ... reality of a kind must come into being when a landscape and a people are subjected to the creative pressures of so many minds, differing in any number of important ways but ultimately controlled by an

---

[13] Swinden, p.73.
[14] This is precisely what Leonard Woolf meant when he said that, while out in the East, he had never been able to decide whether Kipling had described the Anglo-Indians with unique accuracy or whether everybody in the East was behaving like Kipling characters. (cf. Leonard Woolf, *Growing: An Autobiography of the Years 1904 - 1911*. London 1961, p.46.)

> intangible idea of the rightness of their presence - more than that their *superior* presence - in the place they now call home. [15]

Yet this 'reality' was - in the nature of things - both highly precarious and peculiarly impermanent. After all, it could only be sustained for as long as no one - the Indians, or the English at home in England -, actually called the sahibs' bluff. And this is where the fate of an obscure group of British expatriates begins to be really interesting, for their experiences make the concept of reality itself appear doubtful. For, to quote Swinden once more,

> ... if this impermanence is not recognized by those whose reality it is felt to be then reality, however substantial or laden with histories and emblems of those who lived it, itself becomes an illusion. [16]

The India of the British Raj, therefore, Swinden concludes, represents for Scott "the supreme illusion". [17]

In the light of these reflections it is not hard to see why Scott should have felt that the British Raj would make for a singularly appropriate metaphor for contemporary life. Through it he would be able to capture what we have come to regard as the essence of our twentieth century existance: the experience of bewilderment and disorientation, of alienation and deracination, which is the consequence of our having lost all conviction in the metaphysical and humanist certainties of earlier generations. What interested Scott was to see how individuals react when the last ropes that hold things in place are cut.

There are, it seems, only really two kinds of reaction: either to ignore all doubts and stick to one's guns, as Brigadier Reid does quite literally in *Jewel*, or to wake up to reality and try to come to terms with it. And Swinden is right to say that Scott's main interest lies with the latter group,

---

[15] Swinden, p.5.
[16] Ibid.
[17] Ibid., p.3.

> ... because to feel as they do is to loose a part, perhaps a very large part, of their own reality - which has been ... dependent upon their connection with India. How is a man supposed to hold on to a sense of personal reality when he can feel the external props which have sustained it for so long, at first gently, and then violently being pulled away? [18]

Ultimately this kind of experience must threaten a man's identity, perhaps even, as Susan Layton's fate would suggest, his sanity. This, then, is the deadly-serious subtext to the deceptively light-hearted irony of the 'Pankot books'.

"India", Scott says in his lecture to the Royal Society of Literature, "was ... a metaphor for the English pursuit of happiness ... " [19] This being so, the *Quartet* must be 'about' that pursuit of happiness and about the rocks on which that pursuit foundered in our century (and, of course, about the people who were able to make out the rocks on which it would founder). In the context of the 'Pankot books' this translates as the gradual process of enlightenment as to the real reason for Anglo-India's growing malaise in the final decades of the Raj. These are obscured by the superficial irritants of the changes forced on the sahiblog by events outside India. In Pankot these are first felt at the outbreak of war in Europe, and seem comically trivial to the reader - not least because of the exaggerated importance the station attaches to them. And it is this obsession with trivialities in the face of a vast impending tragedy that gives the middle books their distinctive character and lends them full credibility.

At the centre of Scott's hillside cosmos are the Laytons, who when we first meet them are bearing with great fortitude what are, we are told, unusually trying circumstances; tongue firmly lodged in cheek, the narrator proceeds to regale us with a tale of splendidly stiff upper lips, of distressingly unsatisfactory living conditions, and a deplorable lack of understanding on the part of the Army Housing Office resulting in the expenditure of a small fortune in tonga fares to get from an inconveniently-situated home to the club for morning coffee. And here Scott is at his

---

[18] Swinden, p.5.
[19] "A Post-Forsterian View", p.125.

subversive best, almost allowing this tale of truly epic courage in the face of adversity to overshadow the real test of strength with which the Laytons are faced: the absence of their husband and father, the Colonel, who is away in Europe, in a POW-camp to be precise. Only the women, therefore, remain, three generations of them, "to hold the fort". This recurring expression, innocent enough in itself, is another of the clues Scott leaves for the reader; but it will take an unusually sharp reader to spot immediately its true significance: for it has such a convincing ring of upper-middle class argot to it that few people will be sufficiently jolted by it to make the connection with the title of 'Book One' of *Scorpion*, "The Prisoners in the Fort". Ostensibly, that title refers to the Nationalist leaders whose incarceration is related in the first chapters of the book. But with the phrase recurring again and again and the desperate lack of happiness in the Laytons' lives increasingly apparent, it begins to dawn on the reader that Mr Kasim and his Congress friends might not be the only ones to be deprived of their freedom; that the Laytons are, in fact, as much prisoners as they appear to be commanders in their own metaphorical fort.

And this suspicion is confirmed when we find that the deaths of old Mabel Layton and of Susan's husband Teddie Bingham, Susan's madness, and the (initially) secret rebellion of her sister Sarah are all reported in "Orders of Release" - though, again, that title refers ostensibly only to the fate of the Congress detainees.

Like the narrator's tongue-in-cheek description of Pankot, then, the titles of the two 'books' of *Scorpion* amount in themselves to an authorial comment on the Raj, and the moral and political ideas that underpinned it. [20] And it could scarcely have been more trenchant. The actual story-line is no less damning, as the merest glance will bear out: Mabel's silent despair, Susan's attempted infanticide, Teddie's suicidal gesture in the Assamese jungle, Mildred's gin-dazed misanthropy, and Sarah's string of loveless sexual encounters combine to form a wordless, but all the more powerful, indictment of the Raj. Events do indeed speak for themselves, as Mabel foresaw they would. To look at the fates of the

---

[20] The same can be said of the title of the four novels: 'from *The Jewel in the Crown* to *A Division of the Spoils*' is nothing other than a succint summing-up of one man's view of the end of the Raj.

individual members of the Layton clan, then, is to read not just a study in imperial decline but of the corroding effect of imperial rule on the rulers; this is only fully apparent once the proconsular mantle has become threadbare enough to reveal pathetically vulnerable creatures underneath.

The various protagonists in the unfolding Pankot drama all react differently to the threat to their world. Some, like Mabel Layton, do not appear to react at all. This is, as far as the club is concerned, precisely as it should be. For, with the Colonel, the commanding officer of the local regiment away, the station looks to her for support and encouragement in a situation which is generally perceived to be getting more difficult with every passing year. They do so, not just because of the family connection, or her exalted social position (the result of her own and her late husband's distinguished background), but because she represents by virtue of her years, a living link "with an earlier golden age". (*TS,* p.25) Her aloofness from public life, her solitary and taciturn existence at 'Rose Cottage', devoted almost entirely to the upkeep of her garden, only reinforce that image. Pankot sees her as a monument to the past, and to past glories; someone who stands firm and unchanging; who, if rather too forbidding to offer much comfort, does at least provide through her example a much-needed moral shot-in-the-arm. And already the narrator is dropping heavy hints that the price for such splendidly upright imperial backbones might be more than just a degree of emotional sterility. Certainly, there is little in the description of Mabel that suggests much warmth, in her 'imperial' persona at any rate, witness the following passage where she is described as

> ... stony-faced and uncompromising; a bleak point of reference, as it were a marker-buoy above a sunken ship full of treasure that could never be salvaged; a reminder and a warning to shipping still afloat in waters that got more treacherous every year.
>
> (*TS,* p.25)

And though we may feel disinclined to rely too heavily on a passage so obviously tinged with authorial irony, there is also Sarah's evidence: even to the person she loved most, Mabel seemed unapproachable: someone "you could lean against" but "could not embrace". (*DS*, p.319)

However, Mabel's posture - like so much in the *Quartet* - is not quite what it seems. Her silence is real enough, and it is indeed a silence of pursed lips, of deep-felt if unvoiced disapproval; but it is a disapproval directed not at the forces assailing the Raj from every corner, but at its upholders, its institutions, its very nature even. The reader is allowed to guess all this before being told so explicitly. The first intimation of Mabel's true attitude is characteristically oblique: Sarah, then a mere child, draws a family tree and proceeds to ring the individual names with colour crayons - blue for her 'English' relations, Imperial red for her Indian ones; quite unconsciously, she was going to put a blue ring around Mabel's name, before she comes to and picks up the 'correct' red pencil.

For Pankot the process of enlightenment is much slower. Though it does occasionally suffer doubts about Mabel's true motives for her complete withdrawal from the social life of the station, it is inclined to reassure itself in view of her background, and put it all down to pardonable eccentricity: the

> . . . personal idiosyncracy of someone who had lost two husbands in the cause of service to the Empire, one by rifle fire from the Khyber, the other by amoebic infection; and having thus distinguished herself retired from the field of duty to leave room for others.
>
> (*TS*, p.25)

Significantly, it is not Mabel herself who is being lampooned here but those who refuse to recognize the truth about her. This is characteristic of Scott's treatment of the sahiblog throughout. For while he is capable of showing great sympathy for those among them who - like Mabel - bravely try to face up to a reality which threatens to destroy them - a sympathy which even extends in some measure to the 'villains' of the *Quartet*- , he is less indulgent with those who prefer to continue down the much-trodden path of self-deception. There irony comes into play, and though it is usually of the gentle variety, the cumulative effect of it can nonetheless be quite devastating. In the case of the Pankot mems it certainly is. Few readers, one suspects, will take them seriously, once they have witnessed their remarkable double act, so to speak, of simultaneously looking up to the elder and better in Mabel *and* of harbouring dark suspicions about her true motives as an individual.

For to them Mabel's silence smacks uncomfortably of betrayal. And betrayal, one might say, is what the *Quartet* is all about; which will come as no surprise to the seasoned reader of Eastern tales. 'Betrayal', after all, is another of those key words in the vocabulary of the Raj, like 'duty', 'loyalty' and 'honour' (of which three it is the antithesis). And like 'Duty', 'Loyalty' and 'Honour', it is properly spelt with a capital letter. For in India, as any Anglo-Indian novel will tell you, the air is thick with disloyalty. It hangs over the bazaar like a miasma, making the natives uniquely treacherous; and, on occasion, a fatal whiff of it will also blow into the hallowed confines of the cantonment where it will seek out the one weak link in the chain, the one rotten apple in the pile, the one sahib (or his mem) lacking the necessary moral fibre to withstand it: and then the result is 'Betrayal'. Forster had famously poked fun at this hardy perennial of a motif. Scott, too, uses it with subversive intent: contrasting imaginary betrayal with the real thing, which goes unnoticed. Events in and after Amritsar provide a textbook example.

To the sahiblog, Amritsar was a double betrayal: the (not altogether unexpected) disloyalty of the natives compounded by a reaction in England which, it was felt, amounted to a stab in the back. To Mabel Layton - and doubtless she speaks for Scott here - Amritsar also signified an unforgivable double betrayal, but one perpetrated by the rulers: a betrayal both of the trust invested in them by the Indians and of their own imperial ideals. And if originally only General Dyer and a handful of his men had been guilty of it, Anglo-India was quick to share the disgrace by backing the overzealous soldier to the hilt.

In the *Quartet*, firmly anchored as it is in the wartime years, Amritsar seems no more than the fading memory of an already remote past; only dim echoes of it can be heard, often not immediately recognizable - just as the actual name of the scene of the massacre, the Jallianwallah (Bagh), pronounced by Mabel in her restless sleep sounds to an uncomprehending Barbie like a woman's name: Gillian Waller. And yet, for all that, thoughts of it, and the betrayal it epitomizes, are rarely far from the surface. They dictate behaviour, influence decisions and explain entire lives; lastly, they are prompted by history itself, which appears to provide for periodic repetitions of Amritsar. This, indeed, is one of Scott's main points, and one which will interest us later; suffice it for the moment to say that the *Quartet* both opens and ends with, as it were, reenactments of the Jallianwallah: the events surrounding the "Quit India" riots in *Jewel* and the apocalyptic scenes preceeding Partition in *Scorpion* being presented as variations on the theme. And against the background of these actual historical betrayals, we see in the *Quartet* the small unrecorded disloyalties of the individuals. We observe the sahiblog in 1942 praising the conduct of Reid and Merrick and working themselves into a lather about 'that Manners girl' letting the side down; and we glimpse them again five years later, crates and tea chests packed, firmly averting their gaze from the butchery that accompanies their precipitate departure. In the combination of the two, to paraphrase Max Beloff, Scott captures the end of paternalism. And it is Mabel Layton, more than anyone else in Pankot, who symbolizes its passing.

With her impeccable Imperial credentials, she stands for the finest in the old paternalist tradition of the Raj. Indeed, at times, she seems nothing less than the Raj personified. (At her funeral, for instance, the impression is certainly overwhelming that what is hurriedly being dumped in a pit is more than just the body of an old woman.) For Mabel then, as for the Raj as a whole, Amritsar provided a decisive turning point: after the slaughter in the Jallianwallah there could be no more talk of being in India for the good of the natives, nor could there be talk of loyalty and honour. As such, Scott implies, Amritsar was not a last bloody triumph of die-hard autocratic paternalism over enlightened liberalism (as Forster, perhaps, might have been tempted to see it), but the public admission of its intellectual and moral bankruptcy: force now being substituted for conviction, and aspirations, hopes and ideals, all sacrificed to the single-minded pursuit of power politics; far from being a last-ditch attempt to defend the imperial mission, it was in fact the uncerermonious abandonment of it.

For Mabel, therefore, events in and after the Jallianwallah present an existential problem. Having identified more closely with the British enterprise in India than many of her compatriots, her own life threatens to become compromised along with the Raj. The only way to avoid such contagion is to repudiate the Raj publicly. This she feels unable to do so and contents herself with breaking off all contact with the world around her. She becomes, as Weinbaum puts it, an "anachronism", cutting " . . . herself off from . . . the present" so as to " . . . preserve whatever may be left of past values". [21] (An act which finds its echo in an even more extreme form in the attitude of Major Tippit, historian by inclination as much as training and gaoler of M.A. Kasim at Fort Premanagar: preferring the Moghul period to the present day, he cuts himself - and his prisoner - off hermetically from the outside world and suggests that they might both look upon the fort "as a refuge from life's turmoils and disappointments". (*DS*, p.28) Even so, Mabel feels that some act of personal expiation must be carried out. The opportunity for it presents itself when money is being collected to compensate old General Dyer for the loss of his pension rights; Mabel not only refuses to contribute to the fund, she engages in distinctly macabre financial calculations: if there had been between 200 and 300 victims in the Jallianwallah Bagh, and if the money collected for the old general finally amounted to £ 26,000 , the "current price for a dead brown" was now effectively public knowledge; and, by sending a cheque for £100 to the Indian appeal for the victims of the massacre she tries to buy back her own lost innocence.

"After such knowledge, what forgiveness?" - Mahood quotes Eliot in connection with Lady Manner's discovery of the truth about Merrick and the extent of the Raj's guilt in the Kumar case; but the question seems just as appropriate here. [22] Besides, Lady Manners and Mabel Layton are drawn as very similar characters, to the extent that they become, at times, almost indistinguishable from each other.[23] Moreover, they have both stared into the same abyss: they have discovered the dark side of the Raj, and remain haunted by this knowledge to the end of their days. Indeed, the last glimpse Scott allows us of Mabel is scarcely comforting; it is the chilling image of her stroke-contorted body as Barbie sees it in the Pankot morgue: eyes, Mahood points out, as wide open in

---

[21] Weinbaum, *Aspiration*, p.174.
[22] cf. Mahood, p.254.
[23] For a discussion of Scott's characteristic technique of, as it were, merging characters see inter al. Rubin, p.136.

death as they had been in life to the hypocrisy around her. [24] And the mouth "... open too and from it a wail of pain and terror was emitting". (*TS*, p.229) A sight the narrator describes as Barbie's "... first authentic vision of what hell was like". (*TS*, p.230)

The image of the contorted body in the morgue provides final confirmation of Mabel's failure both to find personal happiness and to preserve untainted the old values of the Raj. If in the attempt she has become something of a monument, it is one of despair. Far from being a beneficent mother-and-father, as any upholder of the Raj should be, she is unable to help and comfort even those, like Sarah and Barbie, who are dearest to her. Unexpectedly perhaps, it is the veiled figure of Lady Manners, who - after Mabel's death - steps in to do precisely that, when she slips, ghostlike, into the Pankot church and comforts by her mere presence Barbie and Sarah in the hours of their greatest spiritual need. That she should be able to do so is, we feel, explained by the one major difference in her life and Mabel's. Lady Manners has found in her half-Indian niece Parvati an unexpected way out of the 'fort'. She has overcome the emotional barrenness and paralysing passivity of her kind, and has regained through the defiant adoption of that half-cast child her own individuality, following Scott's interpretation of the term. In the process she has also - incidentally so to speak - fulfilled the unkept promise of the Raj of becoming mother-and-father to the Indians, thus introducing at last genuine love into the 'imperial embrace'. (It is through a similarly selfless love for an Indian child that Barbie, another living embodiment of the Raj, is finally redeemed and rescued from despair.)

Scott's message here is clear: if one is to escape despair in the midst of a disintegrating world one must hold fast to one's own sense of identity and be prepared to stand up to all those who would deny it one. Lady Manners, of course, does precisely that, and does so even in the very citadel of Anglo-India - albeit with due deference to Edwardian decorum. Though she shuns the company of her countrymen, preferring instead to stay in the Indian half of Pankot, she nevertheless insists on formally announcing her presence by signing the visitor's book of the Area Commander and on 'signing out' at the end of her stay. But, as if to emphasize the difference between old-fashioned courtesy and true respect,

---

[24] cf. Mahood, p.249.

she permits herself a splendid gesture of disdain for the new breed of rulers when her car fails to give way on the narrow drive from Flagstaff House, nearly forcing into the ditch the oncoming staff car bearing the General's lady. And with this little scene of a funereal figure from an earlier age in black veil and solar topee, gliding past the speechless dignitaries in her hearselike motor car, it hardly needs her entry in the visitor's book - 'pour prendre congé' - to tell us that, in the words of Mahood, " . . . the best of the past has indeed taken its leave". [25]

And with it have gone all the old certainties that had sustained the Raj all along. This shows immediately in the incident of the disappearance of Mabel's old bearer Aziz. Driven by a wordless grief at his mistress's death, the loyal old retainer abandons Pankot for his native hills; Mildred promptly mistakes grief for guilty conscience, turns Rose Cottage upside down to make sure nothing is missing, and can only just be dissuaded from sending for the police. This, of course, is typical of Mildred, and serves no doubt, in part, to establish her character. But there is much more involved here. What makes the trivial incident noteworthy is that it touches at the idea of 'man-bap' - the relationship central to paternalist ethos of the Raj. If the masters feel they can no longer trust those who have eaten their salt, the very fabric of the Raj is at risk. British rule, after all, rested on the assumption of an unswerving loyalty of its twin pillars: an army of servants and an army of sepoys. Now the loyalties of both are in doubt. For at the time of Aziz's disappearance reports reach Pankot of large numbers of sepoys trading captivity in Japanese camps for the new uniforms of the enemy's so-called 'Indian National Army'. Pankot receives the news with studious unconcern, with disbelief even, but, when confirmed, it adds to the sense of being abandoned all around, emphasizing still further " . . . the grave shifting of the ground beneath one's feet as the layers of authoritarian support from above thinned and those of hostile spirits thickened." (*TS*, p.255) Life for the sahibs would never be the same again.

> Somewhere along the line doubt had entered. Even on a sunny day it lay upon the valley, an invisible mist, a barrier, to the clearer echoes of the conscience. A rifle

---

[25] Ibid., p.254.

shot would no longer whip through the air, slap hard against a hillside and bounce, leaving a penetrating and convincing smell of cordite, sharpening senses and stiffening the blood. It would go muffled, troubled, and its message would be garbled; and the eye would not dart, Khyber-trained, to the hillsides for the tell-tale flick of a mischievous robe, but shift uncomfortably, to observe the condition of the lines, for signs of mutinous movements on the parade grounds ...

(*TS*, p.256)

The evocation here of the Khyber, that supreme symbol of the romantic, Kiplingesque view of India as a place of high adventure and firm moral purpose has a twin objective; it highlights the extent of the loss of conviction, and it is a useful reminder to a reader who has spent much time in the genteel company of the Pankot mems of an aspect of the Raj which he was in danger of forgetting: namely the inordinate amount of the time and effort devoted to the defence, or rather the preparation for the defence of India. For as the years went on and the objectives of the Imperial mission proved ever more irreconcilable with the aspirations of the 'natives', the bewildered sahiblog increasingly cited the commitment to defend India as lending legitimacy to continued British rule until, at last, it became the only argument that could be put forward in the Raj's favour. In the *Quartet* this is faithfully reflected in both plot and structure: while *Jewel* had a firmly civilian setting (with the notable exception of Brigadier Reid's 'Memoirs'), the two middle books introduce us to the lives and preoccupations of Army families until, in *Spoils*, nearly all the protagonists are in khaki. And for Scott the supreme irony of history lay in the fact that even as Anglo-India was winning the fight on the battlegrounds of Burma, the structure of the Raj itself was disintegrating from within: while Teddy Bingham prepares to go to his fiery death reaffirming old values, his mother-in-law Mildred wrongfully suspects a loyal old servant of theft. Scott has a knack of capturing the fate of nations at the level of the fate of the individual. And it is at the level of the individual, he maintains, that things invariably go wrong.

The deciding factor for success or failure in life rests for Scott, as we have seen in the previous chapter, in recognizing individuality in oneself and in others. For Edwina Crane in *Jewel* this recognition had come late in life, too late in fact; Daphne Manners, on the other hand, had derived from it sufficient courage to risk breaking the colour bar; Hari Kumar had found in it a mental refuge from persecution and the only effective weapon against Merrick's perverse philosophy; in Pankot, Sarah Layton, too, discovers in it a haven while her sister, who is denied it, lapses into madness; and it helps Teddie Bingham, Lady Manners, and Mabel Layton to bear what would otherwise be unbearable. And it is Mabel who makes what is perhaps the most explicit remark on the importance of the individual in the entire *Quartet*. Ostensibly, she is talking about her beloved rose bushes:

> no flower is quite like another of the same species. On a single bush one is constantly surprised by the remarkable character shown by each individual rose. But from the house all one sees is a garden . . .
> (*TS*, p.199)

The true significance of these lines will not be lost on the reader as he recalls an earlier scene outside the Pankot Rifles mess: when Mabel had stopped to speak to the aged servant helping her out of her tonga; had alone taken notice of the man, had recognized something familiar about him, and even remembered his name. She had seen an individual, others merely an Indian; or to use the garden imagery, she had bent down to examine the character of the rose, and was rewarded by its unexpected fragrance, while her compatriots had been interested solely in its colour.

This denial of individuality to the subject race results, as Scott shows throughout the *Quartet*, in a corresponding loss of individuality among the rulers: when colour becomes the chief distinguishing mark, all other distinctions become blurred. Inevitably, this influences profoundly the way people see and conduct themselves. The British in India, as Sarah Layton reflects, seem to have lost their belief in themselves as ". . . people who each have something special to contribute. What we shall leave behind is what we have done as a group and not what we could have done as individuals which means it will be second-rate" (*DS*, p.139) Bereft of their own separate identities, they feel a desperate need to emphasize the traits shared by all so as to build up an alternative, corporate, or, dare one say it, tribal identity. Hence the obsession with group solidarity noted by every visitor from Foster onwards; hence also the strange readiness of the British in India to behave like cartoon characters, to project, as Scott puts it " . . . the cartoon image of the Sahib and his Memsahib . . ." [26] That there are strong underlying reasons favouring that process has already been shown in earlier chapters; what interests us here is the effect this has on the ethos of the Raj: permanently alienating the rulers from the ruled and from the land they rule. Lady Manners, striking up a friendship with the Chatterjees, Mabel and her garden, Daphne, who has learned ". . . if not to love, to need" India, and finally Sarah and Ahmed Kasim - these are the exceptions, while the people who created Pankot, their own absurd little bit of England, perched precariously on the edge of the Himalayas, are the rule. (*JC*, p.192)

What might have been achieved is hinted at in another garden image, again prompted by the sight of Mabel's garden, which the reader gradually realizes to be the sum total of her life, and, as such an image of, and comment on, the Raj: this time it is Barbie - like Edwina in *Jewel* increasingly clear-eyed and disillusioned - who realizes that

> . . . each bud was . . . a convoluted statement about . . . the austerity of the vegetable kingdom which was content with the rhythm of the seasons and did not aspire beyond the natural flow of its sap and the firm grip of its root. The bushes from which these roses came had been of English stock but they had travelled well and accepted what was offered. They had not wished to adapt the soil or put a veil across the heat of the sun or spread the rainfall more evenly throughout the year. They had flourished. 'You are now native roses', she said to them. 'Of the country. . . . We are only visitors. That has been our mistake. That is why God has not followed us here.'
>
> (*TS*, p.276)

---

[26] "The Raj", p.75.

The consequences of the British reluctance to accept India as it is are of a fundamental order. [27] And as Paul Beloff remarks, Scott's triumph in the *Quartet* is to capture and "... convey the full tragic significance of the combination between a sense of duty and a sense of permanent alienation from those to whom the duty was owed ... ."[28] This has obvious repercussions on the sense of duty itself, or rather on the interpretation of it. It enables someone like General Dyer - or in the *Quartet* Brigadier Reid - to fire indiscriminately at the very people whom he and his countrymen have pledged to guard and protect. [29] And Reid, it should be stressed, is not described as a monster (or an incarnation of evil like Merrick) - he is no more than a little thick-skinned and uncomprehending but quite capable of asking - bewildered and perturbed by the spectacle of inexorable decline - "How are we at fault?" or even "In what way have I personally failed?" (*JC*, p.309)

The rulers, then, as Christopher Hitchins points out, find they must learn to live with two great fears: "on the one hand ... the fear - in part a guilty fear - of treachery, mutiny and insurrection, of burning and pillage in which even one's servants cannot be trusted" and "on the other ... the fear of having to break the trust oneself; of casting aside the pretence of consent and ruling by force." [30] The consequences for the survival of the Raj are obvious. For whereas the outward structure of British rule

---

[27] Scott summarizes them in the above mentioned essay when he writes, "I cannot doubt that the sight, the smell, the experience of India, of Indian manners, attitudes, heightened the natural feeling of an Englishman had of being English to a point where it stopped being a feeling and became a physical and mental reassurance, a ready-made suit of armour." ("The Raj", p.76)

[28] Beloff, op.cit., p.66.
In "The Raj" Scott describes graphically the extent of this sense of alienation: "From these sanctuaries, constant sources of refreshment (the bungalow, the cantonment, the club), one could sally forth and deal with the alien world one was required to deal with; and those dealings were also heighteners of the consciousness, the necessity of being English; for here were corruption, bribery, false witness, a wild and irritating inablitity to get even the simplest thing right ... (i.e. the English way), endless argument, open emotionalism, revolting personal habits, noise, squalor, filth, religious bigotry, ... ghastly practices, fawning, flattery, terrible cheek and sullen insolence. What could be worse?" ("The Raj", p.76)

[29] Reid is of course modelled on Dyer. In fact, the similarities between the two men are specifically pointed to by the narrator: "There was a rather sordid little joke going round Mayapore Indians that if you spelt Reid backwards it came out sounding like Dyer ... ." (*TS*, p.75)

[30] Hitchins, *After the Raj*, p.188.

remains, for a while, unaffected, the ethos which helped to establish, guide and uphold it is not. What we see in the 'Pankot books', therefore, is not so much the relentless assault on the Raj from without as the sapping of its strength from within: the slackening of the imperial resolve once the spell is broken and the gradual loss of that "calm assurance of always being in the right" which Nehru had noted as a characteristic trait.[31]

Paradoxically, the immediate consequence of this unsettling inner vacuum is a desperate clinging to the traditions of the Raj. For while fewer and fewer still actively believe in an ideal and an ethos that look increasingly threadbare and unconvincing even to its upholders, the outward forms that once symbolized it continue to be adhered to in ritual observance; the imperial mystique has utterly vanished but the rites of Empire with their distinct religious overtones are still solemnized with scrupulous attention to detail, even though they have become devoid of all meaning. For

> ... the god had left the temple, no one knew when, or how, or why. What one was left with were the rites which had once propitiated, once been obligatory, but were now meaningless because the god was no longer there to receive them.
>
> (*TS*, p.255)

In what is one of the imaginative highlights of the entire *Quartet*, Scott further emphasizes this quasi-religious side of the Raj through his description of the regimental function at the officers' mess of the Pankot Rifles, the holiest of holies of the station. We see it through Barbie's eyes, the eyes of an outsider, which allows Scott to convey the full sense of wonder the place produces in the unitiated. (And it is hard not to ape Scott's language here, when he speaks of 'the temple', of 'acolytes' and so on.) Barbie leaves the main party there to go off in search of her friend Mabel, who had been prevailed upon to attend as guest of honour but steels away unobserved, midway through the proceedings; Barbie discovers her eventually in the inner sanctum of the mess, the room where

---

[31] Jawarharlal Nehru, *An Autobiography*. London 1936, p.425.

the battle honours and the regimental silver are kept: there she finds Mabel transfixed

> ... like someone in front of a reliquary. She had become untouchable, unapproachable, protected by the intense and chilling dignity of the room in which (Barbie felt) some kind of absolute certainty had been reached long ago and was now enshrined so perfectly and implacably that it demanded nothing that was not a whole and unquestioning acceptance of the truth on which it was based.
> (*TS,* p.192)

This "whole and unquestioning acceptance" of the rightness of the British presence in India is, of course, the road that had lead to Amritsar. Equally, it precludes all thought of change or adaption to altered circumstances. Not surprisingly, therefore, Mabel remarks that nothing in the mess has changed in all the forty years since she had first set foot in it, and adds, "'I can't even be angry. But someone ought to be.'" (*TS*, p.193)

In the interpretation of this scene critics have tended to concentrate on Anglo-India's ingrained reluctance to accept change. For them it ties in with what they see as Scott's general distrust of unadaptable conservatism, and inevitably, comparisons are attempted with Scott's guiding star Eliot (with, it must be said, startlingly divergent conclusions). [32] Such interpretations are perfectly valid, given Scott's insistence throughout the *Quartet* that the accumulated detritus of history tends to get in our way of dealing with the present; a view which finds graphic expression in Barbie's tonga accident where - in undisguised sympolism - the sheer weight of the personal mementos in her trunk brings about her destruction. It is equally valid to contrast in this context the attitude exhibited in the Pankot Rifles mess with Mabel's own, as manifested in the

---

[32] Jill Bonheim, for instance is moved to declare apodictically, "Anders als der konservative Eliot richtet Scott seinen Angriff nicht gegen den Verlust des Alten, sondern gegen den Versuch, an alten Formen festzuhalten." (Bonheim, op.cit., p.55) Francine Weinbaum, on the other hand, is reminded of the following lines, "There is, it seems to us. / At best only a limited value / In the knowledge derived from experiences. / For knowledge imposes a pattern, and falsifies ..." Surely, in view of the overriding passivity of the sahiblog as Scott describes it in the Pankot books, the obvious quotation reflecting Scott's views must be "And right action is freedom/ From past and future also."

seemingly ruthless trimming to which she annually subjects her beloved rose bushes. And yet to concentrate purely on these aspects is to miss a wider and more fundamental criticism implicit in the scene. And there is no need to speculate on hidden deeper meaning, since it is all spelt out in the text of the *Quartet* itself some sixty pages on, when Pankot reassesses Mabel's behaviour and concludes, rightly, that her unceremonious departure from the mess had been a stinging rebuke to the Raj and its upholders: " . . . a criticism of the foundations of the edifice, of the sense of duty which kept alive the senses of pride and loyalty and honour. (*TS*, p.255)

If the sense of duty is questionable since it takes no account of the feelings and wishes of the Indians (to whom, after all, it was owed), then the sense of pride is unjustified and only devalues the senses of loyalty and honour which are the more redeeming sides of the Raj. What Mabel's gesture at the mess amounts to, therefore, is nothing less than a questioning of the 'truths' on which British rule was based. Her silent exit is her way of asking, 'What are we in India for?' or even, 'By what right are we in India?' And whereas once the answers to those questions would have seemed obvious, so obvious, indeed, that no one would have thought of asking in the first place, the tattered flags and the gleaming silver in the mess are now the only answer the Raj can come up with. The past itself seems to have become the only legitimization for the present. (It is the same train of thought that leads Barbie to refuse to part with the accumulated junk of a lifetime because it seemed to provide the only hold on India.)

Mabel appart, it is indeed Barbie who is the first in Pankot to reconsider the question of the purpose of the Raj. Inevitably, given her background and personal history, she seeks to find the answer in Edwina Crane's old painting of "The Jewel in the Crown". But whereas once it had seemed to be an allegory of Britain triumphant it now suggests an unfulfilled hope. Amid all the pomp and obeissance, in the picture as much as in real life, something "got left out", which Barbie, " . . . not wishing to use that emotive word . . . ", calls "the unknown Indian." (*TS*, p.383) Quite what the "emotive word" is, is never explained; 'love' perhaps, or even 'God': in either case a word denoting something that is wholly absent from the imperial equation.

Barbie, after all, as Tedesco reminds us, had come out to India driven by genuine religious fervour; had come out on an errand of love to save Indian souls, only to find that the authorities temporal and spiritual actually discouraged her from doing so, suggesting instead that she should concentrate on spreading the alphabet. [33] While bowing to the superior wisdom of those in authority, she had nevertheless remained uneasy about the evident divorce of the British enterprise in India from that of disseminating, and living by the very Christian values to which the Raj publicly demonstrated its adherence each Sunday. At the end of her career, or rather at the end of her stay in Pankot, she, too, must realize that she has failed when it dawns on her "... that the unknown Indian was what her life in India had been about." (*TS*, p.69); it impresses itself upon her with the inescapable force of truth, when she leaves the ease and elegance of Rose Cottage and is confronted in the bazaar with "suffering, sweating, stinking, violent humanity." (*TS*, p.71) This, she now realizes, is "... the background against which you had to visualize Jesus working." (*TS*, p.71) And in a poignant Christmas message to her successor in the mission she asks if among the "... gifts [the] ... mission has brought to the children of India ... [there] has ever been the gift of love. I do not mean pity", she adds, "I do not mean compassion, I do not mean instruction nor do I mean devotion to the interests either of the child or the institution. I mean love." (*TS*, p.195) This, indeed, is the yardstick against which all British endeavour in India must be measured: what goes for Barbie's mission clearly goes for the Raj as a whole. And in both cases, the earnest pursuit of the cause of duty and loyalty and honour has pushed aside all thought of love. Barbie - like any other Anglo-Indian - had, in Tedesco's and Popham's pithy American phrase, "... served to feel good, not to do good." [34]

Ultimately, the point is not lost on Barbie. In a mood of stark recognition, of looking unflinchingly at the truth about her own life and the world around her, she is moved to say, speaking both as a missionary and simply as an Englishwoman in India, "I question my existence, my right to it. This is not I trust despair." (*TS*, p.195)

The reader is soon reassured that it is not: Scott allows Barbie a

---

[33] cf. Tedesco, p.132.
[34] Ibid.

brief period of fulfillment, though not before she is ejected by Mildred Layton from Rose Cottage and the ranks of the pukka sahiblog. And once unencumbered by considerations of her status as a memesahib and the need to keep up white prestige, she is free to befriend a tiny orphaned bazaar urchin: to show her love and to have it requited. And though there is illness and even madness yet for her to endure, hers is a good end amidst near-universal desperation and failure. "Do not pity her", we are in fact specifically told by the narrator, "She had had a good life," which, like "its scattered relics", is ultimately "blessed by . . . good intentions." (*TS*, p.391)

Tedesco and Popham are therefore quite right to point to the deeper significance of Barbie's life and to say that " . . . without ever preaching, Scott has established a causal link between a world without God and a world where love is scarce or even impossible." [35] In the immediate context of India, this spells doom for the British Raj. And with delicious irony Scott allows the unsuspecting Pankot rector to say as much, when, on the occasion of the solemn thanksgiving service for the victory over the Japanese in Assam, he has the Rev. Peplow choose a verse from the Prayer Book that proves unintentionally apposite: "'Except the Lord build the house: their labour is but lost that build it. Except the Lord guard the city: the watchman waketh but in vain.'" (*TS*, p.279)

This absence of God, as Tedesco and Popham point out, is further stressed by the deepening silence in the later volumes of the *Quartet*. They are undoubtedly right to remind us in this context of the first verses of St.John's Gospel ("In the beginning was the Word; the Word was with God and God was the Word.") and to conclude: "Without God there is no Word and silence takes on metaphysical dimensions as does Scott's light imagery", which, they suggest, is also founded, at least in part, in St.John's Gospel. [36] Thus Mabel, Barbie, and Lady Manners, who have all been vouchsafed a glimpse of hell - or if not hell, of a world from which God has turned His countenance - are all reduced to silence. [37] Mildred

---

[35] Tedesco, p.126.
[36] Ibid.
[37] The symbolism though is too multi-layered to allow for just one interpretation - the result of Scott's technique of using what Mahood calls "image clusters"; Lady Manner's silence in Pankot, for instance, also carries distinct echoes of Eliot's "Ash Wednesday": the veiled sister who "signed but spoke no word." (cf. Mahood, p.254.)

Layton, too, maintains a kind of silence - an emotional silence, as it were - though for a different reason: she is specifically identified with the forces of evil, when her image and that of Merrick merge in Barbie's vision and are recognized by her as faces of the devil. (On Merrick, of course, is imposed the most complete silence of all: alone among the protagonists, he is denied a voice of his own; is never permitted to address narrator and reader directly, but is only seen through the recollections of the other participants in Scott's Anglo-Indian drama.) Lastly, there is the title of the third book of the *Quartet* itself: *The Towers of Silence*, which, in the opinion of most critics, refers not only to the towers in the Parsee temples but also, metaphorically, to the unapproachable old women of Pankot who stand silent in their recognition of the truth and their resulting despair, towering over those who do not, or will not, comprehend. [38]

There is, it seems to me, however, additional reason for, and added meaning in, this oppressive silence of so many of the major characters; especially if we bear in mind that this silence is most complete in those, like Lady Manners, old Mabel Layton, or Barbie Batchelor, who represent the best of the old Raj. And this has something to do with language itself. For in a world dominated by cant, where the meaning of words like 'duty', 'loyalty', 'honour' etc. has been systematically perverted, speech itself must become suspect and silence the only alternative to being tainted oneself by the corruption of language. The transformation of Barbie Batchelor from garrulous memsahib to the gaunt figure in the Ranpur asylum who lives as if under vow of silence provides a striking illustration of the point. To Barbie words seem so corrupted that they should be left, like the dead of the Parsees, to the vultures glimpsed from her cell. And at the end of her life she has indeed cleansed herself by emptying herself of language, though not, significantly, of memory: "She remembered a great deal. But was unable to say what it was. The birds had picked the words clean." (*TS*, p.391) In this questioning of language the *Quartet* reveals itself, contrary to what some of the critics may say, very much a child of our century. [39]

---

[38] cf. inter al. Parry, p.360.
[39] cf. notably Beretz who regards this as the *Quartet*'s major weekness.
Where Scott shows himself to be less in tune with the spirit of the century, however, is in the way he reacts to this questioning of language. For while he imposes

It is surely no coincidence that the two archvillains of the *Quartet*, Merrick and his alter ego Mildred Layton, are plagued by no such doubts, but are, if anything, crafty manipulators of language. Merrick, certainly, shows himself highly gifted in swaying people through the power of his speech and Mildred is renowned in Pankot for the sting of her tongue. And it squares with Tedesco's and Popham's interpretation of the meaning of silence that these two supreme manipulators of language and people should be clearly identified as exponents of evil.

If such an equation of the main antagonists with the devil may perhaps sound a trifle melodramatic out of context, it seems entirely convincing within the world of these novels - and particularly in *The Towers of Silence*, laden as it is with symbols, allegories and allusions. Nor is this, as Benita Parry thinks it is, a crafty way to let the Raj off the hook by attempting to explain away the dark chapters of British rule in India as the work of demoniacal madmen.[40] On the contrary, the Raj itself is on trial with Mildred and Merrick; for Barbie's devil, after all, " . . . was not a daemon but a fallen angel and his hell no place of fire and brimstone but an image of lost heaven."(*TS*, p.88)

Mildred, indeed, is the one person in Pankot described as existing in a kind of living hell, offering despair, as Barbie says of the devil, " . . . as boundlessly as God offered love." (*TS*, p.89) Unable even to love her own daughters, she remains the proudest of the 'towers of silence'; and - alone in the midst of the general uncertainty - continues to display that complete self-assurance which had been the hallmark of the true memsahib of old: the unshakeable conviction " . . . that she was right, would

---

silence on his characters in a manner reminiscent of Eliot's lines from "The Hollow Men", ("We grope together/ And avoid speech"), he imposes no similar constraints upon himself as a novelist. This robustly old-fashioned attitude is, of course, none too popular with a generation of critics raised in the rarified atmosphere of 'sprachzweifel', and accustomed to the breathtaking linguistical acrobatics of Joyce or Beckett. Compared to the dazzling exploits of these 'artistes' of the novel, Scott's prose must indeed seem stolid and unexciting: the equipment for his raids on the inarticulate disappointingly conventional. But he felt presumably that, when all is said and done, this 'decaying equipment' is still the best we have, and are likely ever to get. So that, for the novelist, there is nothing for it but to get on with his job, which is that of the production of prose; and prose, as Iris Murdoch has reminded us more than once, is " . . . for explanation and exposition, . . . is essentially didactic, documentary, informative . . . [and] ideally transparent." (Iris Murdoch, "Against Dryness: A Polemical Sketch". In: Malcolm Bradbury (ed.), *The Novel Today: Contemporary Writers on Modern Fiction* . Manchester 1977, p.28.)
[40] cf. Parry, op.cit. p.364.

always do right and therefore had nothing to explain even when not done right by, except to people who did not understand this and to such people an explanation was never owing." (*TS*, p.34) It is this, more than anything else, which marks Mildred as one of the chief "antagonists" in the *Quartet*, following Weinbaum's central distinction. As a fully-fledged antagonist, Mildred is rather more than just an unlikeable character; she is someone who swims against the tide of history and does not " ... see through the illusion" in Swinden's use of term, but is " ... conscious mainly of all ... [she has] been sacrificing for India and how poorly she has [been] repaid .... " [41]

Mildred may fail to recognize the truth about the sahiblog's existence in India but this is not to say that she is under any illusions about her own fate and that of her kind; on the contrary, she is perfectly aware that " ... the game that had never been a game was very likely up." (*TS*, p.38) Unlike most of her fellow-Anglo-Indians, however, she refuses to allow this awareness to influence her life unduly or let it weaken her resolve. In fact she feels that suspicions she may entertain about the future do not in any way " ... countermand her duty to the existing order of things if she continued to believe in it." (*TS*, p.38) Her demonstrative observation of 'duty', however, fails to produce the intended effect. She may succeed through her actions to remind people of what lives had been like in the past when they were still ruled by seemingly immutable certainties, but she cannot bring that past back to life any more than can her son-in-law with his impassioned stand in the jungle. She may ride out into the hills to 'comfort' the womenfolk of the Pankot Rifles, whose husbands are, like her own, prisoners of the Germans, but this painstaking observation of past behaviour is now no more than an empty gesture, " ... a charade which neither she nor the women she comforted believed in for a moment." (*TS*, p.35) Nor did anyone else in Pankot believe in it, for that matter. Like Teddie Bingham's equally anachronistic gesture in Assam, it merely emphasizes the extent of the loss of confidence that had already taken place.

Yet for all the superficial similarity, these two acts are fundamentally different. Teddie's is born of true conviction. He still believes in the values of the past and feels that the traditional ties of loyalty still bind

---

[41] Weinbaum, p.108.

him firmly to his men - to the extent that it is nothing less than his duty to go after those who have been led astray and bring them back into the fold. His stand in the jungle, therefore, is a supremely emotional act and in marked contrast to the cool professionalism displayed by Merrick. Mildred, like Merrick, has no such convictions. She is one of those Britons to whom, in D.C. White's phrase, the Indians always appeared "extraneous to the business of living and working" in India. (*JC*, p.314) She may preserve the outward shell of the paternalist tradition, but inside she is hollow, in the same way that her alter ego Merrick is. [42]

Not surprisingly, Mildred achieves the exact opposite of what she sets out to do. Far from reaffirming old certainties and reasserting her claim to a vanishing world, she only succeeds in exposing that world's questionable sides: namely its inherent double standards. Her excursion into the hills merely highlights the fundamental presumption of the imperial enterprise: for ". . . to offer matriarchal wisdom to women older and wiser than [oneself] . . . , that", as Barbie notes, "was an arrogance . . . ". (*TS*, p.236) Mildred's attempt to strip 'Rose Cottage' of what she considers to be the tainting memories of Mabel proves similarly counter-productive: "The aim of restoring its original appearance", had been " . . . to create a setting that would speak for itself and also for . . . her family's claim on history through a long connection." (*DVS*, p.134) The values she had meant to convey were those of "service, sacrifice, integrity." (*DVS*, p.134) What she was unaware of, however, is that the bungalow does, in fact, predate these values by several decades, having been built in Company days by one of the original Nabobs who had came to India not to serve but to amass a great fortune. And so, "unwittingly she had exposed the opposites of those words: self-interest, even corruption." (*DVS*, p.135) This, of course, is the truth about the Raj: "We were in India for what we could get out of it", as D.C. White puts it. (*JC*, p.317) The paternalist ethos, for all the undoubted sincerity of its upholders, had only been a façade disguising the less palatable reasons for British rule. Now that it had worn away, the original and true foundations of Britain's Indian Empire were surfacing once again.

---

[42] The similarities between Merrick and Eliot's "Hollow Men", and, indeed, the original 'hollow man', Conrad's Mr Kurtz, are well-established; cf. notably Bonheim, pp.51-4.

The restored bungalow, then, like the image of the gleaming silver in the regimental mess of the Pankot Rifles, serves to reveal "the material interests behind the self-deception",as Mahood puts it. [43] At the same time, it marks a genuine breakdown of morale and loss of standards. To quote Mahood again, "now that the Anglo-Indians having nothing to live by, now that their self-image has finally failed them, the way is open to pure rapine." [44] It is, after all, a telling coincidence that while Mildred is busy accusing loyal old servants of imaginary thefts, hounding Barbie out of Rose Cottage and trying to deprive her of the annuity left her by Mabel, her brother-in-law in Calcutta should be engaged in the recruiting of a new generation of rulers from the swollen ranks of British soldiers in transit to the Far Eastern theatre of war. This - in the absence of all ideals - he attempts to do by dangling before blitz-deprived young men the tempting prospect of an opulent life-style in the East: "Among them, surely were a few who would get the call, see the vision, understand the hard realities of imperial service and feel the urge to match themselves to them?" (*DS*, p.360) It is the nadir both of Anglo-Indian morale and morality.

Scott's account of the decline of paternalism is almost complete and so is the chronicle of Pankot: from the splendid uprightness of Mabel Layton and Lady Manners to what Tedesco calls the "smokescreen of moral respectability" of Mildred Layton, and from the high idealism of Mildred's first son-in-law Teddie to the perversity of her second son-in-law Merrick. [45] What remains is the description of the bitter end, both on the actual historical level of the demission of power and, on a personal level, of the fates of the last generation of Anglo-Indians: Sarah and Susan Layton.

Sarah, in fact, emerges as the central figure of the later books acting, in the words of Tedesco and Popham, "as a moral guide much like Dante's Virgil". [46] As such, she guides the reader not only through all the nooks and crannies of Scott's 'Inferno' in the hills, she is also present during most of the crises in the plains, which form the bulk of the

---

[43] Mahood, p.249.
[44] Ibid.
[45] Tedesco, p.256.
[46] Ibid., p.57.

material in *A Division of the Spoils*. Indeed, she is the only member of the Pankot set we regularly meet outside the self-contained little world of the station: proof that here is one prisoner who has discovered a secret passageway out of the fort, and intends to make use of her discovery when the moment comes. As a potential survivor, therefore, amid the near-universal wreckage of her generation she is of particular interest to Scott: marooned on an island, she appears to be " ... the only one alive who still wanted to be rescued." (*DS*, p.140)

Of all the characters in the *Quartet* Sarah Layton is perhaps the closest to Scott's heart. His "special tenderness", as Michael Wood observes, always " ... goes to the imprisoned awareness, to taut, private, intelligent and lonely people who know the word or the gesture that would release them, ... , but cannot say it or cannot make it." [47] Sarah Layton is undoubtedly of that kind. Like the lace butterflies of her christening gown, she strains to be free and is yet firmly caught in the meshes of her world.

Steeped in the traditions of the Raj and imbued with its ideals, she can conceive of nothing other for herself than a life in India: anything else is quite literally unimaginable. Besides, like the best of the sahiblog, she feels she still has a duty to discharge: though it is not, she is certain, the traditional one for young mems of lending moral and emotional support to their menfolk, and providing the restfulness of a home for them, in which to recover from their arduous task of ruling India, nor the concomitant one of bearing (male) children so as to safeguard the continuation of the race of sahibs and their way of life. Sarah is realistic enough to realize that nothing could assure that aim; that Anglo-India has in fact reached the end of the road. But she does feel duty-bound to try to keep intact the world of her own immediate family against the day of her father's return. She therefore presents to the world the outward appearance of a sterling young memsahib, a true pillar of the Raj, equally at ease in her sergeant's uniform at the 'daftar' as in a cocktail dress at the club, while becoming at the same time - and unbeknownst to her peers - an almost dispassionately objective observer of the world around her. As such, she is able to make some of the most incisive and memorable comments on Anglo-India in the entire *Quartet*: her " ... deep sense

---

[47] Michael Wood, "The Days of the Scorpion". *The Times*, 7 September 1968.

of inherited identity" giving her, as Swinden remarks, a ". . . hold on her personality" strong enough to allow her " . . . to behave in an unshowily independent way." [48]

It is significant that Sarah follows in effect the example of old Mabel Layton who had ruthlesnessly pruned the bushes in her garden so that new buds might gain strength; in a sense Sarah echoes this course when she sets about pruning her own existence of the outdated relics of the past, the accumulated detritus of her family's two centuries-old connection with India that clutters and burdens down her life and threatens to undo her as surely as the weighty trunk had undone Barbie.

Sarah's rejection of her inheritance - bit by bit, item for item - requires all the more courage since there is nothing, as Tedesco notes, to put in its place. [49] Yet reject it she must if she is to survive in the world after the Raj, and, more immediately, if she is to hold on to her own personal identity. For, as Swinden observes, " . . . Sarah's sense of her own reality depends on her awareness of the unreality of the world the British have built around themselves." [50] Sarah consciously sheds what Tedesco calls the "protective shell" of the sahiblog and emerges strengthened from it. [51] Her sister takes the opposite course, submerging her own identity in the collective one of the 'tribe' in a desperate attempt to belong and to invest her own life with meaning. But by 1942 this is a doomed course, even in the short-term: the "carapace" - the word is Scott's - that surrounded Anglo-India has worn too thin to provide an effective shield against the heat of the hostile world outside.

Susan's eventual recognition of this fact finds its graphic expression in the eponymous scene of *The Day of the Scorpion*, where she stages a gruesome reenactment of the burning of scorpions of her childhood with her own baby boy being substituted for the scorpion. It is the act of a deranged mother, certainly; but there is method, or at any rate, logic in her madness: for when the heat of the surrounding circle of flames gets too great for the scorpion, it arches backward and appears to sting itself to death; the creature, then, appears to hasten the inevitable,

---

[48] Swinden, p.74.
[49] Tedesco, p.72.
[50] Swinden, p.75.
[51] Tedesco, p.71.

choosing to die by its own hand, as it were, and the Indians have traditionally respected it for its apparent courage; but this is not the message Susan wishes to convey. For she is perfectly aware that the scorpion does not actually sting itself to death, that the arching is merely a reflex produced by the heat. Given this knowledge, and the fact that Susan had not actually doused the child with kerosene but had merely placed him in a symbolic ring of fire - on a wet lawn, moreover, where he would be perfectly safe - , there emerges a clear message from Susan's gesture: it amounted, as Pankot realizes, to a "statement about her own life" in India and everybody else's:

> ... a statement which reduced you ... to the size of an insect; an insect entirely surrounded by the destructive element, so that twist, turn, attack, or defend yourself as you might you were doomed; not by the force ranged against you but by the terrible inadequacy of your own armour. And if for armour you read conduct, ideas, principles, the code by which you lived, then the sense to be read into Susan's otherwise meaningless little charade was to say the least of it thought-provoking.
> (*TS*, p.289)

The statement reducing mankind to the size of insects is not Susan's alone; for if she compares her own life to that of a scorpion, Sarah's is repeatedly likened to the lace butterflies struggling to break free from the meshes of her christening shawl. The implications of such a view of humanity for the paternalist outlook of the Raj is clear: for while paternalism shared with enlightened liberalism the conviction that man is master of all he surveys, Scott consistently suggests otherwise in the *Quartet:* from the fate of Daphne's and Hari's love in *Jewel* to the murder of Ahmed Kasim in *Spoils*, from the high idealism of people like District Commissioner White to the grim reality of Partition, from Count Bronowsky's careful plans for the future of his prince's dominion to the image of a Mirat in flames, the suggestion is that forces are at work, larger than man and inimical to his designs, devices and desires. It is this tragic awareness informing Scott's writing that raises the *Quartet* above the level of purely historical fiction to one touching at what are universal truths.

There is, as no critic can fail to spot, more than just an echo of Conrad in Scott's analysis of Susan's act; and since Scott is too conscientious a novelist to use such echoes without some very good reason, we should remind ourselves of the context of the famous line from *Lord Jim*. Indeed, Scott's meaning becomes instantly clear once we remember that Conrad's original "destructive element" - water - served him as a metaphor for life; applied to Pankot, we see Susan shrinking back from the "destructive element" and promptly getting drowned as Conrad suggested one would, while Sarah plunges in with a will and is buoyed up by it. Here, too, the destructive element is life itself, and it is destructive chiefly because it threatens to engulf the Raj. Or, to look at the same thing from the other perspective, the sham world of the sahibs gets into the way of living life.

Sarah is alive to this aspect of British rule from the day of her return to India after her schooling in England: then, she is instantly struck by a feeling of " . . . entering a region of almost childish presumptions - as if everything we are surrounded by is the background for a game." (*DS*, p.68) And if she is reluctant to enter into the spirit of the game, it is not just because of an awareness that presently " . . . someone will come along and tell us to put our toys away," but because of growing realization of the pernicious effect the game has on the players. (*DS*, p.68) For anybody entering into it can no longer behave naturally but is compelled to perform what Orwell in *Burmese Days* had called the "danse du pukka sahib". And just as Orwell had suggested, the ludicrous theatricality of a life spent in defence of the Raj tends to falsify emotions and feeling, especially between men and women. Scott echoes this when he has Sarah reflecting on the curiously surreal attitude of the Anglo-Indian male to the female of the species:

> They approached you first . . . as if you were a member of a species that had to be protected, although from what was not exactly clear if you ruled out extinction: it seemed to be enough that the idea of a collective responsibility for you should be demonstrated, without regard to any actual or likely threat to your welfare. In circumstances where no

> threat seemed to exist the behaviour of the men
> aroused your suspicion that perhaps it did after all but
> in a way men alone had the talent for understanding;
> so you became aware of the need to be grateful to
> them for the constant proof they offered of being
> ready to defend you, if only from yourself.
>
> (*DS,* p.143)

Sarah feels neither the need nor the inclination to be defended from herself; and so proves quite impervious to the blandishments of the young males of her tribe (though not, significantly enough, indifferent to the attentions paid to her by outsiders): Indeed she is deeply suspicious of the true motives of the young sahibs who show an interest in her; suspicious not in the usual sense, but of the attitude underlying their approaches. Do they, she cannot help wondering, regard her as a desirable individual or as an incarnation of an ideal? After all, they tend to approach her in what she calls a "representative frame of mind": "'Well here I am, white, male and pure-bred English, and here you are, pure-bred English, white and female, we ought to be doing something about it.'" (*DS,* p.143) She is understandably disinclined to take such hints - rejecting, for instance, the advances of Teddie Bingham, who, she intuits, merely regards her as the next logical step in his pre-planned life - a mode of existence Sarah describes elsewhere as "a received life". (*DVS,* p.592) Teddie, of course, is entirely unruffled by her rejection and promptly goes on to confirm Sarah's suspicions by transferring his affections - within the hour - to her sister Susan. (Yet curiously enough, he goes on to surprise Sarah by discovering in married life a blissful experience of individuality he had never actively sought, had never, perhaps, even imagined conceivable; which, ironically enough, Susan is unable to share with him, receiving his proofs of love in the same "representative frame of mind" Sarah so abhors.)

And here we touch at another theme that runs through the *Quartet* like a leitmotif, one we have already encountered in Maypore: the singular inability of so many of the major and minor actors in Scott's Anglo-Indian drama to develop and sustain successful loving relationships. It ranges from the extraordinary number of spinsters or childless widows (Edwina Crane, Mabel Layton, Barbie Batchelor, and the bevvies of barren memsahibs of Pankot) to Susan Layton, who remains unresponsive both as wife and mother; from Sarah herself, who undergoes without a word of protest the abortion her mother orders her to have, to the disastrous marriage of her friend and sometime-admirer Nigel Rowan, and the emotional cowardice of Brigadier Reid, who grasps eagerly at a proffered command as a convenient excuse to get away from his dying wife and yet manages to convince himself that this is what she would want him to do. This widespread sterility, this emotional and biological barrenness makes for a "pattern of more extensive significance", as Benita Perry points out. [52] The frequent recourse to the sex motif, then, is not a case of the author pandering to popular taste, or of lightly dabbing his fingers in the murky waters of the Freudian subconscious.

Finally sexuality itself comes to the fore, and, as David Rubin remarks, " . . . sexual excess, deviation, and aberration [emerge] as the near-inevitable correlative of the Imperial process;" for, he adds, "the greed and the moral and ethical blindness that . . . sustain colonialism in the sphere of public action are accompanied by a parallel degeneration in the private sphere, where sexual problems, violence and confusion reveal and symbolize the same moral failures." [53] Mildred's and Kevin Coley's "joyless coupling" (*TS*, p.301), which fills Barbie who had chanced unsuspecting upon them with horror because of the " . . . instantaneous impression of the absence of love and tenderness" is as much an expression of " . . . the world outside the subterranean room . . . dying . . . " as its exact counterpart in a similarly subterranean room in the Mayapore jail, where Ronald Merrick's dark compulsions are acted out. (*TS*, p.300) Together they amount to a statement about the Raj which speaks louder than any direct condemnation might, however long and eloquent.

This, then, is the world from which Sarah must break free. She begins the process with a half-understood gesture at Mirat; while riding out with the Nawab's young kinsman, Ahmed Kasim, she is suddenly reminded of Daphne Manners and Hari Kumar. And at that moment of trying to imagine what it might be like to love an Indian, Daphne

---

[52] Parry, p.361.
cf. also Boyer, p.69 .
[53] Rubin, pp.74-5.

becomes incomprehensible to Sarah, and her own half-hearted attempt "... to confront imaginable but infinitely remote possibilities of profound contentment" remains incomplete. (*DS*, p.439) When the curtain falls, we leave her, in Swinden's phrase, "... with the break half completed, and the man to whom ... she might have turned in order to complete it, slaughtered without sense or reason in the birth-pangs of the new India." [54]

The last we see of her is Sarah kneeling at a water-tap on a station platform decked out end to end with the bodies of dead or dying Indians, the victims of one of the murderous sectarian attacks that darkened the final days of British rule. And, for once, a bloody scene is not reported but presented in grim detail; reality has overtaken the charade and has finally caught up with the Anglo-Indians. This bloodbath is the crowning failure of the Raj, the "total and unforgiveable disaster" Lady Manners had predicted years earlier. (*DS*, p.305) And Sarah, looking up from the brass jugs she was filling with water to wet the lips of the wounded and dying, taking in the incontrovertible evidence around her of the failure of her countrymen, who would have been mother and father to those dying at her feet, recognizes the uselessness of her own "brave little memsahib act." (*DVS*, p.592)

---

[54] Swinden, p.93.

5. 'The Situation': Truth and the *Quartet*

Burrowing one's way through the splendid bulk of the *Quartet*, one cannot fail to be impressed by the range and multiplicity of topics broached in the course of what one first took to be no more than a novelist's view of the final years of the British Raj. So rich is Scott's cosmos, so crammed full with incident, description, reflection and analysis, that it defies easy labelling and makes the critic despair in his habitual attempt at neat definition. Not that this has actually prevented many critics from having a crack at it regardless, it being - to paraphrase Susan Howe's 'mot' about librarians - their nature, and indeed their profession, to define what resists such a tidy process with all its might. The results of such endeavours have been many and varied but rarely neat. What one tends to end up with is more often than not a mere enumeration of disparate items, a list frequently incoherent and almost inevitably incomplete. Francine Weinbaum's gallant attempt to impose an order essentially extraneous to Scott's tetralogy may serve as an illustration of these problems: she describes the *Quartet* as a series of "journeys" - into the historical past, in search of moral responsibility, "into the mind", and so on; in all, she counts five of them, or rather, revealingly, "at least five" of them.[1] Patrick Swinden on the other hand, perhaps the most perceptive of Scott's critics, eschewes such a course. He prefers to concentrate instead on the question of 'truth', which he regards as a central concern of the *Quartet*.

All great literature, it used to be said, is concerned with truth. Cynical voices might therefore be forgiven for suggesting that talk of it here smacks of expediency: that, having failed to pigeonhole the *Quartet*, the critic, ever resourceful and undismayed, is ready to fall back on platitudes and predictable stocks-in-trade. But Swinden's observations - however suspiciously convenient they may seem - really do go to the heart of the matter. This can readily be seen by reconsidering the 'lists' of other critics in the light of his suggestions: for then a discernible pattern begins to emerge, revealing in Weinbaum's list, for instance, unexpected but definite links between most of the 'journeys'. One way of describing

---

[1] Weinbaum, *Aspiration*, p.2.

the *Quartet* therefore - and it seems as good a way as any - is to call it a 'quest for truth'.

This quest is conducted by the narrator through several related investigations (some of which correspond to Weinbaum's 'journeys'). There is first - and doubtless for many readers foremost - an investigation to establish the truth about the chain of events in Mayapore in August 1942, which at times seems almost like a conventional whodunit. However, these central incidents cannot be wholly divorced from events outside Mayapore, and the scope of the narrator's original inquiry must therefore be broadened to examine the wider context; in other words, it must grapple with the thorny issue of historical truth. These two principal investigations lead, incidentally so to speak, to reflections on the truth about human nature and our concept of morality as the founts of individual and collective behaviour; and out of all these grows the ultimate question as to the nature of truth itself.

The heading for this chapter - 'The Situation' - suggested itself because Scott uses it himself in the third book for a key-section in which this complex of questions is crystallized. Central to both that scene in *Towers* and to what we are discussing here is the shadowy figure of Ronald Merrick. Inevitably, then, this is also very much a chapter about Merrick.

Merrick, as we have observed before, is unique among the protagonists in being denied a voice of his own. We hear him speak, to be sure, and are witness to his deeds (which, of course, speak louder than his words), but it is always through the eyes and ears of other characters that we must seek to comprehend him. Yet for all that, he is at the very centre of the plot, and though there clearly is no such thing as a 'central character' in the *Quartet*, he is perhaps the closest approximation to one: being present in the minds and thoughts of the other characters even when he himself is off-stage, as it were. In a manner of speaking, then, the *Quartet* is 'about' him - at least in the way that *Othello*, let us say, is 'about' Iago or the *Duchess of Malfi* is 'about' two scheming brothers. Nor are these comparisons entirely flippant; for Merrick is, like Iago, a villain in the grand tradition - Allen Boyer even calls him "one of literature's most formidable villains" - and, like Webster's dark plotters, he is not just an individual driven by envy and ambition but represents demonstrably a political and social system at the same time. [2] By fusing these two strands of villainy, so to speak, Scott has created a character who, as Boyer points out, "... fits [both] the romantic vision of the British colonial officer, the masterful player of the Great Game, ... [and] the anti-colonialist's view of the colonial administrator", Daphne Manners's unfeeling "white robot" of the night of the Bibighar. [3] In both respects Merrick's identification with British rule in India is convincing and well-established throughout the *Quartet*. And Boyer is right to remind us in this context of the significance of Merrick's Christian name, and of Guy Perron's explicit recognition of it: "... Ronald, like Rex, is cognate with Raj." [4]

In a sense, then, we already have here the answers to the first two of our questions. For if Merrick's personal responsibility for what happened to Hari Kumar was never really in doubt, the brief excursion into the etymology of the name 'Ronald' provides an unambiguous authorial answer to the second question: that of the historical relevance of the man Merrick; an answer, moreover, which should silence those critical voices who have suggested that Scott was effectively letting the Raj off the hook "because of who and what Merrick is ... ". [5] But in order to understand the reasons for such critical reservations, let us examine more closely the character of the man: a rewarding task, since

---

[2] Allen Boyer, "Love, Sex, and History in the 'The Raj Quartet'". *Modern Language Quarterly* 46 (1) 1985, p.73.
[3] Ibid.
[4] Ibid, p.74.
[5] Parry, op.cit., p.364.
Parry adds "... Scott's critique of the imperial relationship is subtly trimmed and the claims of the old tradition [are] subtly reaffirmed". This leads her to accuse him of harbouring "deeply ambiguous attitudes to the Raj" and of suffering from "double vision". (p.367) Scott was familiar with Parry's article - one of the earliest critical reactions to the completed *Quartet* - and found it intensely irritating. He referred to it, in a letter to his American agent, as "much too intellectual for me to understand" and added, in a letter on the same theme to Ms Weinbaum, that the bits he thought he did understand "immediately seem cancelled out by the next paragraph". (Letters to Dorothy Olding and Francine Weinbaum 5 November 1975, quoted by Moore, p.130) Hearing Parry refer to the *Quartet* as "... a muted clebration of a concept rather than a critique of reality" (p.359), and then see her praise its author for an "unspairing critique of the British-Indian interaction" a few pages on (p.367), it is hard indeed not to share Scott's sense of bewilderment.

he is, in Swinden's words, "one of the most fully realised characters in contemporary fiction". [6]

It is indeed not hard to see why misgivings should have been voiced about an unqualified equation of Merrick and the Raj. Merrick, after all, is very much an outsider: a grammar school boy in a solidly public school world, a man without 'family' or 'history' in a community where background is everything, and, above all, a man condemned to remain an outsider on account of what with decorous circumlocution some critics prefer to call his "sexual maladjustment". [7] His is an extreme case, certainly, but extreme cases can sometimes throw into relief what is inherent in a situation. (And already we find ourselves using this word which in connection with Merrick is pregnant with meaning.)

Let us, then, look more closely at "the situation" - the relationship between Merrick and Kumar in other words - and begin by recapitulating what we have already established about it earlier: briefly, it is that of tormentor and victim. Kumar, as we have seen, had been a victim of the Raj even before he first crossed Merrick's path. His uncompleted education, which had merely made him unfit for life in a traditional 'native' environment without offering him access to the ranks of the ruling elite, his complete deracination, which had cut him off even from his family, on whose financial support he yet had to rely in the absence of career openings, all this guaranteed him a life of misery. But he was not just a victim of circumstance, he was, above all, a victim of Ronald Merrick - not at all the same thing; and for him to become that, for Merrick to devote himself single-mindedly to his persecution, there had to be something in him to which Merrick could not fail to respond. It is not, after all, as though he had been picked at random: he was, as Guy Perron insists, "chosen" to be a victim. (*DVS*, p.206) The reasons for this are to be found as much in the two men's differing social background as they are in Merrick's perhaps more obvious "sexual maladjustment". From the moment he first set eyes on a bare-chested Kumar, washing off a hangover in Sister Ludmila's compound, Merrick was of course - like the memsahibs of Pankot - physically attracted to the young man. It was an attraction he was aware of, but could not admit to - not even, or least of all, to himself. If any-

---

[6] Swinden, p.91.
[7] The expression is Allen Boyer's. (cf, p.73)

thing, he resented the feeling and was ready to punish the man who had inspired it: love being out of the question and indifference impossible, hate suggested itself readily enough.

Ever since Forster first gave it dramatic expression in *Passage*, we have come to associate this kind of behaviour with repressed spinsters exposed to the sultry atmosphere of tropical climes and have learnt to accept it as the most likely reason for the mysterious metamorphosis in the East of level-headed Englishwomen into obsessive memsahibs. The acceptance of Forster's views has been so universal that is now hard to imagine how shockingly Lawrentian it must all have sounded to his readers in the twenties. What had been unmentionable, perhaps even unimaginable, has since become a commonplace, and the famous scene in the Marabar Caves is now almost too familiar to produce in us that sudden jolt of recognition of the forces at work in the Anglo-Indian psyche which early readers of *Passage* must have experienced. That Scott found Forster's suggestions persuasive enough and tallying with his own observations we may infer both from Daphne Manners's own diary entires and from Sister Ludmila's remarks on the subject of Englishwomen in India; but he evidently decided that their words alone would not carry sufficient weight. What was necessary was to create in the contemporary reader the same sense of shock and disbelief that Forster had produced fifty years earlier. And this could only be done by taking the issue out of its too-familiar context and having a *man* behave irrationally. 'The situation' - the subterranean scene in *Towers* where Merrick's complex feelings towards Kumar are finally made manifest - is therefore materially related to the events in the Marabar Caves: forcing us, as these had done, to recognize the extent to which the murky world of the subconscious could undermine the rationality of the Westerner and dictate his behaviour in the East. [8] And in this way Merrick's extreme and profoundly unrepresentative activities do indeed throw added light on the relationship between rulers and ruled.

To concentrate on the extremity of events in Mayapore and to argue, as at least one early reviewer did, that Merrick's obsessive

---

[8] It may be noted that in both cases the setting - deep inside a mountain/ in the nether world of Kumar's prison - is perhaps itself suggestive of those darker recesses in the human mind.

behaviour towards Kumar owed something to the fact that both men were wooing the same woman and that Merrick saw his Indian rival succeed where he himself had suffered rejection, is to reduce the core plot of the *Quartet* to the level of sexual rather than power politics and deny it all wider significance. [9] Such an interpretation is contradicted not only by tone and imagery of all four books but, more specifically, by Daphne's own remarks about her suitor's curious lack of ardour and Count Bronowsky's dismissal of Merrick's proposal as something of a red herring. Daphne's preference for Kumar aroused in Merrick not sexual jealousy but social envy. It heightened still further an already pronounced sense of grievance against his elders and supposed betters; which brings us back to the other decisive factor in 'the situation': for if his sexuality was one thing that dictated Merrick's conduct, class was the other.

What sealed Kumar's fate was the overweening arrogance he exuded during his first encounter with Merrick: the unthinking arrogance of the public school boy towards the man who does not quite get his vowels right. And it seems appropriate here to remind ourselves again of Swinden's key observation that what is being abused and humiliated in Kumar " . . . is not only the envious Indian for whom [Merrick] . . . feels contempt, but the contemptuous English public school boy for whose class, accent and perfect manners he feels the deepest . . . envy." [10] Indeed, for once, the issue of race does seem to take second place. This suspicion is borne out when we find Kumar's fate mirrored - in fine structural balance - in Guy Perron's experiences in the concluding volume of the *Quartet*, when the same combination of physical appeal, public school self-assurance, and essential powerlessness (Perron is a mere sergeant, Merrick by then a major) inevitably arouses Merrick's sinister interest. And Scott develops the theme further in a scene where he has Perron trying to imagine what must have been Kumar's feelings: suddenly - by a trick of the evening light - the skin on his arms seems brown not white. But Perron *is* white and as such can escape Merrick's clutches; Kumar cannot. That is the central aspect of "the situation", and

---

[9] The anonymous reviewer of *Jewel* for the *TLS* seems to be taking this view when he says, ". . . to make his [Kumar's] persecution depend on the personal feelings of a police officer is particularly unhappy." ("The Rape of India", op. cit.)
[10] Swinden, p.89.

its relevance clearly goes beyond what passes between two isolated individuals. And so Scott points us back to the constant in the imperial equation; the issue which, as Merrick always maintained, "you couldn't buck": that of race. (*DS*, p.300)

Merrick gets away with murder because he is white. The pukka sahiblog may find him wanting in background, may condescend to him, and on occasion be barely civil to him, but when it is a white man's word against a black man's, then school ties and well-rounded vowels, or lack of them, become irrelevant. Even the enlighted Nigel Rowan, whose old school tie is the same as Kumar's and who heartily detests Merrick, proves no exception: when it comes to the crunch he feels that it goes "against the grain" to hear an Indian accuse an English brother-officer. (*DVS*, p.305) Merrick may not be a gentleman, and the prospect of having him for brother-in-law is sufficiently dismaying for Rowan not to propose to the woman he loves, but dash it all, the man *is* an Englishman, gentleman or no.

The whole issue of class, then, is introduced into the *Quartet* not merely to add greater authenticity to the description of Anglo-Indian life - on the assumption that something that dominates the English scene cannot be wholly absent in a British colony, that where two or three Englishmen are gathered together class consciousness will be among them, - but to underline the strength of racial feeling 'East of Suez'. For the fact that the strongest dividing force in Britain counts for nothing in the presence of a dark skin surely speaks for itself. And when, towards the end of the *Quartet*, Merrick finally attains his social nirvana and is accepted as 'one of us' even by the cream of Pankot society, it is an unmistakable sign of the moral bankruptcy of the Raj.

But in the character of Merrick Scott reveals more than just one home truth about the Raj: Merrick also serves as a living refutation of the comfortable old (self-)delusion that Britain held India for her own good. And here Scott is adamant where Forster had been in a characteristic muddle. Merrick is a perfect illustration of D.C. White's point that "we were in India for what we could get out of it." (*JC*, p.317) He chose to work in the East because a career there offered him openings closed to him at home and a life style which in England would have been not only beyond his means but above his station. And while that went for practically everyone in India from the lowliest 'desk wallah' to the armies of 'younger sons' who made up the higher echelons of the civil and military administration, it is immediately obvious in someone like Merrick with no family tradition of 'service' in India. By his mere presence, then, he explodes the myth of the 'White Man's Burden'. In fact, he is full of contempt for those of his countrymen who believe in the Kiplingesque rhetoric; for him they are people who have gone soft: old fools whose vision is clouded by sentiment and who will probably lack the nous and the pluck to defend the Empire when the moment comes - as come, he knows, it must. And this, of course, is the allied truth about colonial rule which the character of Merrick demonstrates: that the high-flown rhetoric was never more than just that; that empires are upheld not by pious sentiment but through exercise of power.

That had been Orwell's discovery in Burma, where, like Merrick, he had been an imperial policeman and as such had enjoyed access - if 'enjoyed' is the word - to the shady backstage world of the Raj. Orwell was so appalled by what he saw, and was forced to do, that he resigned the service, fairly fled to England, and, as is the custom with men of letters, exorcised his memories with pen and typewriter. Merrick, on the other hand, lacks not only Eric Blair's literary bent but his scruples: he relishes his work. And this, it must be said, is where his "sexual maladjustment", to which early reviewers so objected, fits in neatly: interrogation, after all, is the ideal field for someone with sadistic leanings. Scott is therefore vindicated along with his choice of motif. For it is not hard to see that Merrick's deviant sexuality - "devoid of love", as Rubin puts it, "and full instead of a lust for possession" [11] - acts as a metaphor for the imperial process, while magnifying at the same time (and on another level, as it were) " ... some of the real facts of the Anglo-Indian relationship", as Swinden suggests it does. [12]

These "real facts" cannot fail to have a profound effect on the reader, and they discredit the Raj's moral claims once and for all. "Before Merrick's interpretation of the contemptuous exercise of naked power", as Mahood observes, " ... the cardboard fort of the traditional faith in

---

[11] Rubin, p.144.
[12] Swinden, p.87.

'man-bap' crumbles for good". [13] In this respect Scott emerges - pace Salman Rushdie - as the true anti-Kipling, so to speak, and much more uncompromisingly so than Forster had ever done; and this not just because Scott is ready to include in his narrative scenes "... too bloody and ... too sordid for Forster's pen", but because his fiction is always firmly rooted in "historical actuality", as Rubin puts it. [14] If Scott conjures up in parts of the *Quartet* a sepia-tinted world suffused by the "perpetual seeming" Edwardian sunlight of so much Anglo-Indian fiction, he does so only to contrast it, or dispel it, with a "brighter, honest, light whose heat ... [burns] the old one to a shadow". (*DS*, p.440) Tedesco and Popham, taking up this image from *Scorpion*, speak of a "scorching light of truth" [15], and even Benita Parry must ultimately concede that Scott "... demystifies the myth and undermines the British claim to moral superiority ...". [16]

Scott's triumph in the *Quartet*, then, is to have balanced successfully the potentially conflicting demands of plot and history; and nowhere perhaps is this success more obvious than in the character of Merrick, who, as Jill Bonheim notes, is not just representative of something but is always supremely 'real': almost palpably of flesh and blood. [17] His actions - though made possible only by the nature of the system he serves - convince as the actions of an individual and are explained by his own distinctive psyche as much as by outside circumstance. There is, after all, as Count Bronowsky points out, an obvious "... connection between ... [Merrick's] sado-masochism, ... [his] sense of social inferiority and the grinding defensive belief in his racial superiority," (*DVS*, p.571) Bronowsky's cool assessment will strike an immediate

---

[13] Mahood, p.248.
[14] Rubin, p.134.
[15] Tedesco, op.cit., p.85.
[16] Parry, op.cit., p.359.
  Barbara Hoffmann makes a similar point when she says, "Die Sicht ist unverstellt von Mythen und Legenden." (Barbara Hoffmann, *Paul Scott's "Raj Quartet": Fiktion und Geschichtsschreibung.* (Europäische Hochschulschriften Reihe 14, Angelsächsische Sprache und Literatur 101) Frankfurt / Main 1982, p.193.
[17] cf. Bonheim, op.cit., p.44: "Merrick ist kein Typus, sondern vielmehr eine Inkarnation: er vertritt nicht nur, sondern *ist*." (Bonheim's italics)

chord of recognition in anyone familiar with Mannoni's reflections on the mind of the colonizer. [18]

Francine Weinbaum is therefore right to emphasize that Merrick not only inflicts wounds but is himself psychologically wounded; that Scott portrays him not only as a perpetrator of unspeakable crimes but also as a victim of a system which, in the final analysis, abuses him as surely as it does Kumar. [19] Merrick's persecution of Kumar, therefore, takes on added meaning, since it is part of that wider pattern of 'divide and rule' of which Christopher Hitchins speaks. The Muslim warders feeding Hindu prisoners beef, the political squabbling between the Congress and the Muslim League (explored in the shenanigans surrounding M.A. Kasim), the distrust between the Princes and the Nationalists of whatever hue or creed, are as vital for the survival of the Raj as are Merrick's police activities. [20] Ultimately, of course, Merrick is as helpless as his own victims had been: for as the end of the Raj approaches, so does the end of his career. He has become an embarrassment to the authorities, just as the Raj itself has become an embarrassment to Britain. Both are now expendable and both will be got rid of without compunction. It is Merrick's mistake not to have foreseen this. And to this extent he is not simply another of the "chance victims of ... a colonial ambition" (*JC*, p.71) but, in Weinbaum's words, "... the dupe of his own illusions". [21]

Inevitably, it is left to Guy Perron to make the most explicit comment on the nature of that delusion. And it is not so much a comment of a detached historian as of a self-assured, if eccentric, member of the ruling class: Merrick, he suggests, had failed to take into account that class's innate

---

[18] Philip Mason in his introduction to the English translation of Mannoni's classic study puts it in a nutshell when he says, "To the spirit convinced of its own inferiority, the homage of a dependant is balm and honey and to surround oneself with dependents is perhaps the easiest way of appeasing an ego eager for reassurance. ... The colonial administrator, ... , and the pioneers show themselves, by choosing a colonial career, particularly prone to this weakness, of which the germ is present in every member of a competitive society and which flourishes with peculiar luxuriance in the warm broth of the colonial situation. (Mannoni, op.cit., pp.11-12.)
[19] cf. Weinbaum, p.97: "Like Kumar, Merrick is in his way Philoctetes."
[20] cf. Hitchins, op. cit., p.115.
[21] Weinbaum, p.115.

> ... conviction of class rights and class privileges, of ... [it's] permanence and ... [it's] capacity to trim, to insure against any kind of major upheaval affecting ... [it's] interests, and... [it's] fundamental indifference to the problems towards which ... [it adopts] attitudes of responsibility. Not moral responsibility, ownership responsibility. A moral responsibility would be too trying.
>
> (*DVS*, p.208)

This is Scott's answer to the high-flown imperial rhetoric of Kipling and his ilk: far from regarding India as the White Man's Burden, he suggests, the upholders of the Raj saw the subcontinent as property, pure and simple. And when it was actually beginning to become something like a burden, as the economist Purvis in his exchanges with Perron suggests it had begun to do, it was promptly unshouldered. For property, as Perron observes dryly, " ... can always be got rid of ..." and be replaced by new property: "new property, new responsibility, but the same manner, the same deep inner conviction and the same snug cosy sense of insulation." (DVS, p.208)

Merrick, Perron is saying, is too much of a peasant to understand the subtle difference between appearance and reality. He is the victim of a "middle-class misconception of upper-class 'mores'". (*DVS*, p.209) For all his affected cynicism, he too has been seduced by the grand romanticism of Empire, has

> ... been sucked in by all that Kiplingesque double-talk that transformed India from a place where ordinary greedy Englishmen carved something out for themselves to balance out the more tedious consequences of the law of primogeniture, into one where they appeared to go voluntarily into exile for the good of their souls and the uplift of the native."
>
> (*DVS*, p.209)

By mistaking the true attitude of the pukka sahiblog, Merrick seals his own fate. Having tied himself to the mast of the Raj more firmly than any of his superiors, he must go down with it, while someone like the patrician Nigel Rowan, to whom Perron addresses these remarks, will of course survive unharmed the imminent shipwreck. And in the light of such reflections we must credit Scott's tetralogy not just with a high degree of historical accuracy but with something one might call an awareness of history, which allows him both to portray history's impact on individual lives and to explore through individual lives the drift of history.

There are in the *Quartet* repeatedly instances where the main narrative gives way to a direct discussion of history and even of theories of history, usually in the guise of conversations between various protagonists or of their letters and diary entries. In many of these Emerson's well-known essay on history plays a prominent role. Much of its detail does not immediately concern us here, but one of its central images does: it is the image of a nation - of its individuals and ideas - resembling a wave which, surging upwards and forwards, maintains its shape and outward appearance even though its constituent parts keep changing in its progress. It is this theory which Perron is challenging, or as he puts it, is refuting, as he ponders the differing destinies of people like himself and Nigel Rowan on the one hand, and of Merrick and his kind on the other.

If Merrick's fate is inextricably entwined with that of the institution he serves - so that he cannot hope to survive it and welcomes death when the end of the Raj is imminent - this dependence begins to work both ways as we move further into the *Quartet* and closer to the year 1947. Merrick and his dark world of wanton arrest and secret torture had, of course, always been part of the Raj, however much its more respectable exponents may have tried to ignore it. Only the honest few among them, like Sarah Layton, were prepared to acknowledge him as "our dark side". (*DS*, p.398) But as the pretence of ruling India by consent becomes impossible to sustain (first in the face of the 'Quit India' riots and then of the mass desertions of Indian soldiers to the I.N.A.), Merrick with his unscrupulous but effective methods becomes truly indispensable to his superiors. His meteoric rise through the ranks after his transfer from the police to the army is therefore an indication, a graph almost, of a corresponding decline of the Raj: of a perpetual lowering of standards and a rapid ebbing of morality. As such, Merrick symbolizes the triumph of crude power politics over what idealism there may have been left, both of the liberal and of the older paternalist persuasion.

We see the process also reflected in the steady rise of his social fortunes. In Mayapore he is still on the outer fringes of Anglo-Indian society: by proposing to the ungainly but well-connected Daphne Manners he hopes to enter, through marriage, the ranks of the pukka sahiblog; in the second volume he acts as bestman to a true pukka sahib - albeit only by default, so to speak, (a more obvious candidate for that honour having come down with jaundice); in the third volume he hob-nobs freely with the Laytons, though still outwardly respectful and appearing to mind his place; in *Spoils* finally, now promoted to the rank of a full colonel no less, he realizes his social ambitions by marrying the widowed Susan Bingham (née Layton).

But Merrick's rise (and the concomitant decline of the Raj) finds its most poignant expression - in terms of the central imagery of the *Quartet* - in a little incident on the verandah of a deserted Rose Cottage. It is there that Barbie Batchelor, another of the characters symbolizing the Raj, finally comes face to face with him; and she decides, on the spur of the moment, to part with her cherished copy of "The Jewel in the Crown", handing it over to a surprised Merrick with the wistful words, "One should always share one's hopes. . . . That represents one of the unfulfilled ones." (*TS*, p.382) The symbolism of this little scene above Mabel's devastated rose garden - flattened by Mildred Layton to expunge all memory of the old lady's life - will require no further comment. The hopes of the Raj at its finest will indeed remain unfulfilled now that the best lack, if not actually all conviction, at least the necessary energy to restrain those who are, as ever, full of passionate intensity. [22]

Lady Manners, another of what Benita Parry calls "Scott's sybilline old white women", is vouchsafed an even clearer and more chilling vision of the future: the nature of the disclosures during Nigel Rowan's inquiry into Merrick's conduct in the Kumar case finally convince her that "it will end, . . . , in total and unforgivable disaster; *that* is the situation." (*DS*, p.305. Scott's italics) [23]

---

[22] "For Barbie to give it [i.e. the picture] to Ronald Merrick", notes Margret Scanlan, "means conceding the colonial project to its most ruthless advocate". (Scanlan, op.cit., p.160)

[23] Parry, p.360.

It is significant that Lady Manners should in this context also use again the word 'charade'. She is, of course, refering to the judicial inquiry, but in a wider sense also to the entire, increasingly frantic, British activity in India. The concept of events on the subcontinent amounting to a charade is by now familiar to the reader, and its relevance in a discussion of the character of Merrick will be obvious: for Merrick presents two faces in the *Quartet*. He is on the one hand the only protagonist determined to cut through all the illusion and recreate, stage, or reenact what he perceives to be the truth, the essence of the colonial situation. This is the jailer and torturer Merrick; the Merrick whose subterranean activities are repeatedly likened in their effect to "radium in a mine" - undetectable at first, but all-pervading, unstoppable and ultimately fatal. The other Merrick - the determined social climber - is more than willing to take part in the general charade. And, unsurprisingly, he is, in Tedesco's words, the most "consummate actor" of them all; though his, of course, is a "different play". [24] He is more successful than anyone else because he is consciously acting a part - as a kind of camouflage allowing him to blend in with the people whose social endorsement he craves. Accordingly, he has reshaped himself in the traditional mould of the sahib 'sans peur et sans reproche'. "The outer casing is almost perfect", as Count Bronowsky observes, but inside there is a gaping void: "He is one of your hollow men." (*DVS*, pp.170-1)

This remark provides an important key to the interpretation of the character of Ronald Merrick. For through his identification of Merrick as a 'hollow man', Bronowsky points to a wider significance of the character beyond the immediate narrative world and the historical framework of the *Quartet*. We touch at something more fundamental here: at truths about the nature of mankind. Bronowsky refers us, once again, back to T.S. Eliot, but this time, through him, even further back to the creator of the original 'hollow man': Joseph Conrad himself. For it is Conrad's Mr Kurtz - as no critic can fail or has failed to spot - who provided Scott with some of the inspiration for Merrick. This is not to say that Merrick is a mere copy or a reincarnation, as it were, of the shadowy hero of *Heart of Darkness* ; but the two characters are related, as are their respective

---

[24] Tedesco, pp.69-70.

functions, or rather the 'messages' they are meant to convey to the reader.

There are in the *Quartet*, as Tedesco and Popham observe " ... some fundamental truths ... which the reader repeatedly encounters"; chief among which is the recognition " ... that man, despite his long past, ... , has not really emerged from the jungle", that "the civilized veneer is paper thin." [25] At any moment, and without prior warning, he may revert to the primitive savagery of his remotest ancestors; the mantle of civilization which seems to hang so firmly on our shoulders falls all too easily to reveal a sight of naked barbarism lurking underneath. That, of course, had been the stuff of Conrad's nightmare vision in *Heart of Darkness*, and events in our century have proved it tragically prophetic.

India, Scott said in his address to the Royal Society of Literature, provided him with a metaphor for twentieth century life. It is not hard to see how Merrick fits into this. For we have in Merrick not so much the image of some kind of anthropological throwback as a chillingly convincing portrayal of the totalitarian ruler of our age. Merrick not only breaks every law under the sun, he does not accept the existence of such laws. His is a world, as he explains to his victims, dominated by two overriding emotions: envy and contempt. "A man's personality", he believes, "... [exists] at the point of equilibrium between the degree of his envy and the degree of his contempt." (*DS*, p.330) The concept of a universal "brotherhood of men", on the other hand, he rejects expressly as mere sentimentality. (*DS*, p.298) And he claims for himself not only the right to torture and humiliate those he considers inferior to himself, he regards it his duty to do so. For it is only through such graphic enactments of "the situation" that the truth about the relations between rulers and ruled begins to emerge from the obscuring haze of 'sentimentality': the "calm purity of ... contempt" on the one side and the undisguised envy on the other. (*DS*, p.299) And only once that truth had been faced up to by everyone concerned, could there be any talk of an "obligation" by the rulers to the ruled. (*DS*, p.298)

In one case, that of the unhappy Susan Bingham, Merrick really does accept such an obligation in an outrageous travesty of the paternalist tradition. Having gained access to her medical files, and thus

---

[25] Ibid., p.253.

armed with a professional insight into her injured psyche, he is not content with forcing her into abject submission but eventually manages to inspire in her a simpering gratitude towards him. It is an alarmingly convincing variation on the famous Orwellian theme of the torturer inspiring love for the oppressor in his victims. Merrick, then, attempts to control not merely the bodies but also the minds of his victims. And in this vital respect Kumar eludes him: Hari remembers the reality of Daphne's love, which contradicts Merrick's view of human affairs, and by recognizing his own distinctive individuality as a result of that love, he finds the strength not to behave as Merrick would want him to. And this refusal to play the part Merrick would want him to play is a small but bright ray of hope in the otherwise impenetrable gloom of Scott's view of human affairs.

What makes Merrick so frighteningly convincing is that Scott resists the temptation to paint in black and white. For all his depravity, for all the enormity of his crimes, Merrick is never a one-dimensional villain; he knows and suffers pain and loneliness like any other man and, like other men, is capable of showing genuine consideration. His affected contempt for 'amateur' soldiers like Teddie Bingham notwithstanding, he is, for instance, ready to throw professional caution to the wind and risk his own life in an attempt to save Teddie's. Even Daphne, who has little reason to think well of him, admits that he is fundamentally kind and well-meaning. Through the delineation of a character like Merrick, then, Scott reasserts two of the oldest truths about mankind: that there is in man a boundless capacity for cruelty and hatred or, to use an old-fashioned word, for evil; but, also, that no man is beyond redemption. These truths, or at any rate the first of the two, had been systematically denied, buried and obscured by the Enlightenment and the liberal tradition; it was only the appalling record of our own century which has forced us to reconsider that over-confident verdict of a happier age. And yet, in spite of this renewed recognition, modern literature, as Iris Murdoch once observed, contains remarkably few "convincing pictures of evil". [26] The *Quartet* must surely rank among the honourable exceptions; and Iris Murdoch should be pleased with it also because its chief exponent of evil fulfills her main criterion for verisimilitude in these

---

[26] Murdoch, op.cit., p.30.

matters: he vividly illustrates the infinite "opacity of a person".[27] For if there is in everyone of us a boundless capacity for evil, there is also - and again in everyone of us - an equally unbounded capacity for goodness and love. And that, as Scott demonstrates, even goes for someone like Merrick.

There is indeed throughout the *Quartet*, as Weinbaum among others has noted, a marked strength of belief - not, to be sure, in the religious sense of the word, but belief in the solidity of traditional values - rare in the literature of our day, beset as it is by moral relativism.[28] Indeed, as Weinbaum goes on to say, Scott's novels are informed by an unmistakable stance of "moral certainty".[29] There *is* a right and wrong; and man is able to distinguish, and is free to choose, between them. Scott is the first to agree with Iris Murdoch that " . . . we are not monarchs of all we survey, but benighted creatures sunk in a reality whose nature we are constantly . . . tempted to deform by fantasy."[30] That point is made again and again in the *Quartet*; indeed, the absurd little world of make-believe which was the British Raj is a perfect illustration of it. Yet at the same time, he is adamant that people are able to recognize the truth and act accordingly; that for all the undoubted "complexity of moral life"[31] of which Murdoch speaks and for all the indisputable helplessness of the individual in a hostile world that will inevitably destroy it, there yet remains freedom of choice - though only in the existentialist use of the term.[32]

From this position on firm moral ground - where 'tout comprendre' does not equal 'tout pardonner', Scott is able to feel compassion even for someone like Merrick. This compassion for the declared villain of the piece stems not only from an awareness that Merrick is a victim himself- like Kumar, he is compared to Philoctetes, the wounded archer of antiquity left behind by his companions because of the smell of his wounds - but from genuine sympathy with Merrick's own lack of happiness. And - we have quoted Michael Wood's observation before - it is

---

[27] Ibid., p.29.
[28] cf. Weinbaum, pp.89-91.
[29] Ibid., p.91.
[30] Murdoch, p.29.
[31] Ibid.
[32] cf. Weinbaum, pp.90-1.

always for " . . . intelligent and lonely people who know the word or gesture that would release them ... into love and feeling, but cannot say it or cannot make it" that Scott reserves his especial tenderness. [33] That also goes for Merrick; he, too, eventually confronts his predicament, and knows "in one brief, unbearable moment of honesty", as Tedesco and Popham put it, ". . . that India could make him happy". [34]

That recognition had come, as Count Bronowsky later surmises, after Merrick had for the first time accepted his homosexuality and had made love to an Indian boy. This, Bronowsky suspects, had afforded him "a moment of profound peace", which however soon became unbearable, for accepting this sense of peace with all its implications " . . . meant discarding every belief he had". (*DVS*, p.571) What is at issue for Merrick is not merely owning up to something in himself of the existence of which he can hardly have been unaware, but accepting that these feelings had been inspired by an Indian. The tenderness he had experienced was, after all, in eloquent contradiction to his view of the world as a place ruled exclusively by contempt and envy; indeed, his own feelings towards that boy effectively exploded the idea of one race being superior to another, and thus threatened to demolish for him the very basis of the British Raj. It is a knowledge Merrick decides he cannot live with: it drives him to abuse in the first instance the boy who had produced it and later to seek death at the hands of those who had neither forgiven nor forgotten his role in the Bibighar case.

Merrick's experiences, then, are an illustration of another old truth: that love and the exercise of power do not go together; or, to look at it from a slightly different angle, as Benita Parry does, that the "psychological satisfactions of having power over subjugated peoples" are "ultimately destructive", for they "enslave the masters and paralyse their capacity for choice and the exercise of free will"; and that, Parry adds, is a recognition which " . . . has only emerged in great literature . . . ." [35]

In the *Quartet* Merrick's experiences form part of a general pattern that includes practically every European actor in Scott's imperial pageant from Edwina Crane and Daphne Manners at the beginning of the tetra-

---

[33] Wood, op.cit.
[34] Tedesco, p.254.
[35] Parry, p.366.

logy to Merrick himself at its end. And the pattern is complemented by a handful of examples of people leading happy, fulfilled lives: these range from Sister Ludmila running her hospice for the dying and the quietly efficient Dr.Claus at the Mayapore hospital to Barbie taking the homeless little Ashok under her wings after she herself had been evicted from Rose Cottage, to Sarah Layton educating the Nawab's daughter at the Court of Mirat and enjoying as equal among equals the company of Ahmed Kasim, and lastly to Count Bronowsky serving his prince: what is common to them all is that they have either abdicated as rulers or never had any desire to rule in the first place.

The *Quartet*, then, is indeed more than just "a relentless analysis of decline and ruin"; there is indeed an emphasis on "positive values", as Mahood, for one, had always stressed there was. [36] Amid the shambles of pointless careers and wasted opportunities there is also meaningful work, which makes for meaningful lives. And again the message is that success or no is of little importance: neither Sister Ludmila nor Dr. Claus can ultimately change the appalling social conditions in Mayapore; Barbie can no more safeguard little Ashok's future than Sarah can prevent Ahmed's murder or Count Bronowsky can stop the internecine fighting that destroys Mirat. But they have done their utmost and have invested the whole of their resources. And that is enough. Or in the words of the poet, they have taken " . . . no thought of the harvest / But only of proper sowing." And again we are back to that solidity of values which, Weinbaum noted, distinguished Scott from so much of the literature of our age. Which leads us at last to the question as to the nature of truth itself.

Truth, thought Merrick, as Tedesco and Popham remind us, depended " . . . upon the light in which it was presented rather than how accurately it corresponded to reality". [37] And Merrick certainly appeared to have proved his point. None, after all, could "lie, shade and twist truths and half-truths" as expertly as he, none was more adept at creating " . . . the image he desired, which would change in chameleon fashion with

---

[36] Mahood, p.246.
[37] Tedesco, p.241.

whoever he happened to be dealing." [38] Is this, then, the truth about the truth, as it were: that there is in fact no such thing?

This much is certain: that 'the' truth is no simple matter - neither in the Bibighar case nor in the wider historical sense for which the Bibighar stands paradigmatically; that much is clear by the form of the tetralogy alone. One has only to consider the length of the list of characters, the army of witnesses who are, in the reviewer's resonant phrase, "giving evidence at the bar of history" to recognize this as a central message of the *Quartet*. [39]

The same message also emerges from the myriad discrepancies between the individual recollections of the interviewees and their interpretations of events. To some extent, these are to be expected, given the distorting effect of time on human memory, though there is also a lurking suspicion that some people are being wise after the event, so to speak, with views being subtly changed to fit the now familiar outcome of events. The recognition and faithful recording of these complexities are one of the strengths of the *Quartet*, combining to create what Pollard calls a "subtle and dense" picture of British India. [40]

But to concentrate purely on the aspect of the doubtful reliability of the witnesses is to stay at the surface of the problem. The more perceptive of Scott's protagonists are beset by doubts of a more fundamental order: they find it difficult, as Swinden reminds us, " . . . to offer a truthful account of the part they [themselves] have played in the events recorded." [41] The problem lies in the sheer number of active participants. And here it is perhaps useful to remember that the narrator-investigator is dealing with two sets of events: those that might be called the 'Bibighar case' (including its aftermath) and those of more general historical interest - though the two are, of course, connected. Discovering the truth about the former is a comparatively simple matter. Scott sets about it using a method which, as Bhaskara Rao reminds us, he had explained at the beginning of an earlier novel, *The Mark of the Warrior*: "Three things are to be considered; a man's estimate of himself, the face he presents to

---

[38] Ibid.
[39] Benny Green, "Lost Jewel: 'The Raj Quartet'". *The Spectator* 23 July 1977, p.28.
[40] Arthur Pollard, " Twilight of Empire: Paul Scott's 'Raj Quartet'". In: Daniel Massa (ed.), *Individual and Community in Commonwealth Literature*. Malta 1979, p.171.
[41] Swinden, p.94.

the world, the estimate of that man made by other men. Combined they form an aspect of the truth." [42] In the case of the fates of Merrick and Kumar that method is manifestly successful. The picture may be incomplete in some respects, tantalizingly so because there are no witnesses, for instance, to Merrick's end - where we have to rely solely on the conjecture of those who knew him and his circumstances best - but what emerges is, most readers will feel, a satisfyingly large "aspect of the truth". But what of the more complex events *outside* the Bibighar Gardens? How to reconcile, for instance, such drastically differing accounts of the same incidents as those offered by Brigadier Reid and District Commissioner White if one accepts that both men are relating what they honestly consider to be the truth? And what then are one's hopes of ever establishing a clear overall picture, given that it should reconcile not just those two diverging accounts but - ideally - the individual impressions of all the historical protagonists?

White, in fact, specifically discusses these problems with the novelist-narrator in *Jewel*. He suggests that one can evolve a theory to explain what happened, but when one attempts to relate it " . . . to all the events in the lives of all the people who were concerned with the action . . . " things soon elude one's grasp again: for "the mind simply won't take in the complex of emotions and ambitions and reactions that led, say, to any one of the simple actions that was part of the general describable pattern." (*JC*, p.334) Is the novelist then reduced to sticking to the "describable pattern?" Must he content himself with sincerity, since truth, even if it should exist, would appear to be unattainable? But perhaps, White adds, " . . . the mind can respond to a sense of cumulative, impersonal justice?" (*JC*, p.334)

It is this last point, which, Swinden suggests, rescues the *Quartet* from the fashionable 'relativism' characteristic of " . . . so much inferior modern writing about history" and its facile belief

> . . . that a novelist can go on more or less for ever adding account to account and point of view to point of view until it becomes obvious that there is no such thing as 'the truth' about anything, let alone something as complex as the behaviour of human beings, or the

---

[42] Bhaskara Rao, p.55.

> evolution of societies, or the relation between one of these things or another. In the end the novelist simply has to stand back baffled at the immensity of the task before him and the egotism of the ambition that drove him to try to perform it. ... Scott's attitude to his responsibilities as a novelist will not allow him to make these elegant little surrenders to the mysteries of things.[43]

But has he succeeded? Each reader will ultimately have to decide for himself. The achievement does seem considerable though. Certainly, the verdict of the historians and surviving Anglo-Indians among his readers has been one of generous and near-unanimous praise, and the critics have tended to echo it, (though of course it is debatable whether they are best placed to judge the historical verisimilitude of a novel dealing with events so completely outside their sphere of experience).[44] What the critic can attest to, however, and for that matter any reader of the *Quartet*, is that Scott seems to have been sure he was not merely being truthful, but that the method he was employing did in fact allow him to tell the truth about the Raj.[45] And indeed there emerges from the welter of diverging and conflicting accounts a surprisingly clear picture of what happened and " ... where the fault had lain and why there could have been no other end". (*DS*, p.431)

Swinden reminds us in this context of a conversation in *Spoils* between Governor Malcolm and Nigel Rowan, which he thinks sums up Scott's approach. In it Malcolm expounds what he calls his 'theory of relativity in administration'. This hinges on the fact that

> although people seldom argued a point but argued around it, they sometimes found a solution to the problem they were evading by going round in ever *increasing* circles and disappearing into the centre of

---

[43] Swinden, p.95.
[44] cf. for instance Swinden, p.95: "Here is assembled a large cast ... , whose collective response to the demise of the Raj is in a profound way representative."
[45] cf. for instance Suzanne Kim, "Histoire et Roman". *Etudes Anglaises* 36 (2,3), p.170: "... Scott est persuadé qu'il détient la vérité historique sur les relations entre l'Angleterre et l'Inde par le truchement d'une vérité sur les individus qu'il va donc analyser très finement, puisqu'ils lui fourniront les clés de la grandeur et décadence d'un empire."

those, which, relatively speaking, coincided with the centre of the circle from whose periphery they had evasively spiralled outwards.

(*DVS*, p.318. Scott's italics)

Malcolm, Swinden adds, is talking about administrative problems and their possible solutions, whereas Scott as a novelist is concerned with " . . . the articulation of fundamentally true facts about a complex human situation, which does not require a solution but which does require an appropriate form". [46]

Scott's triumph is to have found it and to have used it in the *Quartet* with a mastery that gives his tetralogy stature and should assure it a permanent place not just within the constricted little world of the colonial novel but in the mainstream of English letters itself.

---

[46] Swinden, p.96.

6. 'An Imperial Embrace': Fiction and History in the *Quartet*

The individual novels comprising *The Raj Quartet*, which, combined, span the last five years of British rule in India, reflect the mood and events of those days as much in style and pace of the narrative as in actual content. Thus in *The Jewel in the Crown* the high drama of Scott's fictional events in Mayapore faithfully mirrors the historical one of the Raj buffetted by the great civil and military storms of the year 1942; the two 'Pankot books' with their mood of introspection and majestic sadness show the ship of Empire lying becalmed, so to speak, in the politically stagnant seas of the war years, gathering barnacles and slowly decaying from within; and in *A Division of the Spoils*, finally, we witness its dying moments when, severely listing and openly adrift, it is abandoned amid all the scenes of anguish, confusion and loss of life attendant on a shipwreck.

There is, then, in *Spoils* - almost from the first page - an unmistakable sense of time running out for the Raj and those connected with it: an almost audible ticking behind the words as of some great clock marking the dwindling hours till Independence; and a corresponding flurry of activity with the protagonists restlessly crisscrossing the land, as if trying to outrun fate. [1] But the greatly accelerated pace of the narrative is not the only thing that sets *Spoils* apart from the preceding novels: for this final act of Scott's imperial drama comes complete with a radical scene change and, perhaps somewhat unexpectedly so late in the day, with a new central character. And while this new protagonist, Guy Perron, can be said to owe his existence in some measure to the demands of plot, or rather to his creator's mounting desperation of ever getting the *Quartet* completed, he is nonetheless an entirely satisfying, well-rounded character who fully engages our interest and sympathy. [2] Indeed, he is,

---

[1] Mahood makes a similar point when she observes that the numerous train journeys in *Spoils* represent " . . . the dangerous speed with which the English are pulling out . . .". (Mahood, p.251)
  Scott himself speaks of train journeys being " . . . part of the narrative pattern of this closing book". (Letter to Rebecca West 15 August 1975, quoted by Robin Moore, *Paul Scott's Raj*. London 1990, p.111)

[2] cf. Scott's remarks to John Baker: "At that point [while working on *Towers*] I couldn't even see the end . . . , and though I was moving towards Independence . . . ,

as David Rubin notes, " . . . the closest we get to a conventional hero in the *Quartet..*" ³

Yet this is no hero earlier generations of Anglo-Indian novelists - let alone their readers - would have approved of. For though Perron cuts a dashing enough figure, cannot be faulted on 'background', has charm aplenty, and wastes little time to do battle with the Forces of Evil (Merrick in our case), it is in his chosen profession that he disappoints: preferring the pen to the sword, his writing desk to the saddle, and the stale air of the world of books to wide-open horizons and an occasional invigorating whiff of cordite: no maker of history he, but a mere on-looker, content to watch and record what others frame. If India was the place "where the English came to the end of themselves", then *A Division of the Spoils* is the book where the traditional Anglo-Indian novel comes to the end of itself. Guy Perron may still retain most of the outer trappings of a Kiplingesque hero and be as 'pukka' as they come, but he is no longer a sahib in the true sense of the word; and far from looking up to those who still are or at least try to be, he finds, as Mahood observes, that he " . . . cannot even take the best of them as seriously as they take themselves".[4] Here, after a century or more of largely unquestioning acceptance in colonial fiction of the imperial ethos, complete with all its more ridiculous outer manifestations, is a protagonist who sees what Fielding saw - that the upholders of the Raj "have no clothes on" - but who, unlike Fielding, will also say as much. [5] It is indeed the end of a genre.

For such a hero there is, of course, nothing left to fight for. Besides, as Teddie Bingham's fate has shown, the fighting days for the Britons in India are over anyway. The sahiblog have become conspicuously unable to influence the course of events, unable even to determine their own personal future. Throughout the 'Pankot books' the mood is one of deepening resignation, bordering in many cases on despair; with the best lacking if not all conviction at least the will to carry on a fight that looks increasingly like tilting at windmills, it is only the worst, like Merrick,

---

I couldn't see how to get there. . . . Finally, by number Four, I had to bring in an outside observer to draw it all into focus for the conclusion." (Baker, op.cit., p.7)

[3] Rubin, p.131.
[4] Mahood, p.250.
[5] Ibid.

who are still full of the passionate intensity of old. The others are, like Perron, the outsider, reduced to the role of spectator and/or victim. And, as is ever the case when people find themselves overwhelmed by events against which there is neither remedy nor redress, their minds concentrate on the one question of 'What went wrong?'

Thus, at the beginning of the concluding volume of Scott's *Quartet*, the perspective is already largely historical and the present little more than a daily reminder of past errors, lost hopes, and missed opportunities. All that remains for the protagonists to do is to brave out the inevitable consequences. When we first meet Guy Perron in Calcutta amid the surreally hectic military activity of the summer of 1945 - preparations for a reconquest of Malaya which, significantly enough, would soon be overtaken by events - the world of the Raj as it has become familiar to us - the world of Mayapore and Pankot, of club and maidan, stiffly-formal functions and relaxed teas on the verandah - already seems remote enough to suggest another country, and the Raj itself so unlikely and outdated as to be of conceivable interest only to an historian.

And so, before an audience of conscripted servicemen scarcely bothering to stifle their yawns, Sgt. Perron of the Army Education Corps delves into the past seeking an explanation for the present. We hear him lecture on the history of the British involvement in India; watch him meditate on it in sleepless small hours; peer over his shoulders to read his diary entries about it or his letters to his Wildeish aunt; overhear him discuss its economic ramifications with the hapless Captain Purvis, and gaily rehearse strategies to counter the more disruptive effects of its impending end on the financial wellbeing of the individual expatriate with an appropriately named Mr Hapgood; observe him chart its moral drift in late night conversations with Nigel Rowan, or ponder its fatefulness in the company of Count Bronowsky. Thus, with an historian as protagonist, history itself moves centrestage.

It had, of course, played an important part all along: forming not only the basis of the narrative structure of the *Quartet* but also, repeatedly, a topic in its own right; D.C.White's and Mr Srinivasan's observations to the narrator in *Jewel*, Governor Malcolm's discussions with M.A. Kasim on the eve of the 'Quit India' riots and, again, after Kasim's release from detention, Barbie's readings of Emerson, and Major

Clark's scathing résumé of two centuries or more of British stewardship in India (an opening gambit in his seduction of Sarah Layton which is as unusual as it proves effective) - these are only the most obvious instances that spring to mind. All this, in a sense, had been part of what Scott calls elsewhere " . . . a moral dialogue such as any Englishman might have with himself . . . ". [6]

With history thus both setting, as it were, and topic, it is surely worth our while to follow Scott's example and examine more closely some of the aspects involved. Three things in particular are to be considered: the treatment of factual history in the *Quartet*; the author's views on the nature of history; and, lastly, in mapping out this borderland between history and fiction which Scott has made his home ground, we also touch on the vexed question of purpose and function of the novel itself.

Now, a writer producing a set of novels with an historical setting as specific and explicit as that of the *Quartet*, can hardly expect it to be judged by literary criteria alone. And since the historian's aims and preoccupations differ from those of the creative artist, as most people would agree they do, it follows that it is impossible almost by definition to reconcile in a novel the constraints of strict academic faithfulness to a codified body of historical facts with the workings of a free-flowing imagination which is at the origin of any work of fiction. Certainly, the number of novels that straddle successfully the dividing line between literature and historiography, satisfying both camps of critics, is quite small. With a steadily growing body of critical work praising the *Quartet* for its literary and its historical merit alike, Scott's tetralogy can now probably be added to that select canon. But be that as it may, it has certainly helped generate sufficient interest in the Raj for both 'tribes' of critics to sit up and take notice not only of a particular work of fiction but of each other and of the subject matter itself.

It is instructive here to remind oneself of the politely puzzled tone with which early reviewers greeted Scott's work and then contrast it with the ready seriousness with which literary journals and the literature columns of the major newspapers now routinely discuss matters relating to the Raj; or to recall the long initial silence of professional historians now that one of them is referring to Scott in a full-length study of the

---

[6] "The Raj", p.74.

Quartet as "the historian's novelist". [7] And it is surely no less remarkable that criticism by an historian of a work of fiction should have been accepted by a main publishing house such as Heinemann with access to every high street bookshop in the land, and not have been consigned to the usual decorous semi-obscurity of a more traditional academic publisher and the learned shelves of half a dozen specialist booksellers up and down the country. To have brought about this change in attitudes is itself a measure of Scott's achievement.

What, then, specifically has won the critics' approval and, indeed, aroused their enthusiasm? The first thing members of the 'historical camp' tend to remark upon is what they usually refer to as Scott's 'firm grasp of detail'. By this they clearly mean to say more than that he has got his facts right. The phrase would seem to imply that Scott is not only familiar with detail but, more importantly, conscious of its historical 'context': of the forces and processes shaping the course of history, of which such detail can only ever be an illustration. And this even though his fictional analysis of the final years of the Raj leads him to conclusions which are in some crucial respects at variance with what was in the sixties and early seventies the received view of events. Indeed, it is this very readiness to challenge conventional views on the Raj and, even more so, the historiography of its day, which has since earned the *Quartet* and its author rare praise and recognition from those professionally concerned with the past. Here is Robin Moore again, speaking as a man of some knowledge in Imperial history: "*The Quartet*", he writes, "and Scott's occasional non-fictional writings, provide a coherent, original and important statement on the later history of British India." [8]

Moore praises Scott particularly for having extended his inquiry in four directions still largely neglected at the time by the common rooms: that of the true importance of the so-called Indian National Army during and after the War, of the role of Indian politicians and officials cooperating with the Raj in persuance of a constitutional (i.e. evolution-

---

[7] Robin Moore, op. cit., p.194.
 Looking back on the time when Scott was active on the *Quartet*, Moore remarks that, "There is indeed insularity in the life of a nation when the fictive and academic analyses of its history run on parallel lines at the same time without meeting". (Ibid., p.133)

[8] Ibid., p.174.

ary) approach to independence, of British policy towards the Princely States, and finally of the true motives for the precipitate British withdrawal and Partition in 1947. What unites these aparently diverse topics is that they are all in a sense variations on the theme of 'loyalty and betrayal', which had become a growing preoccupation with Scott as work on the *Quartet* progressed. He also felt challenged by the peculiar silence that surrounded them. "I write . . . as an insurance against permanent silence", Daphne Manners had inscribed on the front page of her diary of the Bibighar case. (*JC*, p.349) Much the same clearly goes for Scott himself. And nowhere was the public silence cloaking the affairs of the defunct Raj more impenetrable than in the case of the topics above .

Scott's awareness of the Indian National Army actually dates back to the time of the INA trials of 1946, as Moore has recently established, following his research into Scott's private papers. [9] Scott had then, it seems, actually spent a night guarding an INA officer awaiting trial, though he apparently never spoke to the man. This he must have come to regret. For when his interest in the so-called 'Jiffs' revived nearly twenty years later during work on the *Quartet*, he experienced extreme difficulties in getting at sources. Only a handful of books about the INA had been published; none were initially available in England. As for official British documents - these were still closed under the fifty-year rule. This lack of concrete information was one of the reasons for Scott's 'field trip' to India in 1964 (which was to find its fictional echo in *Jewel* in the narrator's inquiries in the Mayapore of that year). In India, he eventually struck oil when friends arranged for him to meet survivors of the INA. His attempts to gain access to Indian archives in Delhi, however, were politely but firmly rebuffed by the authorities. " . . . As a novelist rather than a journalist", he was later to write, " . . . [that] reluctance

---

[9] cf. Moore, p.106.
For a comprehensive list of Scott's sources on the INA and a detailed account of how he eventually managed to secure them see Moore, pp.82-3 and 107-110 and Hilary Spurling, *Paul Scott: A Life*. London 1990, pp.337-340. Spurling's account, in particular, is highly readable with its loving description of the scene of Scott's interview with actual INA survivors: the palatial house and gardens of his fellow-writer Manohar Malgonkar, who " . . . once lost a dog to a panther on a stroll after tea through the trees". Scott's stay was less eventful, though a planned subsequent meeting in Bombay with a former INA defence counsel had to be abandoned when that city erupted in communal rioting, forcing Scott to make " . . . a dramatic exit . . . under armed escort at dead of night . . . " (Ibid., p.340)

interested me almost as much, if not more, than the archives would have done." [10] The information and impressions gained in India resulted in the creation of the character of Major Sayed Kasim in *Scorpion*, repeated references to the INA throughout the later books and, particularly in *Spoils*, its integration into the very fabric of the book: for it is the INA and its aftermath that tie together the various narrative strands of the *Quartet*, linking the fates of Merrick, Susan Bingham, Col. Layton, and the Kasim family. "The effect of the novel's structure", Moore observes, "is to emphasize that the INA problem undermined the Raj." [11] A view, he adds, rarely voiced in Britain before the publication of the *Quartet*, but supported since by historical research.

"The narrator of *The Raj Quartet* is bound to excite fellow feeling among historians", [12] Moore remarks by way of prefacing his reading of the tetralogy, for the method employed to uncover the truth about the events in Mayapore and their aftermath " . . . is that of historical inquiry." [13] Scott's own methods of researching his material were, as becomes obvious from Moore's study and Hilary Spurling's handsome biography, similar to the narrator's and similarly painstaking. Apart from haunting public libraries, ploughing his way through a roomful of books in his own house, dutifully reading stacks of unpublished and, for the most part, unpublishable memoirs that came his way as a literary agent, he pestered a vast network of friends and friends of friends in Britain and India, remorselessly extracting information from them on anything under the Anglo-Indian sun. But when he did find himself frustrated nonetheless, he could, unlike the historian, use his creative imagination to complement the picture. And the results of that intuitive approach have not only been judged to be historically convincing by those in a position to do so but have frequently been corroborated by new research or new testimony. Moore cites as an example the character of Pandit Baba, the mastermind behind the unrest in Mayapore in *Jewel* and the subsequent campaign against Merrick. The character, he says, is clearly fictitious;

---

[10] Letter to J.A.E. Heard 8 Oct. 1975, quoted by Spurling, p.338.
[11] Moore, p.113.
[12] Ibid., p.171.
[13] Ibid., p.172.

there is no evidence to suggest that Scott knew of anyone like him, yet the Pandit is in the light of recent research historically plausible. [14]

This kind of imaginative insight is even more striking in the creation of the Congress politician Mohamed Ali Kasim, which takes us to the second thrust of Scott's inquiry. For it is characters like Kasim, or, on a smaller scale, Srinivasan, Judge Menen or lawyer Gopal, who reveal the extraordinary subtlety of Scott's description of the Indian response to the Raj. His treatment of the Indian players - as opposed to the nameless noisy audience in the street - is not just unrivalled, it is unprecedented. (The merest glance at the cardboard caricatures in Kipling or, for that matter, *A Passage to India* should prove the point.) The secret of their persuasiveness lies, as Moore has suggested, in Scott's keen interest in the way Empire operated.

In the image of 'an imperial embrace' in the opening paragraph of *Jewel*, Moore writes, Scott had discovered " . . . the key to the mechanics of the Raj, "which", he elaborates, "were not confined to the deployment of superior force and racial distance, though those weapons are the dominant ones in *Jewel*". [15] "By contrast", he adds, "the opening section of *Scorpion* shows the importance for the Raj of its attachment of loyal Indians to the process of imperial rule." [16]

Not only the opening section, one might add. For in that second volume of the tetralogy Scott also deals at length with the more traditional expression of such loyalty, 'man-bap', in its twin manifestations of the loyal bearer and the loyal sepoy. In that respect the *Quartet* does not only reflect an essential part of Raj mythology, it also conforms to, or rather uses for its own designs, the stale conventions of the Anglo-Indian novel where such loyalty was as much a stock ingredient as was bazaar treachery. Scott's novel, of course, differs from the classics of the genre in that it is concerned with the exact moment when this loyalty became uncertain: Aziz's 'desertion' after Mabel Layton's death (though there the disloyalty was imaginary: the product of Mildred Layton's poisoned

---

[14] cf. Moore, pp.69-70.

Moore cites the case of one Prof. Radhe Shayam Sharma of Benares University who, having fomented unrest on campus, escaped arrest, disguised as a sadhu, and found safety in his native state of Gwalior. Moore adds, "The parallel with Baba's seeking refuge in Mirat is striking."

[15] Ibid., p.163.

[16] Ibid.

mind) and Teddie Bingham's murder at the hands of 'Jiffs' from his own regiment.

The reason for Moore's singling out the opening section of *Scorpion* is, of course, that it is the supreme example of Scott's attention to another, heretofore neglected side of the 'imperial embrace': the role of the emancipated Indian and nationalist of conviction who cooperates with the Raj not to serve it but to further by constitutional means the cause of independence. What interests Scott here, given his view of the imperial relationship as an embrace ". . . of such long standing it was no longer possible for . . . [the two nations] to know whether they hated or loved one another", (*JC*, p.1) is the Nationalists' adoption of essentially British ideas about statesmenship, the rule of law etc., culminating in India becoming a secular state with a Westminster-style constitution. For Scott this was a clear vindication of the Raj: Gandhi and Nehru sanctioning and legitimizing the British enterprise in India in retrospect, as it were. Lady Chatterjee in *Jewel* had remarked as much to the narrator in her own inimitable way:

> I have a feeling that when it was written into our constitution that we should be a secular state we finally put the lid on our Indian-ness [sic], and admitted the *legality* of our long living in sin with the English. Our so-called independence *was* rather like a shot-gun wedding.
>
> (*JC*, p.68. Scott's italics)

In the opening section of *Scorpion* - and indeed throughout the rest of the Quartet - Scott is directly concerned with British preparations for that 'shot-gun wedding'. Central to his fictional recreation of events is the character of M.A. Kasim. At the beginning of *Scorpion* Governor Malcolm attempts to persuade him to break ranks with the Congress so as to escape the threat of arrest and remain active in the political arena (from which the Congress had first withdrawn three years earlier in an understandable, if counter-productive, fit of pique over the Viceroy's unilateral declaration of war). Kasim declines the proffered olive branch even though he agrees with Malcolm's assessment of the political situation. Another three years and two books later, Malcolm offers him the governorship himself, which, in 1945, in accordance with Congress policy, Kasim must refuse. Another two years later, of course, other Congress politicians would be accepting more than just governorships.

It is because of such unfamiliar angles in its picture of the Raj that the *Quartet* won in Tariq Ali an unlikely ally during the lively public debate that followed the screening of the television version of the novels. Unlike Salman Rushdie in his notorious *Granta* article, Ali discerned considerable merit in Scott's version of events, and nowhere more so than in the scenes with Kasim. These, he felt, did elucidate history for the public, for they helped to explain " . . . the peaceful transition of power from the ruling race to an old/new ruling class". [17] And Ali adds, "It is this side of the British / Indian connection, which has hardly ever been seriously discussed in fiction or history, that gives the *Quartet* its edge." [18] Moore effectively bears him out when he says that professional historians were only beginning to turn their attention to this topic at about the time Scott did. [19]

When Kasim and Malcolm discuss the political scene during their first encounter in *Scorpion*, they do so, Ali observes, "almost as if they belonged to the same party". [20] As in a sense they do. For they share a common aim: independence for India brought about by constitutional means alone. "I would take as my premiss that the Indians wanted to be free, and that we also wished this, but that they wanted to be free for just that much longer than we felt they should be", as D.C. White had put it in *Jewel*, speaking, we can safely assume, for Scott himself. (*JC,* p.333) The conflict between people like Malcolm on the one hand and Kasim on the other was therefore essentially " . . . a result of the lack of syncronisation of the two wishes themselves". (Ibid.) It follows for Scott that the real conflict, the truly unbridgeable gap, must have existed amongst the Indians themselves: between those who, like Gandhi and Nehru, chose the evolutionary approach to independence and those, like Bose and his men in the Indian National Army, who preferred more radical means.

This conflict is crystallized in another imaginative highlight of the 'middle books', Kasim's confrontation with his son Sayed, a former King's

---

[17] Tariq Ali, "Fiction as History, History as Fiction". *Illustrated Weekly of India* 8 July 1984, quoted by Moore, p.163.
[18] Ibid.
[19] cf. Moore, p.166.
[20] Tariq Ali, *Time Out* 5-11 April 1984., p.13.

Commissioned Officer in the Indian Army, who had gone over to the INA after his capture by the Japanese, and had been promoted to the rank of major by his new masters. In this emotionally charged scene between father - recently released from house arrest - and son - awaiting trial for high treason - Scott maps out the diverging roads an independent India and a newly-created Pakistan would take. It is a clash of temperaments, generations and approaches, at the end of which it has become evident that their aims are irreconcilable too. Sayed, with his fresh memories of the sahibs' humiliation in Burma and Malaya at the hands of a lesser race, sees Britain as a spent force incapable of, and therefore unjustified in holding on to India; for him British concepts of legality and loyalty to the Crown had become irrelevant in the lights of events:

> -'What the English feel or don't feel is no longer important.We've finished with them, whether you like it or not' -'Why do you say whether you like it or not? What has my life been then? What have I been doing? Asking them to stay?-'No. Not asking. But perhaps making it possible because you believe so much in the power of the law. Their law.'
>
> (*DVS*, p.423)

Kasim-père, true to his legalist convictions, wishes his son to plead guilty to the charge of treason and when Sayed shows himself unrepentant, the father refuses to defend the son, adding that a free India would have no use for people like him. Richard Johnson, who has made an analysis of this scene with the help of Scott's original note books, feels that it ". . . rings false to Western concepts of father-son relationships" [21], though he does concede that ". . . Kasim's disapproval of his son's position had its genesis . . . in historical sources." [22] Kasim's decision reflected Congress thinking on the matter: "Let into your army one man of the suspect kind", Scott has Kasim confide to Governor Malcolm, " . . . and you plant the seed of a military dictatorship, you nurture a man who will throw away his commission again and challenge and even overthrow

---

[21] Richard M. Johnson, "'Sayed's Trial' in Paul Scott's 'A Division of the Spoils': The Interplay of History, Theme, and Purpose". *Library Chronicle of the University of Texas* 37 1986, p.86.
[22] Ibid., p.91.

a properly constituted civil authority." (DVS, p.443) It is not for nothing, after all, that polite government officials in an independent India should have been embarrassed by Scott's wish to be allowed to unsettle the dust in old INA archives, nor that Sayed Kasim, in the novel, should announce his intention to offer his services to a future Pakistan.

Another long neglected cog in the 'mechanics of the Raj' was that of the Princely States. Where it had cropped up in novels, it had served to emphasize India's perceived inability to rule itself, or, in the Cambridge-and-Bloomsbury view of things, the endearing quaintness of the Indians. Scott, by contrast, was attracted to the topic of the Princely States because, he felt, they were more revealing about the rulers than the ruled: both by virtue of their very existence and because of the way they were eventually abandoned at Independence.

These nominally sovereign states - three hundred odd, ranging from pocket-handkerchief affairs to states the size of France - were anachronistic islands of feudalism in the increasingly progressive sea of British India; and though the Political Department in Delhi kept through a so-called Resident a discreet proconsular eye on their activities (and was not above heavy-handed intervention over the merest trifles), it left unexamined the social, legal and and administrative structures of the various states and undisturbed all but the most scandalous cases of misgovernment. Thus it was that there continued to exist under the unblinking eyes of the Raj corruption, oriental despotism and dire poverty on a monumental scale, evils the combat of which the Raj would blithely cite as its chief raison d'être. From the perspective of the self-appointed Civilizers and Bringers of Law, Peace and Justice, the continued existence of the Princely States after two centuries of British rule was indefensible, indeed a scandal. Yet from the strategist's point of view, they were invaluable. Since the Princes had as much cause to fear the Nationalists as any crusty old sahib, they made natural allies for the Raj, and their backward fiefdoms usually remained islands of stability even in the most turbulent times.

For Scott, then, the Princely States represented another entry on the debit side of the Raj's moral ledger; an example of the British - though perhaps not actively dividing India, nevertheless, failing to unite it, as they were fond of claiming they had done. For while the main body of British India was moving further towards independence and democracy with each new reform, each new reform also cemented further the autocratic structures in the rest of the subcontinent. This schizophrenic policy reached its grotesque climax in the dying days of the Raj in 1947; one arm of the administration in Delhi was busily negotiating the terms for Independence with Nationalists of every hue and creed and studiously ignoring the problem of the Princes as it did so, (accepting tacitly that their dominions, unable to stand alone, would be absorbed into the newly emerging nations), while the other arm of the I.C.S. assured the Princes that old obligations would be honoured to the last, that, as their treaties with the Crown lapsed at the stroke of midnight August 14, they would find themselves fully sovereign, and therefore councelled against accession to India or Pakistan. Both sides felt they were acting on principle and following the traditions of their respective departments. "'Nothing can bring you peace of mind but the triumph of principles'", is Perron's comment: a blisteringly acerbic use of an innocently pious line by Emerson. (*DVS*, p.498) In Scott's own mind, the fate of the Princes always remained a "... lasting monument to the perfidy of Albion". [23]

For this double-dealing in 1947 to emerge as tragic rather than merely farcical, it was necessary that the reader should be able to sympathise with the Princes. Hence Scott's own fictional state of Mirat had to be made a "paradigm of political virtue". [24] Scott was unapologetic, stoutly claiming there were states like Mirat, though they never made the headlines "... because scandal and bad news are always more memorable than virtue and good news". [25] However, it is probably fair to say that Mirat with its Hindu majority ruled by a benevolent Muslim nawab, and his sympathetic European adviser is more a reflection of Scott's idea of what the Raj might have been than what any part of it actually was. Be that as it may, the sense of tragedy is palpable when Mirat is condemned by the 'men of principle' even before it is physically destroyed by the rioters during Partition, when all over India hundreds

---

[23] Scott, "Imagination and the Novel". In: *My Appointment with the Muse*, op.cit., p.19.
[24] Letter to Francine Weinbaum 31 Dec. 1975, quoted by Moore, p.82.
[25] Ibid.

of thousands of people would die, "massacred by other principled people." [26]

Scott discerned the same 'triumph of principle' in each and every aspect of the demission of power: "Pakistan for the Muslims, freedom for Congress, and the fulfillment by Britain of her promise of self-government", as Moore summarizes it; when in realty it was ". . . the mess the Raj had never been able to sort out" (*DVS*, p.592) - Sarah Layton's words, whom Moore rightly identifies as "Scott's authentic voice". [27] *Spoils*, then, was written to demonstrate in dramatic terms what Scott felt to be the truth behind the high-flown rhetoric of 1947; this he had summarized in a letter two years earlier as the decision of " . . . the people at home . . . to hand India back in as many pieces as was necessary so long as it was got rid of", adding, "Which is what happened. No one, that I know of, has yet said so." [28]

It is not hard to see after all this why Moore should call Scott "an historian manqué" as well as 'the historian's novelist.' [29] If it is the novelist who wins out, this is not least because of Scott's inventiveness in getting his views across. He may, for instance, have the narrator parodying the Anglo-Indian view of events as in the following description - nostrils flared with contempt - of the wartime Cripps Mission:

> It was entirely to placate Roosevelt that Churchill (who knew a thing or two, including the fact that the Americans' only interest in India was that the subcontinent should remain a stable threat in the rear to Japanese ambitions in the Pacific) had sent out that Fabian old maid, Stafford Cripps, to do what Churchill knew couldn't be done: put pepper into Indian civilians and politicians by offering them what they'd been offered before, but which a pinko-red like Cripps, unused to office, would see as new, generous, advantageous, a Left-Wing invention. . . .
>
> (*TS*, p.43)

---

[26] Letter to John Willey 11 Nov. 1973, quoted by Moore, p.114.
[27] Moore, pp.114-5.
[28] Letter to Roland Gant 9 May 1973, quoted by Moore, p.172.
[29] Moore, p.177.

Or he may use the voice of Guy Perron, his own private historian, alone or in conversation with the more active players on the scene, as a medium for conveying an aspect of the truth; or, most striking of all, the description in *Spoils* of a series of fictitious political cartoons by an equally fictitious Indian cartoonist. [30] One of these will serve to illustrate the point: it shows prominent members of the newly-elected post-war Labour government before a map of India, nonchalantly speculating as to the likely significance of the shaded areas that seem to make up so much of it (which the reader, unlike H.M. Ministers in the cartoon, knows to indicate the Princely States). As a way of highlighting the wide-spread ignorance in Britain of all things Indian, which for Scott was a key element in the Imperial equation, this is brilliantly effective. And though this is one instance where the historian feels the novelist is exaggerating, he does not deny the overall validity of Scott's point.[31] Indeed throughout his study of the *Quartet* Moore betrays no sign of fearing for historical truth, given that in his own assessment "The world, to a large extent, learns its history of the Raj from the works of Paul Scott." [32]

Scott's remarkable familiarity with the minutiae of Anglo-Indian history, to which Moore attests, enables him to chart authoritatively its larger designs: tracing in each successive volume of the *Quartet* the various stages of the tragic developments that culminated in 1947; each time slightly shifting the angle of investigation, adding yet another perspective or highlighting a different aspect of the same process: so that eventually there emerges a clear overall picture of "why", in the narrator's haunting phrase, "there could have been no other end". (*DS*, p.431)

Taking the question of the manner of the British withdrawal as an example, we might say, for instance, hat D.C. White's succinct account in *Jewel* of the (political) history of the British involvement on the subcontinent is complemented in *Spoils* by Captain Purvis's reflections on the

---

[30] Scott had inherited from several members of his family a considerable graphic talent and had sought, in the years of post-war austerity, to derive an income from it. The 'Halki cartoons' in *Spoils* are perhaps, as Spurling suggests, ". . . a last salute to . . . [his] own ambitions as a cartoonist in London in 1947." (Spurling, p.363)
[31] cf. Moore, p.191.
[32] Ibid., p.6.

economic madness of continued British rule, in *Towers* by Clark's cutting observations about the retrograde mentalitity of Anglo-India and its complete isolation from popular thought in England, to be rounded off and driven home, as it were, by Perron's musings in *Spoils* on the remarkable lack of impact the possession of India had had on the public imagination in Britain. Nor is Scott content to leave it at that. His determination to trace large designs is perhaps most apparent in one scene firmly outside the main time frame of the *Quartet*: the club scene in *Jewel* set in 1964, included by way of comparison of pre- and post-Independence attitudes and of graphic illustration of his point that there are certain psychological constants underlying these historical events which are still visible today. And it is the club scene - if nothing else - that should surely absolve Scott from the indivious charge of producing fictionalized history. For the historical novelist would have been only too happy to follow the historian's example and keep everything in neat little boxes, which makes for tidy chapters with tidy beginnings and, especially, tidy ends. But Scott can never forget that the end of Empire was far from neat. And he fails utterly to comprehend how one " . . . can rule India for two hundred years until midnight August 14, 1947. And then stop." [33]

That, after all, is a central message of his novels. The Indo-Pakistani wars - and the narrator visits Mayapore at the height of the second such war - are as much a legacy, or an 'unfinished business', of the Raj, as are the fears and prejudices made manifest in the behaviour of the 'new memsahibs' in Scott's fictional world or, outside it, in 'Rivers of Blood' speeches by cabinet ministers. The past is still with us, and all around us are the clues that would unlock it for us. But it needs someone with a keen awareness of history and a vivid imagination, like the narrator in *Jewel*, to bring it to life again.

This strong sense of history, however, is not just evident in remarks by the narrator or in the plotting of specific scenes and the overall structure to which they add up. It is equally apparent in the delineation of characters. And it is this ability to bring history dramatically to life in and through the characters which is, according to Lukács's classic views about the historical novel, more important than a meticulously

---

[33] Moorhead, op.cit.

accurate description of historical events: "What matters is that we should re-experience the social and human motives which led men to think, feel and act as they did in historical reality."[34] This Scott achieves by having a vast cast of characters encompassing every possible spectrum of British life in India, every one of whom, as Benny Green observes, " . . . can stand equally well as a person or as an imperial archetype"; [35] or, as Margret Scanlan puts it, by creating protagonists who are, "for all their psychological verisimilitude, . . . in one way or another representative of political movements, or social strata". [36]

If Scott's picture of British India is, therefore, more comprehensive than any attempted before this is not by virtue of the size of his canvas alone but of the careful selection of his sitters: and, most notable, there is the impressive gallery of female portraits, a significant departure from traditional practice in the colonial novel. And here even the historian, noting with satisfaction an as it were sociologically more balanced composition, pauses to bend down and admire the quality of the brushwork - or, to use Lord Beloff's metaphor, - of the engraving: "The stereotype of the 'memsahib' has now been destroyed once and for all, one would hope. For the portraits . . . [Scott] draws of British women in India . . . are all individually etched." [37]

In praising Scott for the vividness of his characters, Beloff is straying less into the territory of the literary critic than it might seem at first: for the characters presumably satisfy him as being historically convincing: in outlook, manners and language as much as in their actual experiences. And here, of course, Scott's objection against being called an 'historical' novelist suddenly does make sense. For such vividness in a novel set in the past does not stem from a sense of history but from what

---

[34] Georg Lukács, *The Historical Novel*. London 1962, p.42.
  Scott himself would probably not have approved of having Lukács thrown in. He always stoutly maintained that he was not in the business of writing historical novels since the events he was dealing with were those of his own lifetime. Though one may disaggree, one certainly would not want to argue with his wish that the *Quartet* should not be approached as a work of "merely historical interest". (cf. Moore, pp.172-3)
[35] Green, op.cit., p.28.
[36] Margret Scanlan, "The Disappearance of History: Paul Scott's 'Raj Quartet'". *Clio: A Journal of Literature, History and the Philosophy of History* 15 (2) Winter 1986, p.57.
[37] Beloff, op.cit., p.66.

Mary Lascelles has called a 'sense of the past'; this, she says, "no documentation, however thorough, will make ... unnecessary, nor will a lively pictorial imagination take its place"; for it - and it alone - "... stretches, an invisible but indispensable web of connection, between writer and reader." [38] But in Scott's case the past he writes about is part of his own past, unlike that of most historical novelists (and certainly those Lascelles had in mind). Nonetheless, it is still tempting to use Mary Lascelles's term - with its meaning changed to describe not a quality in the author, nor even in his work, but something in the reader produced by the novelist through the vividness Beloff noted - for Scott goes beyond the world of verifiable historical fact to capture something of the 'feel' of those days. And here the verdict of the surviving historical protagonists - British and Indian - must be the best gauge of success or failure; and their response has been, as Moore has shown in some detail, almost uniformly appreciative and frequently little short of enthusiastic. [39] "He got us right", exclaims one such admiring voice, "in the big things and in the small, in the traumas as well as in the tea cups". [40]

There is certainly plenty of both in the *Quartet*: traumas and tea cups. And this is where we cross back onto home ground, as it were. For the tea cups (and especially the striking superabundance of them) must concern those who are interested in the artistic merit of this vast literary china cabinet. Is it all, in other words, merely the product of an unchecked magpie instinct in the novelist in question? [41] Or do the objects somehow add up to more than a heap of fascinating curios?

---

[38] Mary Lascelles, *The Story-Teller Retrieves the Past: Historical Fiction and Fictitious History in the Art of Scott, Stevenson, Kipling and Some Others*. Oxford 1980, p.33.

[39] cf.Moore, pp.126-8.

It is, Moore observes, no small tribute to the power of Scott's creative imagination for him to have had on the one hand an enthusiastic letter from General Mohan Singh congratulating him on his description of the INA and of the moral dilemma faced by its members, while at the other end the political spectrum Sir Conrad Corfield, the last head of the Political Department of the old Indian Civil Service, roundly declared at first that 'Paul Scott' was clearly a pseudoym intended to disguise the identity of some high-ranking member of the ICS.

[40] Richard Rhodes James, "In the Steps of Paul Scott". *The Listener* 8 March 1979, p.361.

[41] cf. Scott's own remark, "I have no academic sense of particular periods. It is hit or miss. Like being a magpie. I pick things up when they glitter.", quoted by Johnson, p.82.

Perhaps the most persuasive answer to-date was provided by the reviewer whom the *Quartet* put in mind of a Veronese canvas - both in terms of scale and of composition: in either case the portraits come complete with ". . . household pets and possessions - dogs and horses and rosebushes . . ." and so on, and in either case these are clearly intended to tell us something about their owners. [42]

If Scott has an undeniable penchant for detail, he has an equally undeniable knack of investing even the most unpromising bric-a-brac with unexpected meaning: christening lace, a volume of Urdu poetry, rose bushes, railway trains and a bush shirt draped over a chair all aquire deeper significance and a battered old trunk can end up signifying nothing less than the Raj itself - and do so convincingly.

One further example may illustrate this characteristic technique of turning mundane objects into symbols. Taking us down Victoria Road in Mirat en route for the Bingham wedding, Scott predictably slows down to point out the "inevitable" statue of the Queen-Empress; but in this case - as in others - the apparent garrulousness is redeemed by what is actually being said: for what we see, following his directions, is not the all-too familiar cast-iron embodiment of British triumph we were expecting to see, but an aged Queen whose head seems ". . . bowed under the weight of the dumpling crown and an unspecified sorrow". (*DS*, p.144)

There is an unmistakable verdict in this throwaway sentence, summing up a good deal of what Scott has been endeavouring to tell us about the British Raj; and as a verdict, it is all the more crushing in its brevity. Since Scott is a master of the 'image cluster', as Mahood has observed, we are hardly surprised to find him taking up that image again and again, coaxing more meaning out of it each time. In Ranpur, for instance, we are invited to admire yet another Victoria Monument, which, being cast in bronze, gives the Queen an "unhappy resemblance" to a Rajput princess - a sight which had moved the scandalized members of the Ranpur club to pass a motion calling on the authorities to ensure that future representations of the monarch be made of white marble only. (*DVS*, p.138) Add to this the fact that the area around the statue had become - for various reasons - unpopular with the sahibs, who moved elsewhere, giving rise to the joke among Ranpur Indians that the sahibs

---

[42] Frank Giles, *The Sunday Times* 4 December 1977, p.8.

had abandoned their Queen, and the symbolism becomes obvious. Nor will it be necessary to point out that these tales of royal statues tie in with the various incidents surrounding Edwina Crane's old painting of "The Jewel in the Crown". We are not, of course, concerned here with a detailed analysis of Scott's imagery; this is merely to prove that the 'tea cups' do add up to something more than a well-stocked china cabinet: that Scott was too ambitious a novelist to content himself with the telling of a straightforward historical tale.

For Scott was, of course, *not* primarily concerned with writing historical fiction, and was certainly not interested in producing what has been called fictionalized history. To the reader of his novels that much is obvious, though one would hardly think so, looking at some of the critical analyses of his 'œuvre'. Barbara Hoffmann, for instance, fills many a learned page, tracing parallels between events and characters in the *Quartet* and actual historical occurrences and personages, which yield not altogether unexpected results: she duly identifies M.A. Kasim as Nehru himself and is delighted to discover that the details of M.A.K.'s captivitity correspond faithfully to the Panditji's; Edwina Crane is, of course, none other than poor Marcella Sherwood, the first of many victims associated with the name Amritsar and the immediate cause for Dyer's infamous 'crawling order'; and - lo and behold! - there is the blood-bespattered general himself, in the pleasingly transparent guise of Brigadier Reid. But here Hoffmann pauses. For Amritsar, we may recall, happened in 1919, but in the *Quartet* Reid and Miss Crane are caught up in the riots of '42! What happened? Could the author have become confused? Was his memory for dates perhaps not what it had been? Hoffmann is mystified, disconcerted even, till at last the awful truth dawns on her: perhaps, she wonders, Scott had never even intended to write a fully accurate historical account? [43] One would prefer simply to ignore such silliness, if it did not seem to be symptomatic of a tendency in post-war criticism which is as widespread as it is disturbing: namely a failure to understand the roots of artistic imagination, or even an attempt to deny its legitimacy. Scott himself knew that the writing was on the wall when he heard that the true identity of the original Lord Jim had at last been established and that we must learn to think of the Conradian hero as -

---

[43] cf. Hoffmann, op.cit., pp.32-3.

Augustus Podmore Williams. And while it amused him to reflect that the research culminating in that momentous discovery had "... occupied ... [its] author well in excess of the time it took Conrad to write the novel", he found the implications of the affair altogether more serious: for it seemed to suggest that it was no longer enough for a writer " ... to conjure images of a place which other people familiar with it will immediately recognize as absolutely authentic." [44] Not authenticity, authentication was now required. And this, of course, only the critic might dispense, thus " ... providing a novelist with credentials of proving that he was a serious person who did his best to keep his imagination in check and his powers of observation nicely harnessed to a world of recognizable reality." [45]

It is indeed ironic that an author like Scott who had always emphasized that imagination alone was not enough for writing a novel but had to be complemented by concrete knowledge, [46] that an author who had taken such elaborate care "to get the small things right", should have his knuckles rapped for taking 'artistic liberties'; and not by some crusty old historian, jealously guarding his particular little patch of research, but by a literary critic. [47] Perhaps, though, such murmurings could only have originated in the literary 'camp' - the historians being more aware that Fiction and History are two different things, with different methods and different aims. Nor are they necessarily convinced of the superiority of their own rigorously accurate methods over the more unfettered

---

[44] Scott, "Speech at the Yorkshire Post Fiction Award". In: *My Appointment with the Muse: Essays 1961-1975* (edited and introduced by Shelley C. Reece). London 1986, p.106.
One wonders what Scott would have made of some of the critical efforts that have been lavished on his own work. Take for instance the comical misfortune that befalls Richard Johnson, as he turns his attention to Scott's original notebooks there to sift for undiscovered treasure; one of the things he dredges up and holds up as a sparkling gem, is Emerson's familiar line: "Man is explicable by nothing less than all his history." It is familiar in that it keeps recurring in the *Quartet* and is always clearly identified as being by Emerson. Yet Johnson records Scott as "apparently quoting from an unknown source" (Johnson, op.cit., p.84) - there having been, one supposes, only time for the briefest of cursory glances at the *published* text of the *Quartet*.
[45] Ibid., p.107.
[46] cf. Scott, "Imagination in the Novel". In: *My Appointment with the Muse*, p.19.
[47] quoted by Richard Rhodes James, op.cit., p.361.

approach of the novelist. Indeed, this is a point specifically made by Lord Beloff in his reflections on the *Quartet.*

He begins his observations by stressing the compexity of motives and of individual decisions that lead to the adoption of policies in, and concerning, India, and does so in terms strongly reminiscent of D.C. White's remarks in *Jewel* (which, it will be remembered, dealt with the difficulties of establishing an objective historical truth). The subject, he concludes, is therefore ". . . one to which the historian's techniques, however refined, may not be able to do justice." [48] In fact, Beloff concedes that the novelist enjoys here a clear advantage over the historian, and cites as an example where this becomes evident the topic of the Demission of Power - what led up to it, what followed, and, above all, the question of moral responsibility for what followed - and I quote at length because what Beloff says does seem of great relevance here: "The historian", he writes,

> is always concerned with what happened and so tends to see what happened as inevitable, and from that it is a small step to justifying it. Few historians have treated the fall of the British Empire as something that did not have to happen in the way it did - and as an episode in which some important values (as well as many lives) were sacrificed for motives only partially pure. [49]

This emphasis on the morality (or otherwise) of decisions taken at the time Beloff regards as the most striking difference between Scott's exploration of the end of Empire and the historian's account of it. It is this that makes reading the *Quartet* for him a deeply moving experience and, he adds, " . . . what is the sense of studying history if it is not to move one and widen one's moral sensibilities?" [50]

'To widen people's moral sensibilities' - that is well said. And, though Scott was always careful not to overestimate the novelist's real influence, he might, one imagines, have been happy to go along with that as a definition of his own aims as a writer. Certainly, it squares with what he

---
[48] Beloff, op.cit., p.65.
[49] Ibid., p.70.
[50] Ibid.

himself has said - obliquely in his novels and more directly outside them. In the *Quartet* the character of Perron, whom Scott invented "... *to draw it all into focus*" is, after all, as Beloff rightly stresses, specifically interested in the moral aspects of British rule, and especially in the way it was ended. [51] For Perron (who clearly speaks for his creator) the manner of the British departure - and not the fact of it, an important distinction to make - was a betrayal of every principle previously adhered to, no matter what politicians (and historians) may have tried to make out. "... To the novelist", Scott remarks characteristically, "the smell of betrayal can never smell of roses. He is interested in people, and uncommitted to policies." [52] And pondering in the same address the feelings of those Anglo-Indians (like Nigel Rowan in the *Quartet*) who were left by questionable decisions in England to " . . . survey the ruins of their public lives . . . ", he wonders, "Was there amongst them no man who felt dishonoured?" [53]

This is not a question the historian would ever ask, nor be interested in an answer to it. "History doesn't record the answer or even pose the question", as the narrator in *Jewel* puts it in another context. (*JC*, p.71) The feelings of the individual - love or hate, and such concepts as honour and loyalty - and their influence in deciding that man's actions are all beyond the historian's ken. They do not get through the mesh of the sieve with which - to use D.C. White's image - the historian sifts through the enormous amount of available fact. What emerges at the other side of the mesh is therefore a greatly simplified and, sometimes, sanitized version of events: one that allows historians, for instance, to congratulate Britain's post-war rulers on their speedy disengagement from the subcontinent as the laudable conclusion of longstanding liberal policies, while overlooking such trifles as the breach - in spirit, though not in letter - of solemn undertakings to the Princes or the bloody reality of Partition. And while such a view of events is neither deliberately misleading, nor wholly unjustified, it is one-sided: the result matching or reflecting the historian's original expectations. For much, if not all, depends, as White explains, on the historian's original attitude - on the nature of his

---

[51] Baker, op.cit., p.7 (my emphasis).
[52] Scott, "Imagination in the Novel", op.cit., p.19.
[53] Ibid.

particular sieve, as it were: "The relevance and truth of what gets through the mesh ... depends on the relevance and truth of the attitude ... "; and if one accepts that, one is, as White also points out, " ... at once back on the ground of personal preference - even prejudice - which may or may not have anything to do with 'truth', so-called." (*JC*, p.333)

Something of that kind had also dawned on Lady Manners, prompted, in her case, by the sight of the hidden mechanics of the Raj during the inquiry into Merrick's conduct in the Bibighar affair. "But it isn't the best we should remember", had been her immediate reaction; to which the narrator had added, and surely this is the voice of Scott himself,

> We must remember the worst because the worst is the lives we lead, the best is only our history, and between our history and our lives there is this vast dark plain where the rapt and patient shepherds drive their invisible flocks in expectation of God's forgiveness.
> (*DS*, p.305)

What all this amounts to, underneath the poetic imagery or White's collected dispassionate air, is nothing less than a full-scale attack on the conventional belief in history's ability to explain and illumine for us the past. By insisting that history and "the lives we lead" are two very different things, and by putting such a heavy emphasis on the palpable reality of life, as opposed to an implied airy insubstantiality of 'history' so-called, the narrator relegates its pursuit to the rank of an intellectual exercise of little practical value. Nor are such sentiments limited to the narrator or D.C. White: they reverberate throughout the body of the *Quartet* and are expressed by all those characters, like White or Mr Srinivasan or Count Bronowsky, whose opinions we have been encouraged to trust most; they are also echoed by Guy Perron, his profession notwithstanding. Indeed, Perron even goes one step further: he suggests that history not only fails to get to the roots of the problem, it may itself become an obstacle to our understanding of people and events. His reflections are prompted by the career of Ronald Merrick - history's 'invisible man' - whose nefarious progress remained unchecked, Perron thinks, because his life was in such utter contradiction to the accepted view of the history of the British enterprise in the East (and of the role of the individual Briton ordained by it) that everyone refused to believe the truth about him even when it was staring them in the face. Merrick remained 'invisible' because he ". . . lacked entirely that liberal instinct so dear to historians that they lay it out like a guideline through the unmapped forests of prejudice and self-interest as though this line, and not the forest, is our history." (*DVS*, p.301)

'History', then, as this striking passage implies, can mean one of two things in the *Quartet*: the real events of the past in all their complexity - "the forests of self-interest and prejudice", in other words - and the simplified image of those events which the historian holds up as 'history'. And nothing illustrates the difference between the two more clearly than the central relationship of the *Quartet*, that of Kumar and Merrick.

> Place Merrick at home, in England, and Harry Coomer abroad, in England, and it is Coomer on whom the historian's eye lovingly falls; he is a symbol of our virtue. In England it is Merrick who is invisible. Place them there, in India, and the historian cannot see either of them. They have wandered off the guideline, into the jungle. But throw a spotlight on them and it is Merrick on whom it falls. There he is, the unrecorded man, one of the kind of men we really are . . .
> (*DVS*, p.302)

The fact that Scott puts Merrick and Kumar, these two 'unrecorded men', at the centre of his own investigation into the past is surely eloquent enough in itself. To say therefore that Scott ". . . betrays a deep scepticism about the ways human beings understand, remember and act on their history", as Margret Scanlan does, is almost to understate things. [54] The title she chooses for her fascinating essay - "The Disappearance of History" - captures the state of play in the *Quartet* rather better. Nor is Scott's scepticism limited to history as such. It also extends, as Scanlan points out, " . . . to the genre in which the *Quartet* is written, making its apparent conformity to the conventions of the historical novel a mask for its persistent subversion of them". [55]

---

[54] Scanlan, op.cit., p.153.
[55] Ibid.

Before we go into the details of that "subversion" and the form it takes, let us quickly rehearse again with Scanlan's help the shortcomings of conventional history writing as Scott portrays them in the *Quartet*. There is firstly the matter of open bias: "all the distortions imposed by temperament and rhetoric", highlighted by Brigadier Reid's memoirs or Lili Chatterjee's recollections. [56] And as an even more pointed example Scanlan quotes the narrator's remarks in *Jewel* about a minor actor in the events of 1942, Mr Laxminarayan, who in 1964 is engaged on " ... a history of the origins of Indian nationalism: his aplogia for many years of personal compromise." (*JC*, p.245) Laxminarayan, the narrator adds, is a master of the subtleties of the English language " ... which so readily lent itself to the business of making the cautious middle way sound like common sense instead of like a case of cold feet." (*JC*, p.245) But the problem is of an even more fundamental nature: for "the raw materials of history" are themselves " ... endlessly vulnerable to interpretation". [57] And Scanlan quotes by way of illustration Perron's comment that the history of the relationship between Daphne and Hari " ... could be made to fit almost any theory one could have of Kumar's character and intentions." (*DVS*, p.304) She might equally have quoted D.C. White's remark about Brigadier Reid's memoirs: that one could easily demolish his objectionable " ... foursquare little edifice of simple cause and simple effect in order to redress the balance and present the obverse, and just as inaccurate, picture of a tyrannical ... power grinding the faces of its coloured subjects in the dust." (*JC*, pp.332-3) But, as White suggests to the narrator, " ... that's not what we're after, is it?" (*JC*, p.332)

What then *is* Scott after? Let us approach the matter obliquely, and begin by looking for Scott's answer to a more fundamental question: that of why he writes in the first place? - " ... *Not - certainly not* to solve problems", was his characteristic off-the-cuff reply in an interview with Francine Ringold. [58] Indeed, he always showed himself convinced that, far from being the 'unacknowledged legislator', the writer could never be more than a "legislator manqué". [59] His own aims were more humble, or

---

[56] Ibid., p.155.
[57] Ibid., p.156.
[58] Ringold, op.cit., p.18.
[59] Scott, "Literature and Social Conscience: The Novel". In: *My Appointment*, p.141. Nothing could perhaps illustrate Scott's no-nonsense attitude better than the

183

perhaps one should say more realistic: rather than lay down the law on everything under the sun, all the writer could - and should - do was "... to ask questions;" [60] questions about "... human beings living life [because] - that's what literature is." [61] A line which, were it not for the poignant echo it produces in our ears of the difference between 'history' and "the lives we lead", would have a deceptively ingénue ring about it. But then it is drawn from a chatty interview in America where Scott, one suspects, was being engagingly 'low-brow', engagingly self-deprecating, and engagingly modest about the aims of literature, too. His private notebooks - as far as one can judge from those few tantalizing snippets that have been published - appear to speak a different language. Novels, one reads there, "... are as much a part of academic investigation as science, sociology, ... philosophy, mathematics", a line which, while corroborating his more homely, not to say homespun, remarks to Francine Ringold, does sit somewhat uncomfortably beside them. [62]

But, then, Scott did enjoy cultivating a playfully self-conscious manner about the use of literary terms in capital letters ("When people talk about The Novel, the vision I have is of a sort of literary St. Pancras Station ..."). [63] That did not stop him, however, from being quite forthcoming over the years about his views on The Novel (and Its Purpose). Apart from various interviews touching upon this topic, he gave several addresses at literary conferences and workshops, which invariably carry the words 'The Novel' in their titles. But the most intriguing remark comes, once again, from the notebooks, courtesy Richard Johnson, gallantly battling with Scott's cryptic hand writing:

> Sometimes I feel, quite strongly, that the novel is the only means of conveying, dramatically and in impolite, even inartistic terms, human ... realization [?] of

---

following line, also on the topic of the 'unacknowledged legislator': "On the whole I can't help wishing Shelley had kept his mouth shut. I feel it may be to him we owe that awful word 'commitment'" (Ibid., p.131)
[60] Ringold, p.18.
[61] Ibid., p.31.
[62] Johnson, p.84.
[63] Scott, "The Architecture of the Arts: The Novel". In: *My Appointment*, p.74.

those areas of silence and incomprehension, of failure of communication, that spread so unhappily. [64]

These "areas of silence and incomprehension" which, Scott suggests, the novel alone can explore recall the "thickets of prejudice and self-interest" of the *Quartet*; and the whole passage, therefore, restates his claim to be able to achieve as a novelist what eludes the historian. There is of course nothing original about such a claim: it has been made by novelists of every generation. David Rubin, contemplating the unexpected upsurge in interest among novelists in the Raj decades after its demise, is reminded of Conrad's definition of the novel as being " . . . a conviction of our fellow-men's existence strong enough to take upon itself a form of imagined life clearer than reality and whose accumulated verisimilitude of selected episodes puts to shame the pride of documentary history". [65]

This takes us back to the historical novel and what Margret Scanlan calls Scott's systematic "subversion" of the genre. For, unlike the great historical novels of the European tradition, the *Quartet* contains no famous historical character. These remain firmly off-stage; as do the great historical events of the period. One will look in vain in it even for a glimpse of a Napoleon at Waterloo or a Kutuzov at Borodino. And this is no coyness of the author; it is deliberate design: the consequence of Scott's doubts of the value of any kind of traditional historiography. Fearing " . . . the tendency of written history to drift away from actual lives . . . ", he prefers to hold fast to the certainties of individual lives which he then anchors in the more uncertain seas of general history; thus seeking " . . . to establish an identity between public events and the private experiences of his characters", as Scanlan puts it. [66] Apart from the obvious case of 8 August 1942 - the night of the Bibighar - with its

---

[64] Johnson, p.86.
[65] Joseph Conrad, "A Personal Record", (quoted by Rubin, op.cit., p.ix).
[66] Scanlan, p.157.
It is here surely that the influence of Thackeray, noted by Francine Weinbaum and acknowledged by Scott, is most obvious. The reader of the *Raj Quartet* will recognize instantly in D.J. Taylor's lines on *Vanity Fair* the description of a familiar approach: "In many ways Thackeray's novel is the refraction of an entire society responding to Waterloo . . . . Occasionally this becomes explicit, notably in the role call of historical cause and effect at the end of Volume One when Napoleon lands in France, all England is ablaze, the funds fall and . . . poor John Sedley was ruined". (D.J. Taylor, *A Vain Conceit: British Fiction in the 1980s*. London 1989, p.34)

multiple significance for the lives of all the characters in Jewel, this is, Scanlan points out, especially true of the life of Barbie Batchelor, who retires on the day of the outbreak of the Second World War and dies on the day of Hiroshima; 'D-Day', with its special significance for the Laytons being another case in point: it is the day of Mabel's death, Susan's premature labour and Sarah's loss of virginity. This characteristic technique is, Scanlan suggests, rather more than just a device to 'anchor' fiction in reality: it serves to produce an "alternative idea of history" which ". . . locates the meaning of public events in the lives and consciousnesses of single people".[67] But Scott, she stresses, goes even beyond that. For there is in the *Quartet*, in spite of its much-praised firm "realistic texture", a constant " . . . tendency to turn history into stories and stories into myths that seek to explain history." [68]

The most obvious example of this technique is, of course, the 'central' story of the *Quartet* itself: that of Daphne's love for Hari and of her subsequent rape. This "story of a rape" functions on one level as a straight forward account of a concrete incident with a definite historical setting (the 'Quit India' riots of August 1942) but hints through its distinct echoes of several actual historical occurrences (Cawnpore 1857 and Amritsar 1919) at a wider significance: indeed, the same first page of the *Jewel* suggests, it might also be seen as a metaphor for the entire relationship between England and India, which Scott calls "the imperial embrace".

These, then, are the microscopic-macroscopic correspondencies of which Weinbaum speaks. Mildred Layton's restoration of 'Rose Cottage' to

---

[67] Ibid., p.158.
Suzanne Kim makes a similar point when she says that Scott attempts to establish an historical truth about the Raj as a whole " . . . par le truchement d'une vérité sur les individus . . . " (Kim, op.cit., p.170)
Also, one is again reminded of the great nineteenth century novelists, as practically every critic, from the early reviews onwards, have observed. Here is D.J. Taylor again on the Victorian giants, and one would be perfectly happy to let what he says stand in a discussion of Scott's *Quartet*: "[They] . . . achieved their odd, luxuriant plausibility by appearing to understand how society worked, by anatomising the various forces and interests by which its charaters were directed. . . . Read a novel like *Vanity Fair* and ask yourself why it tells you so much about the society in which it is set. The answer lies not merely in its patient inventory of detail and artefact - and Thackeray is about the only English novelist from whom you could learn how to order a suit of clothes or discount the bill - but in its ability to link individual lives with the great historical processes." (Taylor, p.34)
[68] Scanlan, p.153.

its old nineteenth-century self - with its metaphorical echo of the Viceroy's wartime decision to revert to direct rule - is one [69], her decision to ride roughshod over Mabel's wish to be buried in Ranpur - a foreshadowing of the end of the Raj - is another. What goes for individual scenes, also goes for entire lives: "At any moment", says Weinbaum, the life of any character can zoom into focus as the life of England in India." [70] And the history of such a life can - as in the case of Rowan's uncle, who educated a young maharajah and then outstayed his welcome - encapsulate in allegorical form the entire history of the British involvement in India.

It follows that there must be parallels in the lives of the protagonists; and this is, of course, one of the most obvious characteristics of the narrative technique - and structure - of the *Quartet*. Edwina Crane and Barbie Batchelor, Daphne Manners and Sarah Layton, Hari Kumar and Ahmed Kasim, Guy Perron, or even - in the Philoctetes analogy - Ronald Merrick: this process of blurring or even merging characters' identities and of collapsing stories is repeated throughout the *Quartet* till it becomes clear in the end that it is really always the same story. [71]

What, then, is the message contained in the structure of the *Quartet*? That history is a repetition of errors, as David Rubin sees it? [72] Or, to phrase it differently, that man is apparently unable to learn from the past and thus condemned to make the same mistakes over and over again? The answer, in both cases, is yes. But that is only half the story. It is Eliot, as so often, who seems to provide the key to Scott's thinking here; in "Dry Salvages" he speaks of " . . . the past experiences revived in the meaning / [being] . . . not the experience of one life only / But of many generations . . . " But it is Eliot's next line, the rider he adds to the above, which is even more strikingly apposite: " . . . - not forgetting / Something that is probably quite ineffable: / The backward look behind the assurance / Of recorded history, towards the primitive terror."

There you have the essence of the *Quartet*. This "backward half-look", reducing his characters to speechless despair or even madness, is at

---

[69] Credit for first spotting this parallel goes, as for so many things, to Margret Scanlan. (cf. Scanlan, p.160)
[70] Weinbaum, *Aspiration*, p.165.
[71] cf. Scanlan, p.162.
[72] cf. Rubin, p.145.

the heart of Scott's vision. It is that world beyond history which constitutes the core of his novels: the metaphysical core, if you like, of which Swinden speaks. [73] "In other words," as Swinden suggests, "the historical detail is the outer manifestation of ideas about the world which are felt to be incontrovertible and which are therefore meshed into the episodes of the story so as to bring out a pattern in the way the events develop . . . ." [74] This is why Scott was perhaps justified, after all, to insist that he was not an historical novelist. It certainly helps to explain the ending of *Spoils*, the unexpected poetic postscipt through which, as Margret Scanlan has pointed out, the *Quartet* seems to " . . . empty itself of history":

> When it is all over, when the immediate price for India's freedom is at least a quarter of a million lives . . . , then Scott moves gracefully, almost with relief, to another genre. Time in the lyrics is at last released, as Barbie was in her madness, from the constraints of the calendar. The Indian poet offers timeless images of mutability . . . . [75]

What better way, then, to bring to its conclusion a discusion of the *Quartet* than by emulating the novelist's example and turning to the poet for the last word; the poet, in this case, whose work might at times almost be used as a running commentary to Scott's exploration of the past and whose lines, from "Little Gidding", might well serve as a motto for it:

> And last, the rending pain of re-enanctment
> Of all that you have done, and been; the shame
> Of motives late revealed, and the awareness
> Of things ill done and done to others's harm
> Which once you took for exercise of virtue.
> Then fools' approval stings and honour stains. . . .
>
>   . . . This is the use of memory:
>   For liberation . . .

---

[73] cf. Swinden, p.97.
[74] Ibid.
[75] Scanlan, p.167.

'A MOMENT OF HISTORY' : J.G. FARRELL'S *THE SIEGE OF KRISHNAPUR*

When James Gordon Farrell turned to India to write *The Siege of Krishnapur*, Paul Scott was halfway into his *Quartet* and still unnoticed by the wider reading public, for whom *A Passage to India* remained the last word on the Raj; indeed, the news - only months before - of the death of the Great Man himself had rather revived interest in it by a public amazed that its author should still have been alive and holding court at Cambridge. Farrell, in other words, was probably as much aware of the long Forsterian shadow as Scott had been before him. His way of acknowledging it, however, was very different. For whereas Scott, as we have seen, felt the need to confront the Forsterian image of India and to correct what he considered the unacceptable distortions in Forster's vision, Farrell was driven by no such urge. His own ambitions lay entirely in another direction; and that had consequences for the tone of Farrell's novel as much as for its plot: if Farrell lacks the high seriousness of Scott, he is also free of Scott's occasional self-consciousness. Scott, at times, seems almost anxious to blot out in the minds of his readers all thought of *A Passage to India*. Farrell deliberately refers them back to it at the beginning of his Indian novel; but there is no attempt to engage the topic seriously: a passing nod, as it were, in the direction of his august predecessor, or rather a knowing wink at the reader and he is done with Forster: as is perhaps fitting for a novel which, in terms of its subject matter, is definitely 'pre-Forsterian', so to speak.

The Forsterian echo is, moreover, only the first of many literary allusions in *The Siege of Krishnapur*, most of them delivered with a playfully conspiratorial wink. [1] For though they heighten the period feel

---

[1] For a detailed analysis of these cf. Ronald Binns, " The Novelist as Historian". *Critical Quarterly* 21 (2), p.70. and Binns, *J.G. Farrell* London 1986 (Contemporary Writers), pp.73-75. Binn's list of literary influences, though reading at times like a Who's Who in Nineteenth and Twentieth Century English Literature, is entirely convincing, which is more than can be said of some other critical offerings. Here, for instance, are Allen Greenberger and Edith Piness, detecting shades of Kyauktada in Farrell's Krishnapur: "Farrell's George Fleury is a cousin, at least in a number of external trappings to Orwell's John Flory. Both have dogs which have to be killed and both have a distinguishing mark - Fleury's green coat and Flory's birthmark. ... it is not far fetched to think that Farrell intends his readers to reflect momentarily on Orwell's earlier creation." - Can they be serious? (cf. Allen

of the novel and thus - ostensibly - enhance the authority of the narrative voice, they are in reality a subversive device; Farrell uses them to provide an ironic angle both to the narrator's own story and to those to which he alludes.

The 'Forsterian' opening section of *Krishnapur* provides a perfect illustration of this technique: it is, in some ways, almost a mirror image of the first pages of *Passage*. Both set the scene for the events that follow, and both do so in the leisurely omniscient manner of Victorian or Edwardian travel books: ". . . the same detached and knowledgeable descriptive register, the same calmly assured tone", as Bernard Bergonzi observes. [2] The scene itself is instantly recognizable, too: the immensity of the Indian plain, against which the Works of Man dwindle to insignificance and Man himself even more so. Good familiar stuff. And even a line such as " . . . there does not appear to be anywhere worth walking to . . . ; one part looks quite as good as another" (*SK*, p.9) might pass for Forster in his more irreverent mood. [3] It is only once the narrator remarks on the absence of anything " . . . that a European might recognize as civilization", urges us " . . . to press on, therefore, towards those distant white bricks", and follows this up with, "Bricks are undoubtedly an essential ingredient of civilization; one gets nowhere at all without them", that we begin to suspect that all here is not as it seems. (*SK*, p.10) Nor is it. The bricks turn out to be a deserted Indian cemetery, a so-called 'City of the Silent', and in due course Krishnapur itself is discovered to be equally lifeless and neglected, so that " . . . a visitor might well find himself reminded of the 'City of the Silent' he had passed on his way . . . ". (*SK*, p.11)

By this point, of course, the ironic intent of the oblique allusion to *Passage* has become fully apparent. In Forster's day the sight of a British cantonment had evoked in the beholder a feeling of imperial power and permanence: it was "symbolic of the net Great Britain had thrown over India", with which it shared nothing " . . . except the overarching sky". [4]

J. Greenberger and Edith L. Piness, "J.G. Farrell's 'The Siege of Krishnapur'". *Indo-British Review: A Journal of History* 11 (1) December 1984, p.113)

[2] Bernard Bergonzi, *The Situation of the Novel.* London 1979, pp.230-1.

[3] All page references are to the Penguin edition: Harmondsworth 1975; those for *Troubles* (*T*) are to the original hardcover edition (London 1970) as are those for *The Singapore Grip* (*SG*) London 1978.

[4] *A Passage to India*, p.3.

Fifty years on, we find a deserted and decaying cantonment, now - brick or no brick - very definitely part of the amorphous Indian vastness: slowly dissolving and melting back into it like the remnants of earlier empires which litter the Indian plain. From the outset, then, Farrell's perspective is unambiguously post-imperial: the empire he describes is - in marked contrast to that of most novels about the Raj - a sunken empire. [5]

The word 'empire', or rather 'Empire' with a definite capital E, does in fact provide the key to Farrell's interest in India. Western novelists, as he himself once pointed out, have tended to use the country only as an exotic backdrop or " . . . as a means of expressing whatever it was they wanted to say about some other matter, or about life in general." [6] In Farrell's own case this is certainly true. There are only a handful of Indian characters in his 'Indian' novel - all of them minor figures, sketched rather than drawn - and for the greater part of the narrative Indians are glimpsed only through the telescope which the European defenders trail on their native attackers. Farrell's protagonists betray little interest in what Forster's Adela Quested had called "the real India". Nor does the narrator, for that matter; he may occasionally show himself "aware", in David Rubin's assessment, of India's enigmatic and incomprehensible nature, but never in " . . . the grand manner of those who enjoy being baffled by her philosophies and mysteries". [7] Certainly, there is in Farrell's writing little sign of the 'Continent of Circe' casting its familiar spell. "To Fleury", says the narrator at one point, "India was a mixture of the exotic and the immensely boring" (*SK*, pp.30-1), and one wonders whether that does not also sum up neatly the sentiments of Fleury's creator. [8] *Krishnapur*, in other words, is not what Ronald Binns

---

[5] Farrell's stance is much more uncompromising here than Scott's 'soft focus' approach at the beginning of the *Quartet*.

[6] This, incidentally, in a perceptive review of Scott's *Raj Quartet* in which he contrasts Scott's concerns with those of most British fiction 'on' India: J.G.Farrell, "Indian Identities". *The Times Literary Supplement* May 1975, p.555.

[7] Rubin, op.cit., p.38.

[8] Some critics, worn out perhaps by the epic mysteries and muddles of the India of fiction, note as much with approval and undisguised relief: cf. inter al. David Rubin, who believes that "part of Farrell's success stems from his candid indifference to India as a problem." (Rubin, p.41)

Frances Singh would probably disagree, but she is so far alone in thinking that " . . . the real hero of *The Siege of Krishnapur* is . . . India itself . . . "; her

calls a "condition of India novel", unlike, he adds, *Passage*, or, more recently, *The Raj Quartet*. [9] For if Scott's or Forster's approaches to India were at heart biographical and always deeply personal, Farrell's was detached and his interest incidental, so to speak. He did have Indian connections - his parents met in Burma and lived for a while in Bengal - but this part of his family history appears to have had little bearing on his work as a novelist. [10]

Farrell, one might say, reached India via Ireland. For if his Anglo-Indian connections failed to ignite his creative imagination, his Anglo-Irish background had done so more readily. The resulting book, *Troubles*, not only established Farrell's literary reputation, it also shaped the novelist, channelling his creative energies and bringing his views and concerns into focus. These were now directed towards the past and would remain so for the rest of his life. Turning to the past, however, was not an exercise in nostalgia: *Troubles*, as Elizabeth Bowen noted in a rapturous review, was no " . . . 'period piece' [but] yesterday reflected in today's consciousness". [11] Indeed, work on *Troubles* had brought with it poignant reminders of the strong link between past and present. Farrell later recalled in an interview that while researching for his Irish novel in 1968 he would go out to the Newspaper Library at Colindale to ". . . read *The Irish Times* for 1920 and come back, buying an evening paper on the Tube. It was uncanny: exactly the same things were happening again, sometimes even in the same streets in Belfast". [12]

---

reasoning, though, - that timeless India alone emerges unscathed from the general catalysm - is not without its charm. (cf. Frances B. Singh,"Progress and History in J.G. Farrell's 'The Siege of Krishnapur'". *Chandrabhaga* 2 (1979), pp.36-7.
[9] Binns, J.G. *Farrell*. op.cit., p.64.
[10] Ibid., p.29.
Binns relates that Farrell's father was caught up personally in the decline of the Raj: he was apparently injured in a 'freedom riot' in Chittagong in the thirties.In the same paragraph Binns speaks of Farrell "once again drawing partly on his family history for inspiration". It is of course hard to refute such a conveniently vague statement - or for that matter to prove it; but one cannot help wondering whether it is not perhaps significant that Farrell set neither *Krishnapur* nor his second, unfinished, 'Indian' novel in the twentieth century? It seems to me that notwithstanding the "keen interest in his father's experience" and the fact, also noted by Binns, of the personal dedication to his father of *The Siege of Krishnapur*, Farrell was in fact never tempted to write about the India his parents had known.
[11] Elizabeth Bowen, "Ireland Agonistes", *Europa* 1 (1971), p.59.
[12] George Brock, "Epitaph for the Empire". *Observer Magazine* 24 September 1979, p.73.

The novelist in him was quick to recognize the potential of the past "as a metaphor for today": for, he explained, " . . . however much the superficial details and customs of life may change over the years, . . . life itself does not change very much. Indeed all literature that survives must depend on that assumption." [13] The past, he felt, had the added advantage of being as it were neutral territory: whereas people " . . . as a rule, . . . have already made up their minds what they think about the present [,] about the past they are more susceptible to clarity of vision." [14] Lastly, the yellowing pages of *The Irish Times* had generated in him a wider interest in Britain's then still largely neglected recent history; this, after all, was also the history of Farrell's own generation. "It seemed to me", Farrell observed later, "that the really interesting thing that's happened during my lifetime has been the decline of the British Empire." [15]

It is therefore not altogether surprising that Farrell should have followed up his Irish novel with an Indian one, which, in turn, was succeeded by a novel set in wartime Singapore. These three have generally become known as his 'Empire Trilogy', though he himself prefered " . . . to think of them as a tryptich [,]. . . with each panel presenting a picture of a different kind of historical watershed . . . ". [16]

What was perhaps surprising was the choice of topic, or rather of 'period', for his second 'panel': Mutiny India holding neither the kind of family links for Farrell that the Ireland of *Troubles* held nor the affinity in simple terms of generations that the Fall of Singapore would later offer. In fact, it was not only more remote, it was a less likely subject altogether. Susan Howe, in her classic study of *Novels of Empire*, had memorably described the colonial novel as "the running record of a great defeat". [17] In those terms, too, the Indian Mutiny seemed a less obvious

---

[13] James Vinson, *Contemporary Novelists*. London 1972, p.400.
[14] Ibid.
[15] Brock, op.cit., p.73.
[16] Malcolm Dean, "Grip of Empire". *The Guardian* 13 September 1978, p.10. In the same interview he went on to say that he could not promise not to add another panel or two " . . . and turn it into a polyptych". (Ibid.) This was not to be. A sudden and cruel death overtook him when he was halfway through his fourth 'panel'; this fragment, again with an Indian setting and with some survivors of the siege of Krishnapur amongst its characters, was subsequently published as *The Hill Station*.
[17] Howe, op.cit., p.79.

choice, since the sense of defeat there had not been as pronounced as it was later to be in Ireland or Singapore. Indeed, in the annals of Empire the Mutiny and its suppression are recorded in the gilded lettering reserved for its most glorious moments. But therein, perhaps, lay part of its attraction for Farrell. He was, after all, a novelist who relished the subtle difference between appearance and reality, and, in those terms, the topic must have seemed irresistible. Here was defeat disguised as winged victory; an ugly and messy affair, which, perversely, became a source of intense national pride to the Victorians, inspiring - if that is the word - a whole generation of minor artists and lesser poets to dizzy flights of patriotic fantasy. (Farrell playfully alludes to this at the end of his novel when he has a 'victorious' general make mental notes for some future canvas depicting "The Relief of Krishnapur" - complete with suggestions for desirable artistic licence.)

However, the choice of the Mutiny as setting for another imperial canvas of his own held other, more serious, attractions for Farrell. Anglo-Indian fiction had always tended to portray crises in British rule in India essentially as a consequence of outside influence: either in the guise of elaborate conspiracy theories earlier in the century or, more recently, by charting the loss of British prestige on the subcontinent after each of the major military or political setbacks in the Empire's final decades. [18] Farrell, it is fair to say, was in his own way as much an 'historian manqué' as Paul Scott. [19] And like Scott, Farrell felt that the truth about the decline of the Empire had not yet really emerged. Both were, in fact, working on a similar premiss: that the familiar 'barbarians-at-the-gate' approach of Anglo-Indian fiction missed the point: the point being that the Empire had carried within it the seeds of its own destruction. But whereas Scott, driven by personal memories of India, was grappling with the shades and ambiguities of the Raj 'in extremis', Farrell preferred to go back much further: to the time when, as he put it, " . . . the myth of

---

[18] A memorable example of these conspiracy theories - for lovers of such things - is contained in Edward Candler's *Siri Ram: Revolutionist*, published in London in 1912: "under the snows of Amarnath the Gaelic-American-Indian plot gathered. . . . envelopes with the American postmark fluttered on to the ice lingam." etc.etc. (p.171) - And this from one of the more restrained Anglo-Indian novelists.

[19] A mere glimps at the *The Singapore Grip* with its patient inventory of plantation statistics and its painstaking, not to say plodding, account of the war in Malaya should prove the point.

the grateful and obedient natives being led onwards and upwards by the paternal white ruler" was first exploded. [20] What intrigued Farrell was that this should have happened at a time when "the Empire was at its most energetic thanks to the new technology of the Industrial Revolution and seemed to be offering (in many ways it was offering) a vast range of physical, social and moral benefits". [21] A closer look at the Mutiny, therefore, promised an insight free from the myth which had since sprung up around the Empire, and around the Raj in particular.

Yet myth there certainly was, and the Mutiny was at the heart of it. This Farrell was happy to exploit for his own ends. The ostensible British triumph at Lucknow and Delhi and the legends surrounding it - Sir Charles Crossthwaithe, the Anglo-Indian historian, famously described the Mutiny as "the Epic of the Race" - allowed Farrell to use the conventions of the classic adventure story. There were several advantages in this. Firstly, it suited his own tastes: there is in every line of *Krishnapur* an unmistakable sense of authorial enjoyment (which, incidentally, also helps to defuse the horror of the grislier scenes during the siege by producing a sense of boyish complicity between narrator and reader). Secondly, it avoids the danger of things getting overly didactic: *Krishnapur* was to be "a novel of ideas which could be read at the same time simply as an adventure story . . ."; [22] "adventure", Farrell added, being " . . . what the Victorians most loved after profits and respectability". [23] And the mischievous second half of that sentence is clearly another clue to Farrell's aims and methods: he intended to

---

[20] Malcolm Dean, "An Insight Job", *The Guardian* 1 September 1973.
[21] Ibid.
[22] Ibid.
    Again, a brief glimpse at *The Singapore Grip* is instructive: there the reader soon feels worn out by the onslaught of reports and statistics and begins to be vaguely resentful of the unrelenting preaching, lecturing and sermonizing by various characters acting as mouthpieces for their creator.
[23] Ibid.
    Some recent criticism has followed Farrell's lead in reappraising the importance to the Victorians of the classic adventure story, and arriving at perhaps rather similar conclusions. Martin Green, in particular, has made a study of the genre and speaks of adventure stories being "the energyzing myth of English imperialism". (Green, *Dreams of Adventure, Deeds of Empire*. London 1980, p.3) These tales, he goes on to say, were ". . . collectively, the story England told itself as it went to sleep at night; and, in the form of its dreams, they charged England's will with the energy to go out into the world and explore, conquer and rule". (Ibid.)

approach the world of the Victorians from within, as it were, - but with avowed subversive intent.

Accordingly, the narrative resumes, after the 'Forsterian' prelude, in the familiar tones of a Victorian adventure story: "The first sign of trouble at Krishnapur . . . " or "One evening, in the room he used as a study, the Collector, Mr Hopkins, opened a despatch box and, instead of the documents he had expected, found . . . ". (*SK*, p.11) And for a while, as the plot thickens, so to speak, there hangs in the air the promise of a good old-fashioned tale of villainy and derring-do, of fiendish foreign treachery and stout English hearts: "Just supposing that serious trouble should break out at Krishnapur . . . . Could the Residency, merely as a matter of interest, of course, be defended?" (*SK*, p.13) And we almost bite our lips in anticipation of the nasty surprise in store for the Collector when we read that the sight of the brick walls of the Residency inclines him to be reassured, "One felt very safe here. The walls, which were built of enormous numbers of the pink, wafer-like bricks of British India, were so thick . . . you could see yourself how thick they were." (*SK*, p.13)

This can of course be read as a straightforward adventure story, but the tone - even here - is anything but straightforward: the bricks of the Residency immediately recall the ones the narrator had earlier pointed out on our way to Krishnapur, and to someone of Farrell's own generation, the Collector's naive confidence in "the enormous numbers of the . . . pink bricks of British India" might perhaps also conjure up classroom memories of maps of the world with all those pink bits in them, which had seemed so reassuringly large. It will be many pages - almost half the novel - before the brick walls of the Residency have to stand their test, but Farrell has ensured our interest; the narrative tone of what Binns calls a "pastiche Victorian novel, written from an ironic twentieth century perspective" is firmly established and will prove an effective device throughout to manipulate the reactions of the reader. [24] Manipulation of the reader, of course, is the name of the game in all of Farrell's mature fiction. After all, he had never made a secret of his intention " . . . to create" in his novels "a new world into which I could

---

[24] Binns, *J.G. Farrell*, p.65.

bring what I wanted and control the reaction of the reader. I want to hypnotise the reader." [25]

And hypnotised we are, patiently following Farrell from Krishnapur to Calcutta and back again, sitting down to lengthy dinners and arguing endlessly over port and cigars with grave Victorian gentlemen, going for picknicks or drives with their daughters, attending fashionable dances in the presence of the Governor-General, and all the while never as much as catching sight of a mutinous sepoy. But then sepoys - mutinous or otherwise - are not uppermost in Farrell's mind. In describing in minute detail various functions and the localities in which they take place, he is not just setting the scene for the more dramatic events later on: it is 'the scene' itself that interests Farrell. The actual siege is of less concern to him than what the besieged wore or ate or thought before and during it, and as for the eventual relief of Krishnapur and the campaign that lead to it, they are dismissed in a few throwaway sentences towards the end of the book. This is not just a matter of personal interests and preoccupations, however, but something more fundamental. "It is a common misconception", Farrell wrote about *Troubles,*

> that when the historians have finished with a historical incident there remains nothing but a patch of feathers and a pair of feet; in fact, the most important things, for the very reason that they are trivial, are unsuitable for digestion by historians, who are only able to nourish themselves on the signing of treaties, battle strategies, the formation of Shadow Cabinets and so forth. These matters are quite alien to the life most people lead, which consists of falling in love, or falling off bicycles. . . . One of the things I have tried to do . . . is to show people "undergoing" history, to use an expression of Sartre's. [26]

Clearly, this goes as much for *Krishnapur* as it did for *Troubles*. Farrell, then, seeks not only " . . . to retrieve forgotten or suppressed aspects of our history", as Binns puts it, but to examine that which eludes

---

[25] Brock, p.74.
[26] James Vinson, op.cit. p.399.

the historian in the first place: in Farrell's own words, "the smoke in your eyes" or "the blister on your foot" rather than "pincer movements" and "treaties being signed". [27] His approach, then, is in some ways remarkably like Scott's, as Suzanne Kim, has pointed out. [28] And he shares with Scott the perhaps unfashionable belief that the wealth of detail, of individual experience does add up: that the whole *is* greater than the sum of its parts; that the parts will in fact fall into place, if viewed from the right perspective, to form a coherent picture of the past. This, in his own inimitable terms, he expresses most clearly in the thoughts of one of the main characters of *The Singapore Grip*, Walter Blackwell:

> He found himself, . . . , brooding on what makes up a moment of history. . . . Certainly, it was not easy to see a common principle in the great mass of events occuring at any moment far and near. But Walter believed that that was because you were too close to them. It was like being a single gymnast in a vast stadium with several thousand other gymnasts; your movements and theirs might seem quite baffling from where you stand whereas, viewed from an aeroplane, collectively you are forming letters which spell out 'God Save the King' in a pattern of delightful colours.
> (*SG*, p.424)

The Siege of Krishnapur, then, is not primarily an account of the Indian Mutiny - as the title of the novel might lead one to believe - but something altogether more ambitious: it is concerned with the tracing of a pattern in events to re-create, or perhaps even to create for the first time, a clear view of an earlier age - not in isolation, however, as the historian would, but firmly in relation to our own age. That this is an ambitious undertaking needs hardly to be pointed out. But Farrell, like

---

[27] Binns, "Chronicler of the Thin Red Line". *The Times Higher Education Supplement* 709 6 June 1986, p.15.
[28] "Et leurs méthodes respectives ne sont-elles pas comparables? Même sélection des faits, même concentration sur le détail, même effort de reconstruction de l'interaction des faits événementiels, des idées et des émotions, des actions et des mobiles, même utilisation de l'interdisciplinarité, . . . , même soumission des faits signifiants pertinents au crible des hypothèses et des modèles pour donner sens et cohèrence." (Suzanne Kim, "Histoire et Roman". *Etudes Anglaises* 36 (2,3) 1983, p.168)

Scott, evidently felt that literature should be ambitious; and felt, again like Scott, that the novel in England was languishing in the doldrums because of a collective lack of ambition. (Scott, of course, saw the genre as such under attack by the literary experiments of the 'nouveau roman' in France; and the *Raj Quartet*, defiantly old-fashioned not only in its scope, was in part his reaction to the age of the notorious boxed novel.) Farrell, too, did not like what he saw - at least in English bookshops. "If one turns from reading Solzhenitsyn to our own writers", he observed glumly in *The Spectator* in 1970, " . . . one is immediately struck by the thought that, by comparison, we simply have nothing to write about." [29] That elusive grand theme Farrell discovered in Empire, just as Scott had discovered it in the Raj. Not because it offered an escape from the drabness of the consumer society - though it did that too - but because in Britain as much as in Solzhenitsyn's Russia the forgotten or denied past furnished the key to understanding the present.

The Siege of Krishnapur, then, takes us back to the well-ordered, self-assured and, above all, respectable Britain of Queen Victoria's day. And in it, Farrell assures us, we shall find the germs of our present age. Slowly, over the first chapters - the days before the Mutiny, so to speak - he builds up a picture of high Victorianism: an age buoyant with optimism, intoxicated by progress, yet still confident of the old moral, social, and religious certainties. This Farrell achieves by using India as a contrasting backdrop before which to parade the products of Victorian enterprise, taste and ingenuity. Most of these are united in the focal point of the narrative itself: the Residency at Krishnapur. And the narrator lingers there for quite a while, allowing us to take in the eccentric splendour of the place. An oasis of "coolness and great tranquility" (*SK*, p.13), it is for the weary Empire builders not only a place of physical relaxation but also of spiritual regeneration; appropriately enough, it is built "more or less in the shape of a church" (*SK*, p.13) and from one of its towers " . . . the Union Jack fluttered from dawn to dusk." (*SK*, p.14) It is not just a symbol of Empire, however, but of Western civilization itself: the two being, admittedly, largely synonymous. That point is also made, architecturally, by the façade of the banqueting hall with its giant marble busts of Greek philosophers gazing out into the

---

[29] J.G. Farrell, "No Matter". *The Spectator* 29 August 1970, p.217.

Indian plain. This perhaps rather obvious symbolism might easily have backfired in the hands of a lesser novelist, but Farrell knows his craft and it is the earnest Victorians who end up looking crass and ridiculous. And if he takes up that image again and again, it is not just because it allows him to get considerable comic mileage out of it. Take, for instance, the scene when the British defenders of the besieged Residency seek - literal - shelter behind these twin sentinels of Western civilization: on this as on other occasions during the siege " . . . the giant heads of Plato and Socrates, each with the expression of penetrating wisdom carved on his white features surveyed the river and melon beds beyond". (*SK*, p.149) - A wonderful example of Farrell's absurdist vision and a perfect example, too, of his knack of summing up in one memorable image the essence of a situation. Here it is that of colonialism itself: the ludicrous pretensions of the colonizers; the peculiar mixture of arrogance and hypocrisy that surrounded the whole enterprise as much as its individual exponents; the limited impact of colonial rule on land and people; and, in this case, the colonizers' total incomprehension of India and all things Indian. The lack of comprehension, of course, works both ways:

> All they [the sepoys] could see was the looming shape of the banqueting hall and, startling in their clarity, two vast white faces, calmly gazing towards them with expressions of perfect wisdom, understanding and compassion. The sepoys quailed at the sight of such invincible superiority. [30]
> (*SK*, p.166)

For the time being, of course, there is no fighting at Krishnapur: civilization itself seems deterrent enough against potential attackers. The walls of the Residency, we are told, are " . . . thickly armoured with

---

[30] Lack of comprehension apparently affects some readers too. R.P.J. Williams, analyzing Farrell's treatment of 'the native', writes about this scene (a sepoy attack on the Residency), ". . . and then (being ignorant savages) they seem almost more deterred by the vast marble busts of Plato and Socrates, which flank Harry and Fleury's cannon, than by the effect of the cannon fire". (R.P.J. Williams, "Presenting the Raj: The Politics of Representation". Unpublished thesis. University of Nottingham 1988, p.108) Leaving aside even the small matter of authorial irony, there is a perfectly satisfactory, rational, explanation for the sepoys' crucial hesitation: it is of course due to the smoke of battle, as Williams should know because Farrell actually says so. But, then, the smoke of battle can blind critics, too.

paintings . . . , mirrors and glass cases containing stuffed birds and other wonders . . . ." (SK, p.17) And again Farrell sums up in one sentence a theme he will go on to explore in detail: the inherent and ultimately fatal contradictions of mid-Victorian civilization, reflected here in the grotesque image of a stuffed bird; both slightly pathetic creatures, far removed from their natural habitats, lifeless in fact, and shielded for a time from reality by distinctly fragile glass cases.

Highlighting the minor absurdities of the British presence in the East is, of course, something of a stock-ingredient in Anglo-Indian fiction and Farrell's novel proves no exception: croquet is being played and tea parties are held on a patch of sun-baked mud which is fondly referred to as 'the lawn'; women wear absurd dresses which make no concessions to the climate; architecture, furniture, social mores, etc., all combine to create the illusion that no one has ever left British shores: " . . . indeed", says the narrator at one point, "it was hard to believe that one was in India at all, except for the punkahs." (SK, p.17) But Farrell is not just playing on the all-too familiar incongruities of a Home Counties life style under tropical skies; it is not only Anglo-India, he suggests, which to us seems strange to the point of being incomprehensible but - by extension - the entire Victorian world: the past itself is another country, and they certainly do things differently there.

Admittedly, Farrell lays it on a bit thick. He dwells lovingly on the absurd objects cluttering the various rooms of the Residency (or the Maharajah's palace, or the store rooms during the siege), which has made at least one critic speak of an "antiquarian instinct [threatening] . . . at times . . . to usurp the stage and [resulting] . . . in a chase of the bizarre object or incident for its own sake", [31] and has made another refer to *Krishnapur* as a "drama of objects" - whatever that may be. [32] But, ultimately, these grotesque objects do speak for themselves: 'The Spirit of

---

[31] Lars Hartveit, "Affinity or Influence? Sir Walter Scott and J.G. Farrell as Historical Novelists". In: J.H. Alexander and David Hewitt (eds.), *Scott And His Influence: The Papers of the Aberdeen Scott Conference 1982* . Aberdeen 1983, p.414.
On the whole, Farrell keeps this instinct reasonably well reined-in in *Troubles* and *Krishnapur* ; few readers of *The Singapore Grip* , however, would argue with Hartveit's assessement.

[32] Bronislawa Balutowa, "J.G. Farrell's 'The Siege of Krishnapur': A Pattern of Reversal". In: *Studies in English and American Literature: in Honour of Witold Ostrowski* . Warsaw s.a., p.18.

Science Conquers Ignorance and Prejudice', for instance, - a bas-relief in the Collector's study, notable for " . . . the brutish expression of Ignorance at the moment of being vanquished by Truth's sabre . . . " - tells us as much about its proud owner and the age that produced it as it does about our novelist and that novelist's sense of humour. Indeed, the character of the Collector - "whose official title", Binns drily observes, "carries an ironic metaphorical meaning" - is something of a stroke of genius. [33] His obsession with the Great Exhibition - about which he talks incessantly and mementos of which he has scattered all over the Residency - provides the perfect way into the Victorian mind. The Great Exhibition is, after all, as Nicholas Shrimpton has observed, the supreme expression of the missionary zeal of the times, and Farrell tries, through the Collector's obsession, to recapture something of it for the modern reader. [34] In the process, it is true, *The Siege of Krishnapur* does, at times, come close to resembling the Albert Memorial in its love of detail. (The catalogue of the Great Exhibition, certainly, figures in equal prominence in the bronze hands of the Prince Consort in Kensington Gardens and in the Collector's study and conversations at Krishnapur, where later on it provides, in Binn's words, " . . . an ironic touchstone against which the nightmare of the mutiny is repeatedly measured".) [35]

If the Great Exhibition is the supreme expression of an age, Farrell's Collector is its personification; he synthesizes all aspects of high Victorianism: that strange mixture of art and science, sentimentality and cold reason, philanthropy and brutal capitalism, orthodox religious faith and blind belief in progress. And nothing captures the flavour of the period better than the Collector's own words on his nation's agenda, "Every invention is a prayer to God" (*SK,* p.59) or, more memorably still, "The spreading of the Gospel on the one hand, the spreading of the railways on the other." (*SK,* p.55)

It is perhaps all-too easy for us today to mock at such sentiments and the complacent optimism underlying them, and Farrell cannot

---

[33] Binns, *J.G. Farrell,* p.66.
[34] Nicholas Shimpton, "Talent for Thought". *The New Statesman* 24 April 1981, p.18.
[35] Ibid., p.29.
  Binns observes further that "the location of Farrell's new home, almost next door to the Victoria and Albert Museum, was marvellously appropriate to the subject matter of his new novel."

entirely resist the temptation. Dipping into the catalogue of the Great Exhibition, he points out a few tokens of progress in the Collector's study that tend to undercut that sunny optimism: the model of a train, for instance, " . . . which supplied its own railway, laying it down as it advanced and taking it up again as the wheels passed over" - which causes even the Collector to wonder " . . . why six years should have passed away without one seeing these machines crawling about everywhere" (*SK* p.98) - or the "drinking glass with separate compartments for soda and acid" designed so that " . . . the junction of the two streams should come just at the moment of entering the mouth, causing effervescence", of which the narrator says laconically, "The Collector had only once attempted to use it; all the same, he admired its ingenuity and had grown fond of it, as an object." (*SK*, pp.98-9)

The dice, then, are loaded as much against Victorian ingenuity as against Victorian taste. But the authorial mockery is gentle: an ". . . ironic distancing", as David Rubin observes, "tinged with affection, impartial in its view of everybody concerned but tending towards compassion rather than distaste". [36] Indeed, Farrell's irony is almost exclusively directed against ideas and objects rather than the people who, mistakenly, value and admire them. Thus the Collector's childlike enthusiasm for the products of his age may be exposed to ridicule, but never the man himself. Similarly, when we eavesdrop on a meeting of the Krishnapur Poetry Society, we are invited to laugh at the poem we hear and not at the earnest young lady who ostensibly produced it. [37] The reading and subsequent discussion of this poem is another example of Farrell appearing to chase a comic effect: "If you can't call an elephant 'Afric's wondrous brute' what *can* you call it? Why write poetry at all?" (*SK*, p.19) Yet the three farcical stanzas with their cosy picture of foreign shores, their laboured allusions to inventions and discoveries and their inevitable tribute to the Queen and the Prince Consort ("the Royal Founders of the Scene") do serve a purpose. They leave a lasting impression in the reader's mind of the insulation from reality of the people

---

[36] Rubin, op.cit., p.39.
[37] Farrell mentions in his afterword that the stanzas are, in fact, taken from an epic poem on the Great Exhibition by one Samuel Warren; " . . . a work", Farrell adds, characteristically, "which had a great success in its day, though dismissed by one reviewer as 'the ravings of a madman in the Crystal Palace'. (*SK*, p.346)

inside the Residency and - by extension - of the whole childishly confident age. Later on, during the description of the privations of the siege there will be another literary allusion, to a very different Victorian poem this time: to Mathew Arnold's "Dover Beach", with its receding "Sea of Faith" and its "darkling plain", " . . . where ignorant armies clash by night". [38]   These two poems, then, mark the perimeters of Farrell's investigation: the high and low points respectively of Victorian self-confidence.

By laying it on thick in the first chapters, therefore, Farrell heightens the contrast to what will follow, and to some extent lessens the shock of it. When calamity does eventually befall, the reader feels it is something of a deserved come-uppance. The colonists' earlier claims had not merely been complacent but had smacked of hubris. Things, in fact, had seemed a trifle precarious even without the discreet authorial hints in the 'Forsterian' prelude and elsewhere. The extraordinary insularity and self-centredness of the British community, reflected in the alarming geographical isolation of Krishnapur, the insubstantiality of the tokens of progress in the Residency - some fail to work, others, like the books in the library, gradually disappear, " . . . eaten by the ubiquitous ants . . . or having simply vanished nobody knew where" - had provided all along a sombre counterpoint to the Collector's hymn to Progress. (*SK*, p.13)

The general complacency is eventually challenged by two events: the mysterious appearance of chapatis on the doorsteps of offices and private houses all over the district and the arrival of a young man from England full of enthusiasm and alarmingly unorthodox ideas. The Collector is disconcerted - by the chapatis at least - and orders the digging of a defensive trench around the Residency. No such defences, of course, will avail against the second challenge, which, ironically, he does not take at all seriously at this stage.

Yet heresy, is stirring everywhere. The Magistrate's well-known cynicism the Collector had been able to dismiss. After all, the man had " . . . the red hair and ginger whiskers of the born atheist" (*SK*, p.16) and a face " . . . raked, harrowed, even ploughed up by free-thinking . . .". (*SK*, p.99) But now there are others. There is Dr. McNab for one, " . . . who was known to be in favour of some of the most alarmingly direct

---

[38] cf. Binns, *J.G. Farrell*, pp.74-5.

methods known to civilized medicine" and who in due course is discovered to be another, and altogether more formidable, free-thinker. (*SK*, p.22) And the voices of established Christianity themselves are scarcely more reassuring. News reaches Krishnapur - through Fleury, the young man fresh from England - of theological disputes raging in Europe which distinctly alarm the Padre. Having survived in his undergraduate days at Oxford ". . . Tractarian onslaughts enough to shake the strongest constitution" (*SK*, p.56) by dint of sticking to his rowing, he is not slow to recognize the danger: then, too, " . . . this sort of theological beagling had been very fashionable and had ended, alas, in more than one young man taking a fall and losing his Faith". (*SK* p.57)

This is Farrell up to his old tricks, of course: blinding the reader with the sparklers and firecrackers of his craft while he is smuggling into the narrative the ideological contraband of his novel of ideas. Most readers, of course, will realize quite early on that *Krishnapur* operates on more than one level, and that the fun and jinks on the surface are meant to disguise more unsettling developments below. But on those unacquainted with Farrell's critical utterances it will dawn only gradually what he is really up to in his 'Indian' novel; that India for him is an excuse to analyse the mid-Victorian crisis of ideology, when the advent of Darwinism finally shattered the old certainties.

Here, indeed, are assembled all the dominant strands of thought of the pre-Darwinian period, rather like the incongrous mass of exhibits in the Collector's study. On the one hand the doomed beliefs of the older men: phrenology, the pseudo-science championed by the Magistrate, Dr Dunstable's old-fashioned medicine of mustard plasters and leeches, and the Padre's naive Creationism; on the other hand harbingers of a new age, foreshadowed by Dr McNab's successful cholera treatment, or occasional flashes of inspiration by Fleury: "Could it not be, he wondered, vaguely, trembling on the brink of an idea that would have made him famous, that somehow or other fish designed their own eyes?" (*SK*, p.168) The ingredients for a major conflict of ideas are there: the shock of the siege will be the catalyst for change.

To the list of old beliefs about to be shattered might be added that in Empire and Britain's civilizing mission in the world. One recalls here Scott's definition of the Raj as a metaphor for the age when the British last believed in their own value. Farrell, of course, does not share Scott's nostalgia for those days. But he, too, sees the nexus and explores it throughout his Empire trilogy. In the Ireland of *Troubles* the Empire was already in full retreat and the Anglo-Irish community had the unpleasant suspicion that public opinion in England was no longer entirely on their side; in the Singapore of 1942 calamity would overtake a British community which had long been cut off from public opinion at Home and had realized and, complacently, accepted as much; but no such gulf in aims and perceptions existed between the India on the eve of the Mutiny and the proud Mother Country. Things were still clear-cut then: Empire was by Heaven's Command, the Charter of the Land being to spread and advance a superior culture, to provide an example of superior morality, and to do both to the glory of God and for the benefit of the 'natives'.

Farrell resists the temptation of scoring easy points over the Victorian Empire builders. He does not, for instance, contrast directly their cultural pretensions with the artefacts and traditions of an Indian civilization considerably more ancient than any in the West. Instead, he shows a Western community unaware of the existence of such a thing as Indian culture. When his expatriates stumble upon a Hindu shrine "lurking" in a thicket somewhere they find the experience unpleasant, vaguely unsettling even; Fleury, at least, is feeling decidedly uncomfortable as he finds himself suddenly face to face with a six-armed statue of Lord Bhairava, who, the narrator adds, " . . . appeared to be looking at . . . [him] with malice and amusement". (*SK*, p.61) India - "the real India" - seems at best incomprehensible, often in fact threatening; this not least because it clearly eludes the British grasp. And while this ties in, of course, with the mysterious appearance of the chapatis to heighten the general atmosphere of discreet menace, it is clearly more than just a simple device for creating suspense in an adventure story. Farrell provides little reminders of the limits to British power so often that one might refer to them as recurring motif of the narrative. One of the most memorable of these is the Collector's visit of the so-called Prime Minister of the local maharajah, who is kept detained inside the Residency compound; the prisoner, he finds, has coped with unexpected resilience and seems lost in a blissful religious trance. It is a sight which brings on in the Collector a sudden, overwhelming, " . . . feeling of helplessness. He realized that there was a whole way of life of the people in India which he would never get to know and which was totally indifferent to him and his concerns." (*SK*, p.232) The Collector emerges from this encounter " . . . humbled and depressed by . . . [the] thought" that he and his countrymen could leave " . . . and half India wouldn't notice us leaving just as they didn't notice us arriving. All our reforms of administration might be reforms of the moon for all it has to do with them." (*SK*, p.232) The Mutiny, of course, brings such thoughts to the fore, as it gradually becomes obvious to everyone that the British are - and perhaps always have been - " . . . staging a pantomime of government to an empty theatre". (*SK*, p.119)

Again one is reminded that *Krishnapur* stands firmly outside the traditions of the Anglo-Indian novel. Its - very occasional - moments of self-doubt were invariably overcome by the soothing images of the immutable Indian landscape and the eternally 'toiling ryot', with their implied comfort to the Westerner not to expect too much too quickly. In Farrell's novel the sight of that unchangeable Indian landscape seems decidedly less reassuring: the Collector's prophesies of progress, we are told, "rang emptily over the Indian plain", and the 'toiling ryot' is glimpsed only at the beginning and the very end, when the British cantonment is lying in ruins. (*SK*, p.90) The effect is of the entire novel reflecting the Collector's own humbling recognition of failure; of failure, moreover, in an impossible task; a recognition of what Scott's Barbie Batchelor calls "the essential extraneousness" of British concerns to the business of India, and of the hubris of the whole enterprise; and that idea has emerged only in the finest novels about the Raj.

What the British do achieve is no more than grafting on to India and the Indians a veneer of Western civilization; the new recruits to the Christian faith, for instance, promptly throw away the English sweets they were given " . . . for, though Christians, many of them considered themselves to be Hindus as well, indeed primarily, and had no intention of being defiled like the sepoys and their greased cartridges". (*SK*, p.131) A more determined attempt to instruct and uplift produces a creature like Hari, the maharajah's son, whose education had been supervised by an English tutor. Here, too, the result is comically disastrous, with the emphasis, as always in Farrell, on the comic side of disaster: for there is in Farrell's absurdist vision little room for the pathos surrounding that other Hari of recent Anglo-Indian fiction. [39] Farrell's Hari, cultivating incongruous Western hobbies and spouting half-digested Western thought in the vernacular of comedy Indians, is essentially a caricature, intended, as David Rubin observes, " . . . to underscore the fragility and relative unimportance of these trappings of a superior culture." [40]

Part of the problem, of course, is that many of these trappings are themselves whimsical and ridiculous. The same magistrate who tries - in vain - to fight a local superstition that seeks to prevent flooding by sacrificing a black goat remains wedded to his belief in phrenology and goes on right to the end measuring people's heads in order to determine their characters. And Farrell, being Farrell, cannot resist adding a brief scene in which the villagers, " . . . chuckling nostalgically at the thought of the Magistrate . . . who had tried to make them strengthen the embankments", duly sacrifice their black goat, " . . . and nobody was in the least bit surprised when, little by little, the river began to fall".(SK, p.267)

This, needless to say, is a twentieth century perspective. It is this kind of thing Elizabeth Bowen had in mind when she described the earlier *Troubles* as "yesterday reflected in today's consciousness", adding that "the ironies, the disparities, the dismay, the sense of unavailingness are contemporary". [41] Equally contemporary are the Collector's reflections on the relative value of civilizations. These are prompted by the sight of a sadhu - a naked Hindu who had renounced all possessions: the Collector professes to a reluctant admiration for the "rigour" with which the sadhu is pursuing his beliefs, however erroneous his chosen path may be. (SK, p.89) "One has to admit, . . . , that few Christians follow the right one with as much zeal". (SK, p.90) Inevitably, he adds, ". . . this renders the conversion of the native very difficult for beside his ascetic fervour he sees the Christian priest living in a comfortable house with a wife and family . . . and I fear he's not impressed". (SK, p.90) As so often, Farrell's characteristic light touch here is deceptive, for the same

---

[39] It is intriguing to speculate whether the choice of Hari's name is coincidental or a conscious or perhaps subconscious allusion to *The Raj Quartet*. That Farrell was familiar with Scott's tetralogy we know from his review of it for the *TLS*.
[40] Rubin, p.40
[41] Bowen, op.cit., p.59.

train of thought leads the Collector to the central conundrum of Empire - and perhaps not just of Empire either. "What good is it", he asks, "if we bring the advantages of our civilization to India without also displaying a superior morality?" (*SK*, p.90)

The Collector's words point, once again, to Farrell's narrative technique, or rather to the distinctive quality of his narrative voice. One of its most striking features, which interests us here, is its studied political restraint. And this is where, yet again, *The Siege of Krishnapur* breaks with the traditions of the genre it - ostensibly - emulates. Anglo-Indian literature has always had more than its fair share of political sermonizing, mostly of course by successive generations of self-appointed high-priests of Empire. But the 'opposition' too, Forster and Orwell most famously, could not entirely resist the urge to preach; nor, as we have seen, could Paul Scott, albeit in his own anguished way. There is, it would seem, something about the Raj that makes novelists climb their metaphorical pulpits and soap boxes. And, in a curious way, both the public and the critics seem to expect it of them. Farrell's refusal to do so in his Indian novel is all the more striking therefore, and certainly did not go unnoticed. In fact, it caused quite a few raised critical eyebrows. R.P.J. Williams, who clearly intends not to be taken in by Farrell's liberal credentials and harbours dark suspicions about the ideological 'soundness' of the Empire trilogy, is probably an extreme case. [42] But he is by no means alone. Even Binns, otherwise an open admirer of Farrell, confesses to doubts:

> A criticism which has been levelled against *The Siege of Krishnapur* is that the book is really far too funny to convey effectively the underlying seriousness of Farrell's critique of Empire. Certainly one never feels that Farrell's amiable cast of characters - often 'characters' in the secondary sense of the noun - is seriously or reprehensibly involved in colonial exploitation or repression. [43]

---

[42] cf. Williams, op.cit., particularly pp.92-114.
[43] Binns, *J.G.Farrell*, p.80.

And Binns concludes that "the predomiantly comic tone" of Farrell's narrative effectively "conjures away the problem of evil". [44] But might this not be the price for what Victoria Glendinning calls Farrell's "compassionate ambivalence", which she sees as one of his main strengths as a writer? [45] or for the almost "Tolstoyan objectivity" noted by Charles Palliser, which he thinks stems from Farrell's understanding of the "political, economic and ideological contradictions" shaping his characters, and from his reluctance to patronize them? [46] Ultimately then, it is a matter of the novelist's character as much as of his conscious delight in the narrative "stance of an experienced and mature man of the world". [47] This should not, however, be mistaken for lack of historical awareness or for political apathy. Laurence Bristow-Smith is probably nearer the truth here than most when he says that the choice of the particular historical settings of Farrell's novels " . . . allows him to remain close to his characters . . .", without the need overtly to take sides in a " . . . political conflict, the outcome of which is already common knowledge". [48]

But is there not, anyway, in these objections by mostly academic critics a degree of condescension to the 'common reader' who, it is felt, needs to have things spelt out for him in order to be able to grasp them? It might be worth reminding ourselves that though Farrell uses the conventions of 'Boy's Own' fiction he is very much a 'grown-up' writer, writing for a 'grown-up' audience. One does not, after all, have to drone on about the iniquities of Colonialism in order to damn it. Farrell's method of criticising the past is, I would suggest, at once more elegant and infinitely deadlier: he chooses to take the Victorians at their own word and shows up remorselessly the difference between moral claims made on behalf of the imperial enterprise and actual colonial practice. [49]

---

[44] Ibid.
[45] Victoria Glendinning, "Farrell's Last Words". *The Listener* 23 April 1981, p.548.
[46] Charles Palliser, "J.G. Farrell and the Wisdom of Comedy". *Literary Review* 1 5-18 October 1979, p.14.
[47] Hartveit, "Affinity or Influence?", op.cit., p.419.
[48] Laurence Bristow-Smith, "Tomorrow Is Another Day: The Essential J.G. Farrell".*Critical Quarterly* 25 (2) 1983, p.50.
[49] Williams remains doubtful, as ever, and speaks of a " . . . tension between the apparent authorial ideology and intention and the ideological positions produced by the text . . . ". (Williams, p.92) He does, however, accept that the pervasive authorial irony complicates matters from his point of view. One cannot help feeling that the

Thus one will look in vain in *Krishnapur* for a catalogue of instances of colonial exploitation: the evidence for it is not withheld but it is clearly peripheral to Farrell's purpose. Instead, he homes in on the moral rottenness of the very foundations of the colonial edifice and the corruption of its Victorian upholders, which he presents as it were in their own - Christian - terms.

All contemporary accounts - Thackeray for instance - agree that the Anglo-Indian life style in Company days was not without a certain venal charm. This was the age of millions made in a few years and fortunes lost overnight. The cult of work which sustained a later, dourer, breed of expatriates had not yet been invented and the regulation spine pads had signally failed to stiffen the general moral backbone. To the imperialists of Kipling's generation the excesses of their grandfathers were an embarrassment and best forgotten. Indeed, Parliament itself became alarmed and chipped away at the powers of the Honourable Company as more and more scandals came to light and as the national mood changed with the generations from the ease of the Prince Regent to the respectablity of the Prince Consort. Farrell clearly relishes recreating the colourful scene before the nemesis of the Mutiny. And his brush paints images that seem, at times, like a medieval inventory of cardinal sins. Pride, avarice, gluttony, lust and sloth, all make prominent appearances. The pride here, of course, is primarily that of the ruling caste as a whole, which is collectively riding to a fall; avarice, too, is mainly a collective sin, which denies the native labourers a decent wage; sloth, too seems pretty universal before the Mutiny, especially in the scenes in Calcutta where life is an endless stream of balls and parties and picknicks. Young Fleury, who acts as our guide here, finds it all very agreeable; being a soulful young man, he is, however, slightly taken aback when old Dr Dunstable, his host in Calcutta, turns out to be something of a "jovial libertine" who misses no time in hinting at the "manly pleasures" to be had there in the company of "vivacious young widows". (*SK*, p.26) But it is the gluttony, above all, which is memorable for its

---

anonymous reviewer in the *TLS*, unemcumbered by literary theory is more clearsighted: he speaks of the novel's "caustic" quality, for ". . . it delights in uncovering the opposite of what it purports to say, and is sometimes so blunt as to stop the reader in his tracks." ("Down to the Bone: The Siege of Krishnapur". *The Times Literary Supplement* 21 September 1973, p.1074)

proportions. There is indeed, as Binns observes, "an emphasis on the full stomach of . . . [the] English characters", which makes "food and eating central subjects in *The Siege of Krishnapur*". [50] And Binns is undoubtedly right, too, in seeing in it a reference to the complaceny of the expatriate community in the face of a gathering storm: "the gluttony of these well-fed colonists is destined shortly to give way to the privations of the siege, and within a relatively short time they are reduced to eating almost anything at all."[51]

One cannot help feeling, however, that there is rather more to it than that: that there is, in fact, definite moral judgement involved here. As the colonists feast on imported delicacies in the Botanical Gardens of Calcutta, they are watched by "ragged-looking natives" who had "made an appearance at the edge of a clearing". (*SK*, p.33) A little later it is native bearers who make an appearance to clear away the hampers and are subsequently "cleared away themselves". (*SK*, p.35) Later still, near Krishnapur, we watch "Monkey", Lieutenant Cutter's bearer, fill champagne into a bowl for Lieutenant Cutter's horse to drink. (*SK*, p.66) And, back in Krishnapur, we are not greatly surprised to hear that the Collector " . . . piously gave to the poor, . . . the English poor . . . [for] he had accepted that the poverty of India was beyond redemption". (*SK*, p.158) Indeed, on first landing in India, the native beggars - like the mangey pariah dogs - had seemed to him " . . . like a parody of what Nature had intended". (*SK*, p.158) To which the narrator adds laconically, "The humans he had got used to, . . . the dogs never". (*SK*, p.158) It does not come as much of a surprise therefore to hear it said of a group of young subalterns at the beginning of the siege that they had " . . . never seen a dead person before . . . a dead English person, anyway . . . ", for although "one occasionally bumped into a dead native here and there . . . that was not quite the same". (*SK*, p.106)

This, I would have thought, is a far cry from the habitual talk of 'Duty' and 'The White Man's Burden', of Forster's Anglo-Indian beastliness, or even of Scott's conflicting loyalties. It scarcely needs the sight of poppy juice bubbling in great vats to give us an idea of the origins and the true nature of colonial rule. In the face of such evidence British

---

[50] Binns, *J.G. Farrell*, p.67.
[51] Ibid.

claims to a superior morality are simply untenable, and with them is demolished one of the traditional justifications of empire. There is, morally, no difference between Farrell's rapacious expatriates and his dissolute old maharajah, living off the fat of the land and dividing his time between sleep, food and nautch girls. Similarly, it is clearly not just Fleury who is reminded by the sight of the maharajah's grotesque collections of "the junk the Collector has in the Residency". (*SK*, p.91) [52]

The inference is clear: both worlds are corrupt, both will be swept away. This, of course, is proof of the clear sense of history which Suzanne Kim notices in Farrell's work. [53] And it is in this that he departs most strikingly from the cherished traditions of the imperial novel - perhaps more uncompromisingly even that Scott. Jeffrey Meyers, in his study on the colonial hero, quotes Auden's essay on Kipling in this regard, and since Kipling epitomizes the preoccupations of the traditional Anglo-Indian novel that quotation is perhaps worth repeating at length. While "virtually every other European writer since the fall of the Roman Empire has felt the dangers threatening civilization came from inside that civilization", writes Auden, " . . . Kipling is obsessed by a sense of the dangers threatening it from *outside*. For him civilization and consciousness is a little citadel of light surrounded by a great darkness full of malignant forces . . . " [54]

Kipling's views, reflecting those of all Anglo-Indians, are of course the product of the trauma of the Mutiny, which the Raj collectively never overcame. Farrell's stroke of genius in *The Siege of Krishnapur* was to take up the central image of Anglo-Indian mythology, the Residency at Lucknow, to adapt it for his purposes, and then to turn it ironically inside out. The defenders of Krishnapur, peering anxiously through a telescope at the Forces of Darkness ranged against them, suddenly spot a large group of well-dressed 'natives', picnicking peaceably outside the range of the Residency's guns and watching the bedraggled defenders in turn through opera glasses " . . . like gentlemen returning to their seats in the theatre after the interval". (*SK*, p.305)

---

[52] For once, even Williams has to admit that Farrell is impartial in his judgement here. (cf.Williams, p.111)
[53] cf. Kim, op.cit., p.169.
[54] W.H. Auden, "The Poet of the Encirclement". Quoted by Jeffrey Meyers, op.cit., p.25. (Auden's italics)

Focusing his novelist's glass on the Residency and its increasingly ragged defenders allows Farrell to do several things at the same time: to pursue his investigation, begun in *Troubles*, into the psychological pressures in a community under siege; to drive forward the development of Victorian thought; and, lastly, to look more closely at the notion of civilization itself.

The concept of the siege, Farrell felt, encapsulated twentieth century experience; the sense of inexplicable fate, overwhelming force and arbitrary destruction reflected, however, not only the uncomfortable reality of the present age but, he suggested, that of "the human condition" in general: of "hostility all around you with the individual in a rather temporary shelter". [55] It is a recurring theme in Farrell's 'œuvre' and, as Binns suggests, may have its roots in Farrell's own childhood experiences of the blitz. [56] Certainly, *Krishnapur* adds scenes of the gradual destruction of people's homes and lives as poignant as any in the Empire trilogy, and perhaps only the demands of historical accuracy save the main building of the Residency from the conflagration devouring both the 'Majestic' and much of Singapore in the other two novels.

But it is civilization and the various question marks surrounding it that is clearly Farrell's central concern in *Krishnapur*. This, after all, is the subject of the Collector's musings and perorations, and George Fleury, our guide to the strange world of Anglo-India, is actually commissioned to report on its progress in an India under the beneficient rule of the Honourable East India Company. That there is no very definite agreement amongst the Britons there as to civilization's ultimate aims is soon apparent. Nor is there a shortage of opinions as to what exactly constitutes civilization. And here we quickly get beyond the immediate Victorian context. When Farrell has the Collector refer to the increased revenues from the opium trade and assert that the object of it all is " ... not simply to acquire wealth, but to acquire *through* wealth, that superior way of life we loosely term civilization ... ", he is clearly not just thinking of Victorian practice. (*SK*, p.55. Farrell's italics) In an ironic way the award of the Booker Prize itself proved his point; and Farrell enjoyed causing something of a stir at the prize ceremony by remarking

---

[55] Dean, "An Insight Job", op.cit.
[56] cf. Binns, *J.G. Farrell*, pp.17-8.

that the munificence of the prize's sponsors owed much to the rather modest wages of its third world workforce. It is not hard to see what Farrell meant about the past being a metaphor for today minus the controversy. Nor is it difficult to see why the more perceptive reviewers should have observed that Farrell's fiction was more about the Wilson Years [57] than about the imperial past, or that *The Siege of Krishnapur* was at least as much about 1957 as about 1857. [58] "Colonial novels", says Jeffrey Meyers, writing perhaps not coincidentally in the late 1960s, "offer a vantage point for thinking about the value of our own civilization". [59]

What, though, is civilization? To the Collector it encompasses all aspects of life, taking in its economic, scientific, artistic and moral sides, with religion crowning and illuminating the whole edifice. In this mid-Victorian view " . . . both the poet and the Opium Agent are necessary to our scheme of things"; Brunel's steamship is seen as the "embodiment, by God's grace, of the spirit of mankind" (*SK*, p.55) and "possessions" are nothing less than "a *physical* high water-mark of the *moral* tide". (*SK*, p.140. Farrell's italics) Our laughter here is a little uneasy because, though we are neither willing nor able to subscribe to this view of civilization, we lack a coherent definition with which to replace it. And having for the most part rejected both God's grace and the Opium Agent - at least in his most immediate form - we are left with nothing but the material benefits of our Western civilization. Like Fleury, we feel that this is not enough; that civilization should be " . . . something more than the fashions and customs of one country imported into another . . ."; that it " . . . must be *a superior view of mankind* . . . ". (*SK*, p.45. Farrell's italics) But that does not get us any nearer a clear view of it than it did him. Like the Collector during the siege, we feel that civilization ought to alleviate suffering, and like him, we are not sure it has done so or will do so in any appreciable measure: "He thought again of those hundred and fifty million people living in cruel poverty in India alone . . . . Would Science and Political Economy ever be powerful enough to give them a

---

[57] A.N. Wilson, "An Unfinished Life". *The Spectator* 25 April 1981, pp.20-1.
[58] "Down to the Bone", op.cit.
[59] Meyers, op.cit., p.8.

life of ease and respectability? He no longer believed that they would." (*SK*, p.223)

The Collector, of course, (together with the character of George Fleury) acts as Farrell's moral gauge. And it is the gradual ebbing of the Collector's confidence, as "the foxes of despair" continue to "raid his beliefs", which marks the change in the novel's view of civilization. (*SK*, p.259) The Collector may hold out in public but, increasingly, his upbeat pronouncements are unsupported by conviction, and are little more, in fact, than the phantom twitchings of his "amputated hopes and beliefs". (*SK*, p.237) If earlier on he had assured everyone, in a hail of bullets, that Progress could not be resisted successfully, he is now less sure.

> Even if a relief now came, in many ways it would be too late . . . and not only because so many of the garrison were already dead; India itself was now a different place; the fiction of the happy natives being led forward along the road to civilization could no longer be sustained.
> (*SK* p.249)

But it is not just the belief in Britain's civilizing mission in India that seems unsustainable. When, at the height of the siege, the Collector falls prey to a fevery delirium all that had been suppressed and relegated to the subconscious comes to the fore. "And everywhere he is in chains", we hear him exclaim, to the alarm of the young ladies nursing him. (*SK*, p.245) "But it was nothing", adds the narrator in his familiar 'deadpan' tone, "merely a passing fancy of his overheated brain". (*SK*, p.245) In a curious way, illness in its very delirium restores something like clarity of vision: looking out from his bedroom window the Collector catches sight of jubilant native spectators cheering at a sepoy attack: "'How happy they are!' thought the Collector, in spite of the pain. 'It is good that the natives should be happy for surely that is ultimately what we, . . . , are in India to procure . . . .'" (*SK*, p.237) After this there can be no return to the state of affairs before the siege: for the Collector no more than for anyone else in India. And in a typically Farrellian scene, the Collector, physically restored, discovers, as he rises from his sickbed, that he is sprouting a beard " . . . with an atheistical tint of ginger, only a little darker than the whiskers of the free-thinking Magistrate". (*SK*, p.251) "In a sense", as Binns observes, the disease from which he has recovered is "the disease of civilization". [60]

There is in *Krishnapur*, as in all of Farrell's fiction, a great deal of illness and disease. And while this undoubtedly reflects Farrell's own, understandably sombre, view of life, [61] it also " . . . functions", as Binns points out, "as a metaphor for the rottenness of the imperial order". [62] Repeatedly in the Empire novels this is made explicit, " . . . The coming of Capitalism has really been like the spreading of a disease", says a character in Farrell's Singapore (*SG*, p169); and in *Krishnapur* the fires of the burning cantonment are likened to " . . . some mysterious sign isolating a contagion from the surrounding countryside". (*SK*, p.144) But of course it is much more than just the imperial order that is diseased. If early on Fleury had described civilization as a "beneficial disease" (*SK*, p.42) then, increasingly, it is the use of the epithet and not of the noun that seems ironic. The emaciated Indians working in the opium factory or the pathetic Hari always were rather doubtful tokens of progress and civilization. But now the British themselves fall victim to the way of life they had propagated and imposed. When food gets scarce inside the Residency, the Collector organizes an auction of the remaining personal provisions of the deceased. This promptly unleashes all the least attractive forces of the Free Market, viz. wild speculative buying and profiteering, until, at last, the Collector does the unthinkable and confiscates these supplies on behalf of all. Before long respect for the hallowed concept of private property gets equally short shrift. At the beginning of the siege the British community had brought into the Residency compound as much of their personal possessions as they could move. These - furniture, 'objets d'art', hunting trophies etc. make the defence of the place almost impossible: a case of civilization literally getting in the way of survival. [63] In the end the Collector is forced to

---

[60] Binns, *J.G. Farrell*, p.71.

[61] It is, after all, not surprising that someone who was struck down with polio at nineteen, spent six months in an iron lung, and remained an invalid for the rest of his days, should elaborate in novel after novel on the same theme of "people are insubstantial, they never last". (*T*, p.307)

[62] J.G. Farrell, p.69.

[63] Again, this scene seems as much rooted in Farrell's own wartime experiences as in the historical reality of the Mutiny, "I remember as a child during the blitz how adults in pyjamas would assemble in our air-raid shelter clutching the most extra-

move here to, ordering these physical manifestations of the moral tide to be used for fire wood, the manufacture of munitions, or for use in shoring up the Residency's crumbling perimeter walls. And in charting the public reaction to the "rape of 'the posessions'" - with possessions significantly in inverted commas - the narrator is especially acerbic:

> Very often the last journeys of these beloved objects were accomplished to the tune of distressing protests, or of heartrending pleas for clemency. You would have thought that there was no one better fitted in the world to understand these pleas than the Collector. He, at least, was qualified to perceive the beauty and value of 'the possessions'.
> (*SK*, pp.270-1)

But the Collector is a changed man: " . . . he accompanied their tumbrils without a word, his eyes blank and bloodshot, his fur slicked down, his ears still flattened against his skull". (*SK*, p.271)

In a similarly peremptorary manner are discarded all aspects of 'civilized behaviour' which fail the acid test of usefulness for the survival of the community. To the scandalized amazement of the ladies the Collector is seen doing his own laundry once there is no longer a sufficient number of dhobis to see to the job. But soon they too are hard at work. Indeed, conditions inside the Residency soon foreshadow not only the servantless society of a later age but also the coming emancipation of women. In this respect there remains, however, an ironic contrast between the Collector's convictions and the reality of the ladies' increased, if reluctant, activity and of the garrison's growing dependence on them.

> 'Women are weak, we shall always have to take care of them, just as we shall always have to take care of the natives . . . Even in a hundred years from now . . . ' the Collector feebly tried to imagine 1957 . . . 'It

---

ordinary objects. During the Indian Mutiny, Cawnpore was made almost indefensible by pianos and stuffed owls and other bric-à-brac. I don't mean to sound superior. . . . But I do have a feeling that as human beings property, materialism is our undoing." (Dean, "Grip of Empire", op.cit.)

> will be the same. They are made of a softer substance.' (SK p.175)

However, before long these "scientific observations" of the Collector are balanced by thoughts of a different kind, "'Perhaps it's our fault that we keep them so much in idleness?' (SK, p.175) 'Perhaps we should educate them more in the ways of the world? Perhaps it is us who have made them what they are?'" (SK, p.263)

One by one, the cherished tenets of Victorian civilization succumb to the force of circumstance. Rigid notions of rank and precedence become impossible to uphold in the absence of servants and in the face of a growing shortage even of beds. Social conventions, too, have to be suspended and poor Lucy, 'the fallen woman', ostracised for her earlier affair with a young officer, is allowed to return, if not to the fold, at least to a corner in the ladies' dormitory. Personal appearance, too, ceases to matter as hunger and illness begin to take their toll. Even pretty Louise Dunstaple " ... now looked like some consumptive Irish girl ... walking the London streets"; and "in spite of the angry red spots on her pale brow she no longer wore the poultice of flour ... the temptation had been too much for her and she had eaten it." (SK, p.261) And the Collector himself, ever more ginger-haired and fox-like, provides Farrell with one of the most memorable images of the changes wrought by necessity: we watch him catch a large black beetle, selflessly offering it to the Magistrate, who declines manfully, albeit "with a note of envy in his voice", whereupon "the Collector popped it into his mouth, let himself savour the sensation of it wriggling on his tongue for a moment, then crunched it with as much pleasure as if it had been a chocolate truffle". (SK, pp.313-4)

The inversion of fortunes is now complete; for these are the sights the well-dressed native picnickers see through their opera glasses. And though the horrors in Farrell's description of the siege are historically authentic they also foreshadow a similar experience, on a much wider scale, by his contrymen in Burma, Malaya and China less than a century later. Then the recognition by the subject races that whites, too, can starve, stink and look like untouchables would end their dominion in the East. At the end of The Indian Mutiny, however, there appear on the horizon the relieving forces - in keeping with the best conventions of the classic adventure story - to rescue the besieged, to avenge the dead, and to restore the order of things.

But before the army of General Sinclair reaches Krishnapur the last act of Farrell's "drama of objects" has to be played out." [64] As munitions run low, any remaining household object made of metal or stone is requisitioned and fired as grapeshot from the Residency's cannon - including marble chippings from 'The Spirit of Science Conquers Ignorance and Prejudice' which we had met earlier in the Collector's study. And now, as Frances Singh puts it, these " . . . very implements of civilization become missiles of pain, horror and death". [65] It is here that Farrell's predilection for the grotesque and macabre reaches an unforgettable climax. As the shot is fired, deathly silence descends over Krishnapur:

> Below nothing was moving, but there appeared to be a carpet of dead bodies. But then he realized that many of these bodies were indeed moving, but not very much. A sepoy here was trying to remove a silver fork from one of his lungs, another had received a piece of lightning conductor in his kidneys. A sepoy with a green turban had had his spine shattered by 'The Spirit of Science'; others had been struck down by tea-spoons, by fish-knives, by marbles; an unfortunate 'subadar' had been plucked from this world by the silver sugar-tongs embedded in his brain. . . . 'How terrible!' said the Collector . . . 'I mean, I had no idea that anything like that would happen.'
>
> (*SK*, pp.318-9)

It is the Collector's reaction to the carnage, I think, which absolves Farrell here from the charge of gratuitous fictionalized violence; and while there is, undeniably, a touch of schoolboy humour about these gruesome descriptions (and perhaps also something of the schoolboy's sadistic streak), Farrell's underlying purpose is serious and honourable. For as an image of the unforeseen and unforeseeable consequences of exporting one country's way of life into another, this scene is supremely

---

[64] The term is Bronislawa Balutowa's. (cf. Balutowa, op.cit.)
[65] Singh, op.cit., p.29.

effective; all the more so if one bears in mind that the Mutiny had started for *cultural* reasons, namely the introduction of the new greased cartridges and the sepoys' fear of being forceably converted to Christianity.

Equally effective, and equally memorable, is the description of another stage of the cannonade. One of the last shots fired by the besieged contained the filed-off heads of the Collector's electrometal figures. "And of the heads, perhaps not surprisingly, the most effective had been Shakespeare's; it had scythed its way through a whole platoon of astonished sepoys . . ." (*SK*, p.335) - As a sardonic reflection on the triumph of English civilization this is probably unsurpassed (and is complemented - in a neat allusion to Anglo-French rivalry, and its outcome both in India and on a wider stage - by the image of the head of the "French cynic", Voltaire, becoming jammed in the gun). [66] In this slightly underhand way Farrell makes his final point: that ultimately civilization depends on guns. In fact, the Collector himself admits ruefully that of all his cherished momentos of the Great Exhibition the most useful were the two revolvers he had purchased there. And, as if to tie together the various strings of Farrell's scrutiny of civilization, the two giant busts of the banqueting hall make a final appearance: glimpsed, this time, by a Briton, the advance guard of the relief:

> . . . Lieutenant Stapleton noticed two giant white faces smiling at him with understanding and compassion. There was something about those faces, however, that made him uneasy and coming nearer he saw that they had been terribly pocked by round shot and musket fire, as if by a disfiguring disease.
>
> (*SK*, p.340)

---

[66] However, as the rest of the scene demonstrates, it is, on another level, an example of the novel's charactersistic mixture of realism and Farrell's own anarchic sense of humour: "The Collector suspected that the Bard's success in this respect might have something to do with the ballistic advantages stemming from his baldness. The head of Keats, for example, wildly festooned with metal locks which it had been impossible to file smooth had flown very erratically indeed, killing only a fat money-lender and a camel standing at some distance from the field of action." (*SK*, p.335)

And with this uncomfortably apposite image of Plato and Aristotle serenely contemplating the slaughter, Farrell's tale might be done. Yet he still has one surprise in store for the reader: in a type of epilogue he gives us a telescoped view of the time after the Mutiny. And how quickly everything returns to 'normality'! Young love flourishes as happy couples are united, life for the survivors resumes its quiet flow, and

> only sometimes in dreams the terrible days of the siege, which were like the dark foundation of the civilized life they had returned to, would return years later to visit them: then they would awake, terrified and sweating, to find themselves in white starched linen, in a comfortable bed, in peaceful England. And all would be well.
>
> (*SK*, p.343)

This, then, is Farrell's final ironic twist: to show how quickly - and how completely - most of his protagonists return to the comfortable cocoon of an upper middle class existence. And with the significant exception of the Collector, who took to pacing the streets in the poorer parts of London, "staring as if he had never seen a poor person in his life before", they have gained nothing at all from their experience. (*SK*, p.344) To drive home that point we are offered on the last pages of *Krishnapur* a glimpse of a middle-aged George Fleury: a florid, opiniated and supremely complacent Victorian 'pater familias', complete with private art collection, 'ideals', and mistress. "And all would be well."

This, of course, is the hallmark of the man who would juxtapose in his last, unfinished, novel the merry goings-on in rarefied Simla with the image " ... a few thousand miles away in London [of] a familiar bearded leonine figure ... [turning] a little in his seat in the British Museum to see the hands of the clock at the northern quarter of the Reading Room, ... [thinking], 'Soon it will be closing time.'" (*HS*, p.92)

And so, inevitably, we return to thoughts of history and that which Walter Blackwell in *The Singapore Grip* calls its "organizing principle"; for that, in a deeper sense, is what Farrell's fiction is all about. Walter, of course, is "vague" about its precise nature, "He believed that each individual event in a historical moment was subtly modified by an intangible mechanism which he could only think of as 'the spirit of the time'". (*SG*, p.424) In Walter's Singapore, as much as in the Collector's India that 'spirit of the time' is bringing about dramatic upheaval. But what, in turn, determines this 'spirit'? The Collector in his well-appointed dining room before the siege is in no doubt: it is shaped by conscious human endeavour and by the ideas and ideals which motivate each individual to exert himself on behalf of all mankind. But events during the Mutiny destroy that conviction. "Perhaps", speculates the narrator, "by the very end of his life, ... , he had come to believe that a people, a nation, does not create itself according to its own best ideas, but is shaped by other forces, of which it has little knowledge". (*SK*, p.345)

What, then, of the events in and around the Residency? Here the narrator is more explicit. As the Collector slowly makes his way back to England over the vast expanse of the Indian plain, he realizes " ... because of the widening perspective, what a small affair the siege of Krishnapur had been, how unimportant, how devoid of significance". (*SK*, p.343) And that is Farrell's final, characteristic, gesture: to deny the importance of the Mutiny and, in a wider perspective, of the Raj and perhaps of the whole imperial enterprise. What to contemporary spectators and those caught up in it had seemed momentous was only momentary: no more, in fact, than a brief moment of history.

'AN ATTEMPT TO REMAIN STANDING': RUTH PRAWER JHABVALA'S
HEAT AND DUST

When Ruth Prawer Jhabvala won the Booker Prize for *Heat and Dust* in 1975, the 'Anglo-Indian revival' which Salman Rushdie so deplores was already well under way. J.G. Farrell had won Booker laurels two years earlier for his 'Indian' novel and Paul Scott would soon do so with *Staying On,* the 'coda' to his *Raj Quartet.* In the cases of Scott and Farrell the sudden glare of media attention had surprised two authors who had been quietly engaged in two of the most ambitious literary enterprises of the sixties and seventies. Ruth Jhabvala's own case was different. Though perhaps not at the centre of literary life for most of her career, she had nonetheless attracted critical attention early on and somehow never seems to have known the struggle for recognition which had so much shaped the life of Paul Scott. The contrast between these two literary careers is all the more striking as they were in a sense contemporaneous. In the same twenty years or so that saw Scott both explore his craft and theme in a series of prentice pieces and then write the four great tomes of the *Quartet,* there had appeared, at decorously spaced intervals, about half a dozen elegant slim volumes bearing Ruth Jhabvala's name: novels for the most part, their number augmented once or twice a decade by a collection of crisp short stories. All had been reviewed favourably in the serious papers, had in polite terms been discussed in arts broadcasts and over literary dinner tables, had found their way into public libraries and provincial bookshops, and had won their author the loyalty of a readership large enough to keep her in print and thus in the public eye. This quiet success had owed much to the calm ironic tone and measured elegance of her narrative voice. Indeed, there was in all her writing a distinctive restraint, which might be said to have extended even to the choice of topic. All her books and short stories were set in India - contemporary and mostly urban India, that is - , with the plot often revolving about European expatriates. [1]

---

[1] This is especially true of her more recent work; while in the early novels Westerners are protrayed only on the extreme fringes of the narrative, they progressively move inward until, by the time of *Heat and Dust,* they command the centrestage. It is hard to believe that this strikingly linear process should be accidental. And while it is possible to put it down to changing artistic interests ("I

It was a world she knew well. She was, after all, very much an expatriate herself. Born in Germany of Jewish parents, she had as a child in the thirties escaped to safety in England, where she later met and married an Indian architect whom in 1951 she followed to Delhi. This varied life makes it difficult for critics with tidy minds and habits to 'place' her, and for some years there was a great deal of earnest debate as to whether it made her an 'Indo-British' writer (an 'insider', as some would have it) or an 'Anglo-Indian' writer (an 'outsider'), or neither of these or indeed some combination of the two. [2] She herself was noticeably less worried about labels, though she never sought to disguise her Western origin and outlook: "If I must be considered anything, then let it be as one of those Europeans who have written about India." [3] What is more, she has since put matters beyond all doubt by leaving India and settling in New York - almost as if out of consideration for anguished critical souls. [4]

Heat and Dust, then, written at the very end of her Indian years, brought Ruth Jhabvala unprecedented public acclaim. It also broke new ground for her artistically: both in its narrative technique and, more importantly for our purpose, in its choice of time frame. The setting was India, as ever, but for the first time she widened her perspective to take in the days of the Raj. The plot centres on parallel events fifty years

---

get fascinated by certain subjects and then write about them till I'm bored or exhausted"), it is tempting to see in it a reflection of Ruth Jhabvala's evolving attitude to India. (Ramlal Agrawal, "An Interview with Ruth Prawer Jhabvala". *Quest* 91 September/October 1974, p.35)

[2] For a lucid analysis see Vasant A. Shahane, "An Artist's Experience of India: Ruth Prawer Jhabvala's Fiction". In: M. Manuel and K. Ayyappa Paniker, *English and India: Essays Presented to Prof Samuel Mathai on His 70th Birthday*. Madras 1978, pp.1-2.

[3] Agarwal, op.cit., p.36.

[4] This tortuous biography, one imagines, might also have occasioned much mental agony amongst librarians, compilers of annual bibliographies and the like. Happily, however, there exists a convenient term for eccentric people like Ruth Jhabvala: that of 'Commonwealth author'. This felicitous appellation, of course, also made her eligible for the Booker Prize. The empire of Commonwealth letters is, it must be said, more far-flung than any Clive or Rhodes or Raffles ever dared dream of. Americans alone remain debarred from it. Inevitably, this produces envy amongst those thus singled out. The novelist Paul Theroux - London-based, but born on the wrong side of the Atlantic, so to speak - explicitly mentioned Ruth Jhabvala in his famous outburst about unlikely recruits to the imperial colours and the sheer unfairness of it all. This, of course, was before Ruth Jhabvala muddied the waters even further by moving to New York. In taking American citizenship she may, however, have finally gone too far.

apart. Briefly, it may be summarized as the story of Olivia Rivers's affair and eventual elopement with an Indian ruler in the 1920s, and that of the nameless seventies narrator - the granddaughter of Olivia's deserted husband - who has come to India to visit the scene of the old scandal. The two narrative threads are closely and cleverly interwoven; indeed, much of the novel's effect stems from the adroit juxtapositioning of individual scenes. This technique of swift intercutting has put one critic in mind of the strict rules of polyphony; she speaks of a plot which is "fugal and antiphonal: past and present . . . [echoing] each other as subject and counter subject in a fugue". [5] Clearly, neither the 'subject' nor the 'counter subject' are meant to be seen in isolation. For our purpose here it will be useful, however, to concentrate for the moment on only one of the two - and leave until later the question of which is which so to speak.

The events surrounding Olivia and Douglas Rivers and the Nawab of Khatm are set in 1923. This, as no critic worth his salt can fail to spot, lands us squarely in 'Forsterland'. And chasing after Forsterian (or, for that matter, Kiplingesque) quarry is of course one of the most cherished traditions of 'Anglo-Indian' criticism. Any new novel with an Eastern setting seems to elicit the same old response: packs of critics can soon be seen beagling across its pages in almost single-minded pursuit of Kiplingesque foxes and tired Forsterian hares. A novel set in 1923 promised excellent sport.

In the end, however, *Heat and Dust* proved something of a disappointment. That there was no shortage of Forsterian echoes was soon apparent: they ranged from individual character traits to the inventory of the store rooms of the palace of Khatm; but they were so glaringly obvious that all excitement of the chase vanished utterly. Ruth Jhabvala, the unspoken feeling went, would have had every right to turn to Forster for a bit of local colour, since her own experience of India had been limited to post-imperial drabness; but she had clearly gone beyond borrowing mere bits of colour here. Yet simple imitation seemed unlikely in a novelist of her proven skill. It was all deeply puzzling. Her "indebtedness to Forster", intoned one critical voice darkly, was "not

---

[5] Laurie Sucher, *The Fiction of Ruth Prawer Jhabvala: The Politics of Passion*. London 1989, p.107.

straightforward".[6] What, then, lay behind it all? "Could it be", wondered the more mystically-minded, "... that Forster [had] touched upon the core of Anglo-Indian experience, and no writer dealing with that era ... is able to transcend the archetypes created by him"?[7] A more persuasive, if rather more prosaic, explanation was put forward in an article in the *Partisan Review* under the playful title of "White Writers' Burden". The burden in question, the author suggested, was one shared by all Western novelists dealing with the Eastern scene and it bears forever the familiar features of the Sage of King's: for, "even after fifty years, an 'enlightened' white experience of such countries can scarcely be rendered in fiction without evoking for the reader, if not for the writer, the presence of E.M. Forster."[8] What is inevitable may however be actively embraced; the "strategy" of the author of *Heat and Dust* "... is to confront the Forsterian ghost boldly and, if not to exorcise it, to weaken its influence by public exposure".[9] The novelist John Updike, encroaching on critical territory, arrives at a similar conclusion: he speaks - with an almost audible chuckle - of Ruth Jhabvala having "deliberately invaded" sacred literary precincts.[10]

Updike's hint at mild mischievousness behind the sober face of *Heat and Dust* may seem particularly appropriate in the light of one of the novel's minor characters: that of Olivia's friend Harry. The portrait of this camp and ineffectual young Englishman at the court of Khatm carries familiar, indeed famous, traits. This, some critics evidently felt, is where Ruth Jhabvala had gone too far; and, though generally keen to note similarities with Forster's writings, they preserve a tightlipped silence as to those with the man himself.[11] Yet - sacrilegious conception apart -

---

[6] Shirley Chew, "Fictions of Princely States and Empire". *Ariel: A Review of International English Literature* 17 (3) 1986, p.113.
I am being unfair, of course; Shirley Chew is entirely clear-sighted about the nature of the literary connection between Ruth Jhabvala and E.M. Forster.
[7] Meenakshi Mukherjee, "Journey's End for Jhabvala". In: R.K. Dhawan, *Explorations in Modern Indo-English Fiction*. New Delhi 1982, p.211.
[8] Anon., "White Writers' Burden". *Partisan Review* 44 (2) 1977, p.310.
[9] Ibid., p.311.
[10] John Updike, "Raman and Daisy and Olivia and the Nawab". In: *Hugging the Shore: Essays and Criticism*. London 1984, p.714.
"Perhaps", Updike muses, tongue agreeably wedged in cheek, "she grew tired of being interviewed in terms of *A Passage to India?*" (ibid.)
[11] There are only a few exceptions, notably Laurie Sucher, Shirley Chew and Richard Cronin (of whom more later).

there is little enough to offend in the character of Harry: his portrayal is good-humoured, affectionate even, and free of the condescension that dripped so readily from Forster's own pen. [12]

Harry, we said, was only a minor player in the events of 1923. In a sense he owes his very existence to the demands of plot and the expediencies of narrative technique: acting as a kind of go-between in the early stages of Olivia's association with the Nawab and later as a commentator on events (both retrospectively, in the 1970s, and while they are unfolding). In this second capacity he shows himself capable of shrewd judgement and occasionally of genuine insight. Yet the most memorable thing about him remains his intriguing similarity to the author of *A Passage to India*; or, more to the point perhaps, to the author of *The Hill of Devi*. That someone possessed of Ruth Jhabvala's sense of humour must have relished the sheer naughtiness of it all seems beyond question; to see in Harry merely the reflection of a broad authorial smile, however, as Shirley Chew appears to do, is a more doubtful approach. [13] For one thing, it seems a little out of character. A novelist as disciplined as Ruth Jhabvala is unlikely, one would have thought, to permit herself the self-indulgence of extended literary jokes, however witty. Using a good joke to drive home a serious point is another matter.

That there is indeed in the 1923 section of *Heat and Dust* more than meets the eye is the contention of Richard Cronin in a long and closely argued article. The thrust of his investigation already finds expression in its title: "'The Hill of Devi' and 'Heat and Dust'". Ruth Jhabvala's novel, Cronin suggests, " . . . is concerned not only with the relationship of two Indias" - those of 1923 and 1973 - "but with . . . [her own] relationship with her literary predecessors, the Englishmen who described life in Indian princely states in the 1920s". [14] In itself this is hardly sensational stuff, and the first paragraph or so of Cronin's article almost misleads one into expecting another tiresome half-hour in the company of a member of the Anglo-Indian 'hunting circles'.

---

[12] Which makes all the more curious the critics' display of sensibility - if sensibility it is.
[13] cf. Chew, op.cit., p.113.
[14] Richard Cronin, "The Hill of Devi' and 'Heat and Dust'". *Essays in Criticism* 36 (2) 1986, p.142.

"Behind Ruth Jhabvala's Khatm", Cronin declares, thereby fuelling one's worst suspicions, "lies Chhatarpur as it is presented in J.R. Ackerley's *Hindoo Holiday*, and Dewas as it is described by Malcolm Darling and by E.M. Forster." [15] This he proceeds to back up by a rapid rehearsal of the similarities between Khatm and its denizens and those of Dewas. [16] But Cronin is only going through the motions. His real interest lies not with the maharajah's rotting pianos, nor with the moral rot of the man himself, but with the character of Harry. Here, too, Cronin is in no doubt as to its source of inspiration. Yet *Heat and Dust*, he concedes, is no potted biography of E.M. Forster, and Harry not an accurate likeness: "For one thing, Harry is utterly without genius. He is a talentless Forster . . . ", but - and here is the surprising twist in Cronin's argument - this makes him in the eyes of Jhabvala "the more trustworthy witness." [17] If this should sound puzzling, Cronin soon makes his meaning clearer. *Heat and Dust*, he writes, "implies that Forster, Ackerley and their like got India wrong: they were deflected from it by their literary sophistication." [18]

High Bloomsbury polish, then, Cronin contrasts not only with Ruth Jhabvala's talentless Harry but also with the distinctly unsophisticated narrator in the modern section of her novel; the young woman in question strikes him very much as "the product of a meagre culture". [19] Yet for all that, he insists, she is not without intellectual curiosity; through the "gauche, unimaginative prose" of her diary entries he sees her groping

> . . . , however clumsily, in an effort to reach out to her experience. Forster and Ackerley are never clumsy, never grope. Their experience never seems to lie outside the language in which they record it. Which is to say, of course, that they are accomplished writers, but which may suggest also that writers are not wholly to be trusted. [20]

---

[15] Ibid.
[16] As for Chhatarpur/ Chhokrapur, it is - to the reader's relief - never again explicitly invoked.
[17] Cronin, p.144.
[18] Ibid.
[19] Ibid.
[20] Ibid.

We shall leave unexamined for the moment the nature of that gauche girl's experience of India (and the intriguing implications of this paragraph for Ruth Jhabvala herself as writer and expatriate) and follow Cronin back to Dewas in the 1920s. And Cronin asks us to consider particularly Forster's famous description of it in *The Hill of Devi*: "The oddest corner in the world outside *Alice in Wonderland*: it has no parallel except in a Gilbert and Sullivan opera." These twin points of reference, Cronin suggests, are not quite as innocent as they may sound; they are more in the nature of a literary sleight of hand, controlling Forster's Indian reminiscences and allowing him ". . . to present his liking for Dewas and his ruler as a properly English relish for eccentricity . . . ".[21] Cronin's concern, however, lies not so much with what might be called the mechanics of Forster's approach as with its consequences. Forster may well have described Dewas as he saw it; but, Cronin insists, he saw what he wished to see. "Before he ever went out to India he thought of it pre-eminently as a school of the heart."[22] He, and his fellow-Kingsmen Darling and Ackerley, went there

> . . . predisposed to find in another country what they could not find in Britain, somewhere where understanding took second place to affection, judgement was subordinate to sympathy, and people were bound to one another not by political and economic inter-dependence but by bonds of love.[23]

Cronin's main interest in all this evidently lies with Forster; ours does not. If we quote him at length, it is because his observations have a distinct resonance for the reader of Ruth Jhabvala's novels. Our novelist too is, for instance, not generally noted for her preoccupation with "the political and economic interdependence" of her characters. This stance

---
[21] Ibid., p.144.
By the same token, Cronin adds, they allow Forster " . . . to impute to the English officials who . . . stripped Tukoji Rao of his ruling powers, . . . a humourless and self-righteous rectitude that Forster's readers would be happy to accept as a less congenial expression of the English national character." (ibid., p.144-5) This, as we shall see, is not without relevance in a discussion of *Heat and Dust*.
[22] Ibid., p.147.
[23] Ibid.

has in fact drawn critical fire (some of it directed specifically at *Heat and Dust*).[24] In this, then, as in other things Ruth Jhabvala would appear to be following in famous footsteps.[25] Personal relationships, certainly, are at the heart of her fiction too. In fact, she has created over the years a long line of characters who might be said to be wearing their 'Forsterian' hearts on their sleeves. But let us recall Shirley Chew's words of caution: that with Ruth Jhabvala things are rarely straightforward; that, while she may give "the impression of echoing" Forster, "... she always maintains an ironical distance".[26] Usually this takes the form of giving her 'Forsterian' characters plenty of rope with which to hang themselves.[27] Some come to grief dramatically; others, leading more charmed existences, escape unharmed and go on viewing the world through a rosy haze of benevolence; both are shown to have failed utterly in their oh-so-earnest attempts to comprehend the Indian reality. The example of the egregious Hochstadts in *A Backward Place*, and the high comedy that surrounds their blundering subcontinental progress, may suffice to illustrate the point.

And this, of course, leads us back once more to Cronin and Forster and a splendidly barbed paragraph on the 'Bloomsbury' perception of India. Its relevance to our purpose will, I think, be readily apparent:

> The better to liberate the heart, India assaults the intellect. . . . Perfectly ordinary mistakes become

---

[24] cf. inter al. Eunice de Souza's dismissive appraisal: "... there is no progress towards a deepening of insights about the social forces at work in the country, no striving to understand these. Indeed, the writer shows no inclination whatsoever even to attempt to go beyond the facile emotional reactions to what she observes on the Indian social scene". (Eunice de Souza, "The Blinds Drawn and the Air Conditioner on". *World Literature Written in English* 17 (1) 1978, p.219.

[25] Forster's is not the only perceived literary influence on Ruth Jhabvala; Chekov and Jane Austen are the other names most commonly bandied about. As for the comparison with Jane Austen, H. Summerfield rightly calls this an "occupational hazard" faced by "any woman who writes witty novels in English about courtship and family life". (H. Summerfield, "Holy Women and Unholy Men: Ruth Prawer Jhabvala Confronts the Non-rational". *Ariel: A Review of International English Literature* 17 (3) 1986, p.85) *Heat and Dust* and its unblinking description of degredation, death and disease has probably put paid to the comparison with Jane Austen.

[26] Chew, op.cit., p.113.

[27] Perhaps this is what Meenakshi Mukherjee means when she says, "Her standard method is to diminish her subject by making it ridiculous and at the same time to appear to treat it with concern." (Mukherjee, op.cit., pp.209-10)

symptomatic of the fallibility of the understanding . . .
A 'small dead tree' is mistaken for a snake, an 'exciting
and typical adventure', so typical that Forster included
it in *A Passage to India*. . . . His mind must become
foggy so that he is forced to trust his heart, so that he
may realize: 'It doesn't do to think. To follow the
promptings of the eye is quite enough.' Presiding over
all this, as its ideal embodiment, is the Maharajah . . .
With him Forster touches the full extasy of freedom
from the intellect. 'Quite often I did not understand
him - he was too incalculable - but it was possible
with him to reach a platform where calculations were
unnecessary. It would not be possible with an
Englishman.' [28]

It will have become clear by now, I think, why Cronin's 'lateral' approach to *Heat and Dust* actually touches the novel's core. The loss of rationality - or rather the conscious abdication of the Western intellect in the hope of achieving mystical (Eastern) communion - is after all a recurring theme in Ruth Jhabvala's fiction. If anything, it has with the passing years become even more prominent. In her novels, and especially in her short stories, she has created a small army of characters who reach in India "the full extasy of freedom from the intellect", and who have indeed come to India expressly in order to do so. It is a spectacle Ruth Jhabvala does not enjoy. The obsessiveness with which she returns to it again and again is itself a measure of her dismay. And it is surely no coincidence that the very first pages of *Heat and Dust* should vouchsafe us a glimpse of such spiritual flotsam. [29] The Europeans in question are pointed out to the narrator by a desiccated old missionary woman - "a ghost with backbone", the narrator calls her in fine Jhabvalian irony. (*HD*, p.6) But there is a notable absence of authorial irony in the description of those blond and blue-eyed beggars: in fact, the narrator is inclined to agree with the old lady that their eyes are indeed the eyes of "souls in hell". (*HD*, p.6)

This brief scene at the beginning of the book is easily overlooked as the reader is swept up by the gathering tide of events at Khatm and

---
[28] Cronin, pp.147-8.
[29] All page references to *Heat and Dust* are to the Futura paperback edition (London 1976), refered to hereafter as *HD*.

their present day echo. Laurie Sucher is practically alone in examining it more closely. And she is undoubtedly right in emphasizing the ironical element in it: the old missionary as a "Dantean angel", the naughty pun of the "S.M. (Society of Missionaries) hostel" etc. [30] She is surely right also to see in it "the traditional Gothic beginning: a young woman arrives in an exotic place, naively fearless; she is warned by one who knows more; she scoffs . . .". [31] But is Sucher right to add quite so unequivocally that "the warning voice represents a past system of values no longer valid or applicable . . . "? [32] – If we see in the missionary nothing other than a narrowly religious representative of Western values, perhaps; but Sucher herself notes the incident of the old lady guarding the narrator's watch while its owner is asleep, and had earlier identified that watch as a " . . . symbol of Western rationalism, efficiency and temporal linearity . . . ". [33] Can we then, knowing as we do about Ruth Jhabvala's preoccupation with Western rationality, really dismiss the whole scene as an exercise in authorial playfulness: mere fun and jinks, so to speak?

The answer, surely, comes in the guise of a character we encounter a few pages later. Chidananga, or 'Chid' as he is more usually referred to, is one European who has divested himself of more than just the trappings of Western civilization: having burnt his possessions on a ceremonial pyre, he has shaved his head, donned saffron robes and has acquired with his Hindu name the begging bowl of the Hindu holy man. He is not very successful at his new calling, however, and has to fire off regular telegraphic demands to England for life-saving money orders: a character, in short, calculated to invite sardonic comment. Certainly, the missionary lady from the 'S.M.' would have given him short shrift. The narrator, on the other hand, is more tolerant. She does not seem to find Chid's brand of second-hand spirituality particularly convincing, it is true; hers, after all, is a robust attitude even to the genuine, Indian, sadhus: "On the whole they look a sturdy set of rascals to me . . . ". (*HD*, p.63) Yet judgement, while not perhaps subordinate to sympathy, does remain suspended for a time, as she patiently satisfies Chid's various demands on

---

[30] Sucher, op.cit., p.105.
[31] Ibid., pp.105-6.
[32] Ibid., p.106.
[33] Ibid.

her time, property, and person. This remarkable passivity should not, however, be mistaken for inertia; nor is it saintlike forbearance: it has about it a strong element of curiosity - something almost of the calm detachment of the ethnologist - as well as more orthodox compassion and a readiness to give anyone the benefit of the doubt. [34] Eventually, however, some unfavourable conclusion is clearly reached and Chid is thrown out. At which point Laurie Sucher's tired "system of past values no longer valid or applicable" would seem to stage a remarkable recovery. For something has finally snapped in the narrator, and it is not just her patience with her guest's exploitative antics. The reasons for her rejection of Chid and all his works go deeper than that, and they are very much along familiar Jhabvalian lines: "What most disturbs the narrator - and here she seems to be the author's mouthpiece - ", observes H. Summerfield in this context, "is his flight from reason". [35]

If a wrist watch in a dormitory in Bombay was symbolic of the Western sense of order, then Chid's unstructured life beyond time and reason clearly stands for the opposite; and as for the narrator, it is not for nothing, one would have thought, that she keeps a diary in which to mark the passing of time and to record - and analyse - her experiences. There is much in this young woman's life that would meet at best with incomprehension from the missionary glimpsed at the beginning; but here, surely, we may imagine the old lady claiming kinship and vigorously nodding her approval.

If, then, in *Heat and Dust* we see Ruth Jhabvala once again mounting the melting ramparts of Western rationality we are bound to

---

[34] To some extent the narrator is prepared to grant that benefit of the doubt also in the question of the value for Westerners of Indian religion itself. Ruth Jhabvala never really commits herself either way in *Heat and Dust*, but an underlying scepticism does shines through; certainly, the ironizing urge is not entirely kept in check. The narrator finds, for instance, that Chid's voracious sexual appetite - suprising in one otherwise so weakened - puts her in mind of " . . . the Lord Shiva whose huge member is worshipped by devout Hindu women. At such times it seems to me that his sex is engendered by his spiritual practices, by all that chanting of mantras he does . . . ". (*HD*, p.65) It is presumably with this in mind that Vasant Shahane writes: "the narrator has only vague intimations of immortality flowing from a sexual experience with Chid". (Vasant A Shahane, "Jhabvala's 'Heat and Dust': A Cross-Cultural Encounter". In: M.K. Naik (ed.), *Aspects of Indian Writing in English: Essays in Honour of Prof. K.R. Srininvasan Iyenagar*. Madras 1979, p.226) The ironic mode is evidently catching.
[35] Summerfield, op.cit., p.93.

ask what it is in particular she is defending it against. For Summerfield the matter is clear-cut: a Westerner marooned in the East has taken up arms against something that is alien to her - and thus to our - traditions: Ruth Jhabvala "to a considerable extent, . . . identifies the outlook she regards as non-European with the predominance of emotion over reason". [36]

It is easy to see how, given the Indian setting of her novels, one might arrive at this conclusion. Nor is it wholly erroneous. But it does perhaps invite misunderstanding. For one thing, it implies criticism of the Indians for as it were getting their metaphysical priorities wrong. Yet there is, to my knowledge, no attempt anywhere in Ruth Jhabvala's writing to stricture those whose religious beliefs, she knows, will always elude her understanding. Condemnation she reserves for those she does comprehend: the manipulators - Indian or European - on the one hand, and on the other those ready to abdicate all responsibility: not out of weakness but out of intellectual, emotional, and - dare one say it - moral torpor. She knows about the temptation of dulling one's mind to that around us which is unpleasant or disquieting. And she knows, too, about the consequences of yielding to such temptation. With every "turning away from reality", as Summerfield rightly stresses, there comes in Ruth Jhabvala's world "a passive acceptance of evil and suffering". [37] Chid, as Summerfield goes on to observe, is a case in point: when the narrator's house is filled with the screams of her landlord's deranged young wife and everyone stirs in alarm or sympathy, there is from him no reaction whatsoever; he keeps up his moronic chanting throughout, as if nothing were amiss. [38]

It is this scene, more perhaps than any other, that crystallizes Ruth Jhabvala's true concern. For the point here, surely, is not that Chid wears Eastern robes and is chanting Eastern mantras - he is never anything other than a European affecting Indian disguise - but that he is using these trappings of Eastern religion as a convenient excuse for inaction: in the face an unpleasant reality he has chosen the easy option of shutting his eyes to it. Later, when reality catches up with him

---

[36] Ibid.
[37] Ibid., p.95.
[38] cf. ibid.

personally in the form of serious tropical illness, he is quite ready to discard his now inconvenient Eastern sainthood, and slips back, effortlessly, into his old Western identity. (Contrast this with the portrayal of Maji, the narrator's friend and discrete guardian angel, who - to the author's undisguised admiration - manages to combine traditional Hindu piety with clarity of thought, robust good sense and a life of action.)

The East- West tags, then, are largely beside the point. *Heat and Dust* in any case is not really concerned with the familiar niceties of 'the East-West Encounter' (and not everyone, it has to be said, shares Eunice de Souza's regret at the absence in this novel of an italicised experience to point the moral and adorn the tale). [39] Ruth Jhabvala, let us recall, is a Western writer writing for a Western audience, and she is grappling here with something which - for herself as much as for her readership - is both larger and more immediate: the question of how we as Westerners in the second half of the twentieth century should live our lives. Chid, the young narrator, and indeed the entire cast of characters allow her to explore our contemporary world. India, in a sense, merely provides the setting for this exploration; and it does so only because at the time it provided the setting for Ruth Jhabvala's own life - and had done so for close on a quarter of a century. (Accordingly, we find ourselves translated in her most recent novels to the unwonted surroundings of the American East Coast; the underlying concerns, however, are instantly recognizable.) Ruth Jhabvala's interest in the Indian scene is therefore personal but not parochial: India is the prism through which she sees the world. David Rubin is right to remind us in this context of a revealing passage in Ruth Jhabvala's contribution to James Vinson's anthology *Contemporary Novelists*. [40] The key sentences in this authorial self-portrait bear repeating:

> My books may appear to be objective but really I think they are the opposite; for I describe the Indian scene not for its own sake but for mine. . . . My work

---

[39] cf. de Souza, op.cit., 222.
[40] cf. David Rubin, *After the Raj*, op.cit., p.680.

is only one individual European's attempt to compound the puzzling process of living in India. [41]

Therein, depending on one's point of view, lies the attraction or the shortcoming of Ruth Jhabvala's art. For what to some is evidence of a superficial approach, is a refreshing lack of pretension to others. [42] Certainly, it is difficult to argue with Haydn Moore Williams's remark that "India is not a 'problem' to her, as it appears to be to so many earnest investigators, but a life." [43]

An individual experience must, of course, in some way be viewed against related experiences if it is to be transmuted successfully into fiction: that is to say, if it is to be both of interest to the reader and of use to the author by somehow illuminating that which had originally exercised the author's mind and had, as it were, first planted the seed for the book. In *Out of India*, Ruth Jhabvala's own selection of her short stories, one finds included by way of introduction her celebrated autobiographical essay "Myself in India"; and 'Jhabvala in India', clearly, is the soil from which *Heat and Dust*, like most of her fiction, has sprung. Yet through its extended time frame alone, it also reaches more overtly than any other work beyond her immediate sphere of experience. Here, for the first time, she looks back at what one might call her own pre-history: the experience of India of the generation that preceded her own. Turning to the past is therefore no exercise in nostalgia. Nor is it, as unkind voices have intimated, a cunning ruse to 'cash in' on the renewed popularity of imperial romance without attracting the critical opprobrium that attaches to its more overt purveyors. [44]

---

[41] James Vinson, *Contemporary Novelists*. London 1972, p.678.
[42] As for the former, see for instance M.K. Naik: "R.P. Jhabvala . . . is content to dwell elegantly on the surface . . . ." ("Post-Independence Indo-English Fiction". In: R.K. Dhawan, *Commonwealth Fiction* 1. New Delhi 1988, p.65)
[43] Haydn Moore Williams, *The Fiction of Ruth Prawer Jhabvala*. Calcutta 1973, p.10.
[44] Such suspicions were principally voiced by Indian reviewers. J.S. Lall's words best capture the flavour of most of the initial Indian reaction to the award of the Booker Prize: "This is only partly a book about India. It hardly matters; clearly it is written for markets that pay." ("No Heat, Little Dust". *The Illustrated Weekly of India* 8 Feb 1976, p.35) Such sentiments, though widespread, were not universal. No less eminent a literary figure than Anita Desai rushed to Ruth Jhabvala's defence, turning Lall's sarcastic line "a sure winner" into the heading of her reply (cf. "Jhabvala: A Sure Winner". *The Illustrated Weekly of India* 7 March 1976, p.32)

Some of Ruth Jhabvala's own utterances have added to the confusion (compounded by the fact that much Jhabvala criticism favours an excessively literal approach). Thus too many critics have shown themselves ready to take at face value her self-deprecating remarks made in *The Times* in the wake of the great critical success of *Heat and Dust*. She was turning to the past, she confided to her interviewer, " . . . because the present . . . [was] too new and unpredictable" and the subject of "the new India with the old still inside like a fossil" was one she felt unable to handle. [45] (That this is, in part at least, contradicted by the very structure of *Heat and Dust* appears to have escaped her rapt interviewer.) It seems necessary, therefore, or at any rate pardonable, to state here what should surely be obvious: For all her colourful evocation of the Raj, Ruth Jhabvala remains firmly rooted in the present. The past is of interest only in as much as it might provide the key to understanding the present. Ruth Jhabvala has no personal connection with imperial India, and her novel duly reflects this. It displays, for instance, a complete lack of interest in the pathos of the dying Raj that fired Paul Scott's imagination. [46] If she turns to the 1920s it is because something in that sepia-tinted world must have stood out and caught her eye: some faded photograph or other revealing unexpectedly familiar features.

As to the perceived potency of the charge of peddling Raj-escapism, one can best get the measure of it from Salman Rushdie's diatribe against the *Raj Quartet*. Here insult replaces argument and guilt is established by association; thus Rushdie makes much play of Scott's friendship with Molly Hamilton, who as M.M. Kaye writes commercially successful Eastern fantasies.

[45] Caroline Moorhead, "Interview with Ruth Prawer Jhabvala". *The Times* 20 November 1975.
Mining this interview for arguments supporting various critical views remains problematical. What is more, there is now the added complication of "the new India with the old one still inside it" having become the land on which Salman Rushdie has staked his claim. To read Ruth Jhabvala's innocent remark now is, inevitably, to see anticipated the plot of *Midnight's Children*. Rushdie, of course, in his own way, has changed the literary landscape of India for the Western reader as much as Forster did in the twenties. Ruth Jhabvala's comparative reticence on India, post-*Heat and Dust*, therefore assumes, in conjunction with this interview, a significance which, perhaps, it does not merit.

[46] cf. Inge Winterberg, "An Experience of India: Zu den Indienromanen von Ruth Prawer Jhabvala". *Arcadia* 17 (2) 1982, pp.193-4: "Ein zentrales Thema, das Verhältnis zum British Empire . . . , stellt sich für Jhabvala nicht. . . . Der Konflikt, das Verstricktsein des geborenen Engländers bleiben Jhabvala fremd. . . . [British India] ist nur der Hintergrund, auf dem sich ihr eigentliches Thema entwickelt: 'Myself in India' oder 'Was kann Indien einem Europäer heute bedeuten?'"

We might do worse, therefore, than to follow our author's lead and return to the India of the Raj. And it is, one suspects, with a degree of relief that most readers will do so: happy to trade the sight of emaciated young Englishmen in saffron robes for scenes suffused with the reassuring glow of cultured endeavour and "only connect"; Bloomsbury versus the hippie ashram, as it were. Unsurprisingly, the comparison yields signs of sad decline everywhere. The later generation somehow seem as diminished in person as in their circumstances: possessed, as Brijraj Singh drily observes, of "neither the charisma nor the charm" of their grandparents, they lack "depth and complexity". [47] Above all, one might add, they lack 'style'.

Ruth Jhabvala, of course, is laying it on with a trowel. Whereas we get disease, dirt and poverty in modern India, the past is all polish and starch: shiny limousines gliding over dusty roads, and in the evenings the crinkle of silk and crinoline and the discrete turbaned presence of an army of bearers. "Olivia's world", as John Updike observes, " . . . has a formal grandeur that supports her stylized romance and preordains it from the first page to its pattern of fascination and fall and flight and unutterable disgrace". [48] That inner logic of the narrative is certainly central to Jhabvala's evocation of the Raj; (and it goes a long way towards explaining the novel's popular success). But the essence of *Heat and Dust* lies not in the conjuring trick that produces a shimmering vision of imperial India but in the juxtaposing of it with the sights, smells and sounds of our own day. "Throughout", as Laurie Sucher observes, "the colonial past is almost playfully contrasted to the grubby present, its golden patina now tarnished to reveal the reality underneath". [49]

The key word here is, of course, that familiar awkward word 'reality'. It is in a way as much part of the everyday exchange of post-colonial literature as were such terms as 'snares' and 'delusions' in the

---

[47] Brijraj Singh, "Ruth Prawer Jhabvala: 'Heat and Dust'". In: N.S. Pradhan (ed.), *Major Indian Novels: An Evaluation*. New Delhi 1985, p.197.
Singh specifically refers to Inder Lal and the Nawab, but his observations hold equally true of everyone else in the 1970s section.
[48] Updike, op.cit., p.714.
[49] Laura Sucher, "Quest and Disillusion: The Fiction of Ruth Prawer Jhabvala". Unpublished thesis. State University of New York at Stony Brook 1985, p.127.

days of classical Anglo-Indian romance. [50] Today's preoccupation with 'reality' and yesterday's with 'delusion' might, of course, be seen as essentially two sides of the same coin. David Rubin would seem to be thinking along those lines when he describes Ruth Jhabvala as continuing "... the traditions of colonial British novelists of the half-century preceding Indian independence". [51] Ruth Jhabvala's work constitutes for him "a clever and disarming set of variations on the long tradition of the Anglo-Indian novelists" (and though he is prepared to acknowledge differences between *Heat and Dust* and Ruth Jhabvala's earlier novels he clearly wishes us to apply to it his general observations). [52]

While it is hard to dismiss Rubin's claims outright, they do throw up several questions. Firstly, rather a lot seems to hinge on where in his pronouncements one chooses to place the emphasis: on the idea of continuing a tradition or on that of providing variations on it. Secondly, exactly which tradition of delusion and disillusion do we place *Heat and Dust* in? For there is surely more than one. There is, certainly, that of the clichéd seeker-after-Eastern enlightenment, who - we know - is doomed to be disabused by the cruel reality of India; this, of course, is the deeply insular view which sustained the imperial enterprise, and the Anglo-Indian romance that identified with it. But is there not a second tradition, at least since Forster, which locates illusion primarily among the upholders of the Raj? the "real India", famously, escaping them? Rubin seems to place *Heat and Dust* in the former tradition; and with characters like the nameless English girl who came to India "to find peace" - "but all ... [she] found was dysentery", it is hard to argue with this. (*HD*, p.21) Yet somehow that reading seems too neat - and too one-dimensional - to convince. If to demonstrate India's capacity for delivering blows to starry-eyed Westerners had been Ruth Jhabvala's sole or even her principal purpose it is hard to see why this should have required the complex structure of the twin-narrative. Why not keep things safely in the present and thus in Ruth Jhabvala's own realm of experience? And if

---

[50] These latter terms, of course, also form the title of V.S. Pritchett's essay on Ruth Jhabvala, and describing them as 'everyday exchange' is not meant to suggest that Sir Victor's observations are in any way quotidian.
[51] Rubin, op.cit., p.70.
[52] Ibid., p.99.
cf. also David Rubin, "Ruth Prawer Jhabvala in India". *Modern Fiction Studies* 30 (4) 1984, p.682.

there was an urge to amplify, to trace the same pattern in an earlier age, why of all years choose 1923? a year of such singular significance in the annals of Anglo-Indian letters? why, in a word, all those allusions to E.M. Forster?

The answers, surely, do not require much speculation. They are all there in the novel itself. Let us start by examining the reasons for moving beyond the present. Obviously, the twin-plot structure encourages comparisons between then and now, and these in turn yield three things: first and foremost, they provide evidence of parallels in people's behaviour and expectations. These are in fact central to the structure of *Heat and Dust*. [53] Frequently they take the form of misunderstandings - interracial or intercultural misunderstandings that is - and their "persistence ... across half a century" are, as Sucher notes, one of the main sources of Jhabvalian comedy. [54] (The uneasy combination of drastic change and unexpected continuity in post-Independence Satipur also gives Ruth Jhabvala scope for a few gentle jibes against the contemporary India she had made her home.) [55]

---

[53] For concrete instances of such parallels see inter al. Sucher, "Quest and Disillusion", op.cit., p.127.

[54] Sucher, *The Fiction of Ruth Prawer Jhabvala*, op.cit., 109.
Vasant Shahane is essentially referring to the same thing when he describes Ruth Jhabvala as excelling in the description of life's "incongruities": "These incongruities", he writes, "have social, familial and cultural implications and consequently they become the source of the comic." (Vasant A. Shahane, *Ruth Prawer Jhabvala*. (Indian Writers Series 9) New Delhi 1976, p.15)

[55] The almost uniformly negative tone of Indian criticism towards Ruth Jhabvala, and towards *Heat and Dust* in particular, clearly owes much to offended national sensibilities. Perhaps it is this ability to touch raw subcontinental nerves that is being alluded to in S.N. Kumar's splendidly guarded remark about "Mrs Jhabvala's writings [having] ... attracted attention in drawing room conversations of state capitals ... ". (S.N. Kumar, "Review of Heat and Dust". *Literary Criterion* 12 (2,3) 1976, p.226) However, Ruth Jhabvala does also have champions on the subcontinent. Apart from Anita Desai, one thinks of N.S. Pradhan, who mounts a spirited and comprehensive defence in: N.S. Pradhan, "The Problem of Focus in Jhabvala's 'Heat and Dust'". *The Indian Literary Review* May 1978, pp.15-17.
What remains puzzling is not just the extent of the divergence of views but why most Indian critics should have taken such umbrage in the first place? Haydn Moore Williams probably sums up the reaction of most of Ruth Jhabvala's Western readers in calling her treatment of India one of "tactful comedy". (Williams, op.cit., p.10). Is it her use of irony, then, that is at the root of the problem? Yet, surely, the ironic mode is not alien to India. One thinks of R.K. Narayan, and in particular of the deliciously naughty circus scene in *A Tiger for Malgudi*; (a tiger and a goat sharing a bowl of milk to symbolize the Gandhian tradition of non-violence: a scene that goes horribly wrong when the tamer's attention is momentarily distracted). Compared to *that*, Jhabvalian irony is pretty tame stuff. But, if Feroza Jussawalla is

Secondly, and here things patently move beyond David Rubin's 'Great Tradition', the two-plot structure draws attention to the protective cocoon that in the days of the Raj surrounded expatriates in the East. It does so in two ways: by playing up the elegant luxuriousness of Olivia's age on the one hand; and on the other by contrasting it, two generations on, with the threadbare remains of that old cloak of privilege, now hanging rather more loosely on European shoulders. (Again this occasions wry authorial smiles: this time at our collectively reduced Western circumstances. In a scene of ringing metaphorical echo we observe English travelers camping out on the verandah of the dak bungalow in what were formerly the British Civil Lines; inside, a portrait of George V is still in situ, quietly gathering dust.)

Thirdly, and perhaps most importantly of all, the structure of *Heat and Dust* forces the reader to reexamine his own expectations and perception of India. And through the use of the self-consciously literary format of the narrator's diary, and the obvious literary allusions in Olivia's story, it reaches as it were beyond itself to point at and question other familiar visions of the East.

Most immediately, of course, it queries the reader's own views: certainly, our earlier relief at being whisked off to the enchanted 1920s turns out to have been somewhat premature. For the parallels in the twin story lines suggest that the two experiences of India are being not so much contrasted as firmly yoked together. And, for all the outward differences between glamorous yesteryear and down-at-heel present, the similiarities are unmistakable. Nor are they limited to the lives of Olivia and her 1970s counterpart; they are true of all those earnest seekers - fictional or real-life - who, as they step ashore at Bombay or off the 'plane at Delhi, proceed to cast off the ways of the West. The preferred

---

to be believed, satire is not the issue anyway. Jussawalla, writing from the safety of American shores, suggests that it is "the realistic aspect" of Ruth Jhabvala's description of India which embarrasses and thus offends. (Feroza F Jussawalla, *Family Quarrels: Towards a Criticism of Indian Writing in English*. (American University Studies. Series 4: English Language and Literature 17) New York 1985, p.134) However, there may be yet another factor at play. Ruth Jhabvala reserves the full sting of her irony for Westernized Indians; especially those living abroad who, like the Nawab's descendents in *Heat and Dust*, wax lyrical about India but find the country too strong for their delicate constitutions. One wonders, therefore, whether N.S. Pradhan might not have put his finger on it by reminding us that Ruth Jhabvala has spent more of her life in India than some of her Indian critics? (cf. "The Problem of Focus", op.cit., p.15)

methods may have changed in fifty years; the consequences, Ruth Jhabvala suggests, are not all that dissimilar. In *Heat and Dust* a fictional young Englishman wanders through India untouched by the sights and sounds of suffering around him. Half a century earlier, and in real life, the novelist E.M. Forster notes in passing the grinding poverty of the ordinary subjects of his 'Gilbert and Sullivan' India. It does not seem to have occasioned him too much disquiet; nor would it appear to have dimmed in any appreciable measure his admiration for the man who presided over it. In fact, when that man finally succeeded in bankrupting his state, forcing the Viceroy to strip him of his ruling powers, Forster promptly deplored the officiousness of the Government of India. This was not, we may be sure, patrician disdain. It was affection, trust and love of a kind that would have been impossible in England. The pitiful scenes outside the palace were, in truth, as extraneous to Forster's consciousness as are a young woman's screams to the fictional shaven-headed English youth of a later generation.

Not that the portrayal of the poverty and suffering of India are in any way Ruth Jhabvala's main concern. Fiction, she knows, is not sociology, and *Heat and Dust* is certainly no political tract. However, as she peers out wearily from her room of her own into the glare outside, she does not avert her gaze from what she sees:

> The most salient fact about India is that it is very poor and very backward. There are so many other things to be said about it but this must remain the basis of them all. We may praise Indian democracy, go into raptures over Indian music, admire Indian intellectuals - but whatever we say, not for one moment should we lose sight of the fact that a very great number of Indians never get enough to eat. Literally that: from birth to death they never for one day cease to suffer from hunger. *Can* one lose sight of that fact? God knows I've tried. But after seeing what one has to see here every day, it is not really possible to go on living one's life the way one is used to. [56]

---

[56] Ruth Prawer Jhabvala, "Myself in India". In: *Out of India: Selected Stories*. Harmondsworth 1989, p.14. (Jhabvala's italics)

And though she does not believe in "... making a catalogue of the horrors with which one lives, on which one lives, as on the back of an animal", her awareness of the grim reality of life for the vast majority of the people around her informs her vision of India; this much the merest glimpse at the modern section of *Heat and Dust* will bear out. [57] If such awareness is lacking in the other half of the novel, it must be intentional. As indeed it is. What we see of the India of the Raj, after all, we see through Olivia's eyes: at one remove so to speak. And though this clearly is something of an authorial ploy, it is not one intended to allow Ruth Jhabvala to get away with romanticising the past, exonerating the Raj, and all the other nonsense of which she has been accused. [58] Those critics pointing out an imbalance, a certain subjectiveness in the two visions of India are quite right. And they are right, too, to query it. But they are mistaken in locating the bias in the author. Ironically, they are behaving exactly as Ruth Jhabvala would have her readers react: they are questioning the veracity of what they are being told. For if the contrast between Satipur in the 1970s and that of the twenties contains a veiled authorial criticism, it is not one directed against independent India. It is a criticism of Olivia's way of seeing things, and thus, by extension, an elegantly oblique querying of that other 1920s vision of India, perhaps the most famous vision of India of them all: that of E.M. Forster.

The liberal use of the clichés of imperial opulence surrounding Olivia is part of the same strategy. In highlighting the existence of this protective cocoon, Ruth Jhabvala indirectly draws our attention to the more insidious consequences for those thus insulated from the world outside: chief amongst them, its inevitable tendency to filter out the more disturbing sights of the East. This effect is most pronounced in expatriates

---

[57] Ibid. (Jhabvala's italics)
Her approach here, as in other things, is best summed up in Haydn Moore Williams's words: "... sympathy and not anger dominate ... "; "she does not preach" and "scarcely ever exaggerates". (Williams, op.cit., p.12)
[58] For what is perhaps the most comprehensive list of such accusations see Zahir Jang Khattak, "British Novelists Writing about India-Pakistan's Independence: Christine Weston, John Masters, Ruth Prawer Jhabvala and Paul Scott". Unpublished thesis. Tufts University 1987.
The true gauge for Khattak of the quality of any British novel on India is the attitude to Independence of its author; and here not only Ruth Jhabvala has been found wanting: the Western readership of these novels, too, cannot hope to escape censure. (cf. Khattak, op.cit., pp.1-2)

cast in the role of passive onlookers: those who, like Olivia, are excluded by gender from the transactions and deliberations of the Raj, or those, like Harry (and E.M. Forster), who choose to exclude themselves. The irony, of course, is that Olivia is aware of the limits Anglo-India would impose on her and rebels against them. "It's a man's game, strictly", observes her husband and promptly misunderstands her rejoinder "What isn't?" (*HD*, p.39) Yet failure to understand is not limited to Olivia's slow-witted husband. She is supremely guilty of it herself. For in a universe devoted to beauty, love and friendship there is no room for cold rationality. Olivia is not interested in *understanding* the world around her but eager only to *experience* it. This is not without consequences. For one thing, it does not give her the freedom for which she yearns, but merely replaces one set of limits with another. Only now it is the Nawab who decides what she shall and shall not see and not her husband and his peers. She is, then, not so much the liberated young woman striking out on her own as a largely passive participant in events: a memsahib, in other words; a somewhat unorthodox memsahib, perhaps, but shielded, like all memsahibs, from reality. At the Nawab's palace she may get to see different sights, but - such is the price of "only connect" - she sees them just as uncomprehendingly as any memsahib would from safely inside the cantonment. Yet unlike the memsahibs in the cantonment, Olivia has ventured beyond the palisade into a world of politics as well as passion: a world, in other words, where there be dragons.

    Olivia's blindness to reality leads inexorably to disaster. Yet, in a sense, there is nothing inevitable about it. At any moment in her association with the Nawab - almost to the end - rational thought might set her free. Harry several times obliquely urges her to confront the truth. If she refuses to do so, she has her reasons for it. She is charmed by the Nawab; yet what emerges about him, is scarcely encouraging. Unwelcome evidence, therefore, must be discounted; the stronger the force of the arguments against him, the more firmly rational thought itself must be rejected. That Olivia is temperamentally inclined to do so is first advertised in the famous 'suttee' scene. In it we observe her defending the indefensible: the self-immolation on their husbands' funeral pyres of Hindu widows. She does so partly, of course, to rile her stuffy compatriots. But she is also genuinely seduced by the perceived romanticism of an Eastern 'Liebestod'. It is not for nothing, after all, that her drawing room resounds to lush operatic scores. This grand romantic vision of life leaves no room for the less seductive aspects of 'suttee': the eagerness of relations to push at the lit pyre rather than to hold back, and the stark economic consideration underlying the custom of widow-burning: that of 'one-less-mouth-to-feed'. [59]

The 'suttee' scene also serves to make another point, however. It demonstrates that, through her rejection of rational thought, Olivia ironically ends up sharing the memsahibs' traditional approach to India; an approach characterized by a pronounced capacity of turning what has the potential to disturb into harmless images of the exotic [60] and the picturesque. [61] Life for Olivia is a series of set pieces (in some ways not unlike the stylized scenes which Paul Scott's Sarah Layton saw her countrymen - and especially her countrywomen - act out in India): 'the

---

[59] The 'suttee' scene is one which attracted particularly scathing comment from Indian critics. They point out that the custom of 'suttee' is scarcely representative of twentieth century subcontinental practice and see in it evidence of the sensationalist and anti-Indian approach which, for them, characterizes *Heat and Dust*. This reading ignores several points: firstly, the fact that the incident creates such a sensation precisely because nothing like it had happened in Satipur in living memory; secondly, it makes for a greater, and highly comlimentary, contrast to modern Satipur, which is home to what John Updike calls Ruth Jhabvala's "happy pack of vigorous widows". (Updike, op.cit., p.716) Lastly, but most importantly, the 'suttee' scene is surely meant to tell us more about Olivia than about India?

[60] Vasant Shahane would also appear to be confusing Olivia's vision of India with Ruth Jhabvala's own when he speaks of "Jhabvala's attempts to recreate India [sic] of the twenties and thirties . . . [being] marked more by a flair for the exotic than by the palpable, rigid realities of the situation. The incidence [sic] of the riots at Khatm, of the 'suttee', of the dacoits and the Nawab's involvement with them, the gay parties, the 'hijras' - all these events depict India . . . as exotic, strange and peculiar . . . ". ("Jhabvala's 'Heat and Dust'", op.cit., p.225)
These remarks are all the more surprising as Shahane had, only a page earlier, described *Heat and Dust* as "essentially a story of Olivia alternating with the story of the narrator"; what is more, he had quoted on the same page the narrator's telling remark that Olivia's approach to life was that of the aesthete. (ibid., p.224)

[61] For a detailed analysis of the 'picturesque' as narrative mode in Anglo-Indian letters see "The Feminine Picturesque" in Sarah Suleri, *The Rhetoric of English India*. Chicago 1992, pp.75-110.
Suleri's remarks frequently remind one of Olivia's approach to life in India, and none perhaps more than the following: "For the female colonizer the picturesque assumes an ideological urgency through which all subcontinental threats could be temporarily converted into watercolours . . . ". (ibid., p.75) An extraordinary final echo of this approach is provided at the very end of *Heat and Dust*: the narrator, visiting the house in the hills where Olivia spent the rest of her life after her flight to the Nawab's palace, finds next to the grand window opening on to the India outside an empty embroidery frame.

royal visitor', 'the drive with the Nawab', 'the picnic' etc.; the irony of it is that these echo, and indeed complement, the italicised experiences of the other Englishwomen at Satipur ('the visit to the zenana', the 'state banquet' etc.). Real life, even when it interrupts such scenes, is inevitably seen through the same glass and assumes a characteristic sense of theatricality. In Olivia's world every crisis turns into melodrama. Thus, the Nawab remains a figure of romance even when surprised in the preparation of intercommunal slaughter; he is evidently arranging for a spot of theft and extortion to replenish state coffers in the process, which makes it difficult even for Olivia to regard him as a benevolent prince, and so in her eyes he assumes the picturesque guise of the dacoit. Even as her own life disintegrates, following the discovery of her secret pregnancy and abortion, the only thing that remains intact is the aura of theatricality surrounding her. To Harry, who sees her breathless and in native dress at the palace doors, she seems to have stepped out of the Raj's most famously melodramatic canvas: 'Mrs. Secombe in Flight from the Mutineers':

> Mrs Secombe was also in native dress and in a state of great agitation, with her hair awry and smears of dirt on her face: naturally since she was flying for her life from the mutineers ... to the safety of the British Residency at Lucknow. Olivia was also in flight - but, as Harry pointed out, in the opposite direction.
> (*HD*, p.172)

This, of course, is the final ironic twist in Ruth Jhabvala's 'twenties' tale. The story of Olivia's life in India may have conformed to the conventions of Anglo-Indian romance only to turn them inside out at end. For, unlike the traditional heroines 'undone' by India, Olivia does not return to the fold or flee back to England: she flies "in the opposite direction". And that movement away from the pukka sahibs is one usually associated with the name of the author who represents the antithesis of Anglo-Indian romance: that of E.M. Forster. But the Jhabvalian irony does not stop there. For there is this difference between Dewas and Khatm: what in Forster was an exercise in free will is dire necessity for Olivia.

And thus, just as Olivia's view of India can be regarded as a discrete question mark against Forster's, so can her fate itself be seen as an ironic comment on Forster's own personal experiences in India. The spectacle of Olivia and Harry enjoying the hospitality of the Nawab against the advice, and indeed the expressed wish, of their countrymen is clearly reminiscent of the circumstances surrounding Forster's stay in Dewas. But whereas Forster's epistolary recollections are the story of a great friendship transcending all barriers of race, birth and culture, Ruth Jhabvala puts those issues firmly at the centre of her novel. Olivia finds access to the palace at Khatm not because of her charm or personality but because of her marriage to a government official. Even after she has become an habituée of the palace, and sees herself as secretly in league with the Nawab against the stuffy and tiresome Anglo-Indians, she and Harry never cease to be members of the ruling race; as such they are on a par with Indian royalty and enjoy as of right the luxuries and courtesies otherwise reserved at Khatm for members of the royal house. As for the India outside the palace, they see it only through the window of the Nawab's Rolls-Royce. Olivia and Harry, in other words, may have eschewed the company of their countrymen and relish a sense of adventure and of being different, but neither has left what Paul Scott's Barbie Batchelor called 'the charmed circle of privilege'. Much the same, Ruth Jhabvala suggests, goes for the author of The Hill of Devi. He was in his own way as much an expatriate shielded from experiencing "the real India" as any memsahib safely cooped up at the club for a rubber and a chota peg. Moreover, like Olivia at Khatm, he had found access to the court of Dewas not *in spite* of his being English but *because* of it. Indeed, it is the dubious nature of that hospitality - so famously in contrast to the Anglo-Indian 'beastliness' - that is as central to Ruth Jhabvala's tale as it is peripheral to that of the author of The Hill of Devi.

    To refresh our memory on the factual - as opposed to the fictional - events that concern us here, let us enlist one more time the help of Richard Cronin and of his splendid aide-mémoire on Forster, Tukoji Rao and the politics of Empire. [62] Forster's appointment as H.H.'s private secretary, it will be remembered, did not meet with universal enthusiasm. There was, as every reader of The Hill of Devi will recall, the

---

[62] cf. Cronin, pp.151-2.

incident of the so-called Insult, which so vividly demonstrated the feelings of the Government of India. These strong views on Forster's presence on the subcontinent, Cronin reminds us, were of several years' standing. When in 1916 Forster's name had first been muted in connection with a post at Dewas a mildly compromising letter from him to Syed Masood had apparently been intercepted by the postal censor and duly passed on the Political Department. To the missive had been appended a comment describing the letter's author as "a decadent coward and apparently a sexual pervert". [63] Letter and cover note had then been handed on to the very same official who famously insulted Forster five years later. In 1916, in the middle of the War, it had not been difficult for Delhi to block unwelcome appointments. After the War, in an atmosphere of nationalist agitation and constitutional reform, this was no longer possible. Tukoji Rao's renewed invitation to Forster was, therefore, Cronin suggests, "a calculated gesture of independence"; "Forster", in other words, "was entering a complex political world - but", Cronin tartly adds, "[he] gives little impression of understanding it." [64] Still less does he appear to have realized how much his own personality, and - it must be added - sexuality, were part of these political skirmishes. Cronin in fact points us specifically to *Heat and Dust* and the Nawab's court for what he calls "an indirect clue" to the tragicomedy enacted at Dewas. [65]

> Douglas [Olivia's husband] and colleagues . . . are perfect exemplars of slow-witted public school rectitude. They embody all that is a threat to the Nawab's unrestrained enjoyment of his power. For this the Nawab hates them. He seeks to establish himself as the ideal antithesis of all the British in India stand for, responding with cunning to their affection of frankness, with style to their stolidity, with triumphant malice to their protestations of even-handed justice. He prizes Harry as a parody of all those English virtues from which he suffers. . . . He retains as his court buffoon a homosexual Englishman of weak character. . . [as] a deliberate racial affront. [66]

---

[63] quoted by Cronin, p.151.
[64] Ibid.
[65] Ibid., p.155.
[66] Ibid., p.156-7.

That Ruth Jhabvala's oblique description of the court of Dewas was substantially correct, Cronin proves by referring us to a less-known incident in Fortster's Indian days: one that, significantly, did not find its way into *The Hill of Devi*.

Tukoji Rao was not unaware of Forster's sexuality; that much we may infer from the accounts of mild ribaldry at his expense which Forster so fondly relates. What was never published in Forster's lifetime was an altogether more disturbing memory: a memory of a sordid little charade played out at the beginning of his stay there. It seems a sexual encounter involving Forster was engineered and quickly followed by royal fulminations against the presence of deviants at court whose identity would not go undetected. [67] What appears to have ensued was a humiliating admission by an understandably frightened Forster and a grand theatrical gesture by Tukoji Rao combining a friend's understanding with the forgiveness of a prince. Thus, Cronin suggests, was cemented the famous friendship celebrated in *The Hill of Devi*. [68]

Certainly, the point would not have been lost on a body of men as obsessed with their proconsular, masculine, dignity as was that of the Political Department. For an illustration of the extent of the Raj's racial and sexual paranoia in its dealings with the Princes see Kenneth Ballhatchet, *Race, Sex and Class under the Raj: Imperial Attitudes and Policies and Their Critics, 1793-1905*. London 1980.

Two particularly choice examples related by Ballhatchet may suffice: "There was anxious consultation among officials in 1893, when it was learnt that the Maharajah of Patiala intended to marry a Miss Florry Bryan. The idea threatened the racial and social hierarchy in various ways. First, there was the disturbing thought of an Indian man marrying a white woman. She was of the ruling race and he was not. Yet he belonged to a ruling class and she was of a lower class. It was deeply worrying." (ibid., p.116) The marriage, Ballhatchet notes, could not be prevented; but the Government of India had learnt its lesson. To avoid any danger of repetition, Lord Curzon issued a viceregal ban on all princely travel to Britain or the Continent of Europe. There remained, alas, the unavoidable dilemma of the Indian regiments going to London for the celebration of Queen Victoria's Diamond Jubilee: " . . . handsome men might be a problem. The Viceroy and the Secretary of State conferred anxiously about the tastes of Englishwomen". (ibid., p.119)

[67] To appreciate the full nastiness of this it is worth recalling that homosexual acts were punishable under British law, and that prosecutions could and did result in draconian sentences. Dewas, as a Princely State, was admittedly outside immediate British jurisdiction and the prospect of legal proceedings against a British subject by local courts was probably remote, but nonetheless Forster's position would have been highly uncomfortable.

[68] Cronin's speculations about Forster's part in all this, that is to say about his reaction to all this, are themselves of interest to the reader of *Heat and Dust*. Perhaps, Cronin surmises, Forster saw it as a "test", a "crucial act of faith"; perhaps " . . . Forster believed Tukoji Rao because the alternative was too horrible for him to

Inevitably, one wonders what first drew Jhabvala's attention to all this. The answer is: we do not know. But this much is certain: in re-creating it in *Heat and Dust*, Ruth Jhabvala was not moved by the biographer's impulse, nor was she driven to 'set the record straight' on India. To understand her interest in Dewas and its ruler we need remind ourselves only of the structure of her novel: of the parallels, in other words, between then and now. Forster's 'ingénu' approach in the 1920s was one that struck a chord: she had seen it replicated a thousand times in her own day by young Westerners eager to *experience* India. She herself had described and ironized it repeatedly. And having observed the consequences of such naiveté all around her, she was well-equipped to detect the disturbing subplot to Forster's sun-lit Indian recollections.

But there is one further element in the equation. That of gender. Jhabvala is a woman novelist and her protagonists tend to be female. Women critics seem more aware of this fact than their male colleagues. Laurie Sucher, for instance, suggests that *Heat and Dust* "provides an alternative, woman-centred perspective" to Forster's India. [69] Sucher clearly means to praise. But does she not accidentally achieve the opposite? Surely Ruth Jhabvala, the defender of rationality and plain old-fashioned common sense, is not so much driven to provide "an alternative" perspective as the *true* perspective. Being a woman might well be part of that. In some ways, it may give her perhaps greater perspicacity.

Let us approach that question of perspicacity by way of another Sucher quotation: "Jhabvala's fiction", Sucher observes elsewhere, "seems to be about India: it is really about the desires of women". [70] There is more than just a degree of truth in that. But one might add, echoing

---

contemplate. Vicious behaviour in Forster's fiction results almost always from lack of imagination and lack of sympathy. In order to understand the Maharajah's behaviour in the way that I have suggested it ought to be understood, he would have been forced to contemplate something quite different, something that finds no place in his novels, and that he was perhaps temperamentally incapable of conceiving, an idea of evil". (Cronin, p.115)

[69] Sucher, "Quest and Disillusion", op.cit., p.118.
And, warming to her subject, Sucher is moved to declare elsewhere: "*Heat and Dust* attempts to capture a subject for which no forerunner exists, simply because it is so new: the unattached, non-aristocratic woman in the Third World. In this it is a sort of Heart of Darkness 'au féminin'". (*The Fiction of Ruth Prawer Jhabvala,* op.cit., p.120)
[70] "Quest and Disillusion", p.27.

Sucher, 'Forster's Indian fiction seems to be about India, but is really about the desires of its author.' And that, surely, is the point in *Heat and Dust*. Neither Olivia, who stands paradigmatically for many Jhabvalian characters, nor E.M. Forster ever allow reality to get in the way of their pursuit of happiness. Both suffer an uncomfortable collision with that long-ignored reality. But there the similarity ends. Olivia, being a woman, has to pay the price for her naiveté while Forster is able to put a disagreeable moment behind him and to return to England, cherishing precious Indian memories. And that, too, is Ruth Jhabvala's point. The self-deception, in other words, at the heart of "only connect" is one which perhaps only a male writer could sustain. The author of *Heat and Dust* may be chided by some critics for showing insufficient political awareness, but she more than makes up for it by her recognition of the politics - and of the power politics - inherent in the relationships between men and women. The events at Khatm provide a memorable illustration of these uncomfortable truths.

The Nawab's interest in Harry, as we have seen, is in itself far from innocent. His interest in Olivia, however, is even more ambiguous. Attraction, and even affection, certainly play their part, but from the start there is an unmistakable political angle to this relationship; for it involves, visibly, a third party: that of the 'wronged' husband. The inverted commas seem appropriate. Ruth Jhabvala, after all, is not remotely interested in Douglas Rivers. He is a cipher, an authorial means to an end: his only function to infuriate Olivia sufficiently with his good-natured obtuseness to drive her into the ready arms of the Nawab, and thus to provide a conduit for the Nawab's otherwise impotent rage. What Ruth Jhabvala is doing, then, is to use the hackneyed plot device of the 'love triangle', and with it all the other conventions of the 'tragic love story', to provide an, as it were, anti-romantic vision of human relationships. She is no feminist, but one does not have to be a feminist to see that, in Laurie Sucher's words, "the transaction is not so much between him and her as between him and her ... husband ... ".[71]

It is in fact possible to look on Olivia's fate as a paradigm of more things than one. Laurie Sucher, writing from a feminist standpoint, hears in *Heat and Dust* the reverberations of the "twin themes of sexuality and

---

[71] Ibid., p.100.

colonialism", and sees in Olivia's marriage the "connection between . . . racist paternalism and . . . sexist paternalism" made manifest. [72] This is perfectly valid. It is, however, also somewhat peripheral to Ruth Jhabvala's purpose. For she is clearly no more driven to castigate male exploitation of women than she is concerned about the iniquities of colonialism. What motivates her, as ever, is not anger but a slightly melancholy sense of comedy. Looking around her, she perceives a familiar pattern in Western behaviour in the East, and, interlocking with it, a recurring pattern in the affairs of men and women.

This is not a popular message. In fact, to say it opens one up to a host of accusations: that of being an imperial apologist, a cultural imperialist, an inveterate hater of all things Indian, or even of being somehow personally defective. For one anonymous critic, Ruth Jhabvala is just another neurotic Western woman in India. [73] This psychological insight would appear to be based mainly on the evidence of one of her short stories, "An Experience of India", a story about the hapless, and largely mindless, subcontinental progress of a young Western woman. It contains a recurring scene which, the nameless critic suggests, gives the game away: " . . . a moment of frenzied coupling culminating always in insult, rejection, and disgust"; this, we are told, Jhabvala " . . . has come more and more to represent as if it were *the* experience of India". [74]

Thus the wheel has come full circle: Ruth Jhabvala, a latter-day Adela Quested, fantasizing about Indian men and crying 'rape!' every time she settles down at her writer's desk. It is a thoroughly unedifying spectacle, but not without its ironies: observe the politically correct critic unwittingly resurrecting that old Anglo-Indian bogey, the memsahib; (but for whose presence we men would be getting on so splendidly). The fact that these are women's and a woman writer's experiences of India, and that they inevitably reflect such things as women's social position on the subcontinent, and male perceptions and attitudes towards them, surely deserves a little more thought than that.

In fact this is where - unnoticed by most critics - Ruth Jhabvala does, after all, reveal an awareness of the 'social and economic forces',

---

[72] *The Fiction of Ruth Prawer Jhabvala*, p.111.
[73] cf. Anon, "Sex and the Indian Novel". *Cencrastus: Scottish and International Literature, Arts and Affairs.* 25 Spring 1987, pp.34-40.
[74] Ibid., p.39.

and the extent to which they will impinge on individual relationships. At its most benign we see this in the case of Inder Lal and the narrator. Theirs is in many ways a happy relationship, yet even so, it is informed by the recognition by both partners that, though a woman, the narrator enjoys as a Westerner in India a degree of financial and social independence far in excess of her Indian lover's. The nameless central character of "An Experience of India", whose experiences so enraged the anonymous critic of *Cencrastus*, enjoys a similarly high degree of autonomy; this cannot be without consequences in her relations with her various Indian 'pick-ups': her life style is not only in contrast to the subservience of their wives and daughters but is a direct challenge to their own sense of self-worth. Laurie Sucher is surely right to point out that such autonomy had traditionally been the prerogative of the male. [75] Their pathetic, crowing, triumph during sexual congress is therefore - pace *Cencrastus* - all too credible.

The nameless author of the article in *Cencrastus* does, however, raise one valid point: he (and it is surely a he?) notes the extent to which the 'East-West' encounter is represented in sexual terms, and the fact that in these various encounters the European partner is almost invariably cast as a woman. He offers this explanation for it:

> As an imperial possession India is a challenge to the British ablility to organise. As an independent country it is a challenge to the Westerner's ability to experience. . . . Within the Indian novel sexual stereotypes are alive and well. Men organise, women experience, homosexuals are betwixt and between. [76]

Perhaps there is a degree of truth in what he says about stereotyping. (Although one might point out that in *Heat and Dust*, at any rate, the most efficient organizer, Maji, is very definitely female, and that Chid - in some ways the most helpless creature - is unquestionably male, and without a trace of the homosexual about him.) Where the anonymous critic is on surer ground is in his emphasis on (passive) experience as opposed to leading an active life. And he is right, too, to see a link with

---

[75] *The Fiction of Ruth Prawer Jhabvala*, p.133.
[76] "Sex and the Indian Novel", op.cit., p.39.

Independence. But he is mistaking cause and effect: Independence does not rob the Europeans of their sense of purpose but is merely the outer sign of their loss of purpose and self-confidence. Douglas and his colleagues are leading active, and apparently fulfilled, lives not just because they know what it is they want to do in India, and why they are doing it, but because this knowledge stems from a clear sense of their own identity. Question that and you pull down the whole edifice. That, surely, is what Major Minnies's famous warning about "going too far" in one's love of India ultimately boils down to. (*HD*, p.150)

In the modern section the missionary lady alone radiates these old certainties. But hers are religious certainties; the secular equivalents have vanished utterly. Again, one needs only to look at Satipur in the 1920s to see what has been lost. Olivia Rivers may not have shared her husband's views on India and the Indians; on the contrary, her liberal humanist ideals were in opposition to Douglas's paternalist convictions. But her beliefs - like his - were recognizably *European* beliefs. Even after she has left her husband for the Nawab she remains defined by these beliefs. We are told little about her later life, except that " . . . she did not live so very differently from the way she had done in Satipur, and might have done in London. (*HD*, pp.179-80)

But Olivia's and Douglas's is the last generation to be thus defined. Their grandchildren, in India and elsewhere, are largely bereft of philosophical or metaphysical moorings. The narrator of *Heat and Dust* is as good an example of this as any. She is, as has been widely noted, a curiously flat and passive character. Brijraj Singh remarks on this and, noting how easily she seems to adapt to the alien Indian surroundings, wonders whether the two things might not be connected: if that process is such a smooth and effortless affair, " . . . is it not because there is nothing in her that she has first to subdue or lay aside? Is not her passive acceptance nothing but a general characterlessness?" [77] Strangely enough, this is more perceptive than Singh himself appears to realize; for the indignant rhetorical question with which he follows this up, "Does Jhabvala wish to suggest that only such a person is fit for salvation through India?" clearly misses the point. [78] Or, rather it hits

---

[77] Singh, op.cit., p.215.
[78] Ibid., p.217.

home in a way Singh does not intend: for it reflects not on the author but on the people she portrays: on the rootless Europeans who might feel in need of "salvation through India". Singh speaks of failure, and locates it in Ruth Jhabvala's apparent inability to imagine what he calls a "favourable character".[79] But the failure lies with the modern Europeans and their inability to develop and sustain a clear sense of identity. India brings that failure into sharp relief. Inevitably, one is reminded of Paul Scott's view of India as metaphor for European endeavour and of the Western sense of self-worth. And one is reminded especially of his Count Brononowsky, who, though landless, found a home in his work in India; and finally of the Count's despairing remark as Mirat goes up in flames - and with it his life's work: "we're all émigrés now".

There, surely, we have the essence of Ruth Jhabvala's work. Her own sense of exile for one thing; but also the lack of orientation, the air of aimlessness and powerlessness that surrounds so many of her characters. Take Scott's vision of an exiled Russian count, overtaken by events and despairing of his inability to *do* anything, and finding solace only in the unchanging beauty of Pushkin's verse; superimpose on that the image of Olivia in her lonely mountain exile, dividing her time between the piano (and the great Romantic composers) and her embroidery. And, lastly, there is the image of Ruth Jhabvala herself which she has so often drawn in interviews and essays: that of the Western writer in her room in Delhi, the blinds drawn against the sights outside of suffering beyond hope, finding comfort and strength in the great masters of the European novel.

Is it too fanciful, then, to see in the narrator of *Heat and Dust* an echo of an earlier, youthful incarnation of Ruth Jhabvala herself? of a young woman emptied of Europe by the War, eager to embrace India as her new home? But the twenty-five years between Ruth Jhabvala's own arrival in India and that of the young woman in her novel have taken their toll. The enthusiasm for India of her earlier books has been gradually worn down by the grim reality around her and by a haunting suspicion, hardening to certainty, that she does not belong in India, and never can do - because, unlike the Western visitor, the Indians possess a clear sense of identity, and one which is forever closed to the outsider.

---

[79] Ibid.

> Once somebody said to me: "Just see how sweet is the Indian soul that can see God in a cow!" But when I try to assume this sweetness, it turns sour: for, however much I may try to fool myself, whatever veils I may try, for the sake of peace of mind, to draw over my eyes, it is soon enough clear to me that the cow *is* a cow, and a very scrawny, underfed, diseased one at that. And then I feel that I want to keep this knowledge, however painful it is, and not exchange it for some other that may be true for an Indian but can never quite become that for me. [80]

"I have been thinking lately about inheritance in general, and what it means . . . ", says a character in *Three Continents*, one of Ruth Jhabvala's more recent novels. [81] Much the same clearly goes for the author herself. In fact, in this long search for her own identity *Heat and Dust* marks a critical stage. In it Ruth Jhabvala tries for a final time to rehearse - to herself perhaps as much as to her readers - the attract of becoming fully Indian. But in this task her imagination quite liter fails her, and the book ends with only the vaguest promise of future subcontinental happiness for the narrator. Yet Olivia's final years, shrouded as they are in Himalayan mist, offer no obvious alternative either. This emptiness at the core of *Heat and Dust* has - rightly perhaps - been regarded as a major weakness of the novel. But in this it probably mirrors faithfully the uncertainty in Ruth Jhabvala's own life at the time.

It is indeed tempting to see in *Heat and Dust* Ruth Jhabvala's own final reaction to India: her attempt to define herself not merely in, but against, the land in which she had been living but which had never completely become home; to see in this last of her Indian books made manifest her determination to cling to what is left of her, and our collective, European identity. Nostalgia, she knows, will not help in the task: the enviable certainty of Douglas Rivers and his peers is as irrecoverably lost as the Raj they served. The high idealism of Olivia (and, one might add, of E.M. Forster) she feels she must also reject, for it is a false idealism based on self-deception, and its modern equivalent, the mindless apeing of various Eastern religions, is an even greater negation

---

[80] "Myself in India", p.21. (Jhabvala's italics)
[81] Ruth Prawer Jhabvala, *Three Continents*. London 1987, p.83.

of reality. What is left is the European mind alone: and *Heat and Dust* is its perfect product. Thus in a land of amorphous vastness Ruth Jhabvala can create something small, well-proportioned, and perfectly shaped; she chooses as a writer not to bare her own or her characters' souls while all around her life and suffering and death itself occur in public; to reply to her own exasperation in measured prose, to surging emotion with irony and cooly rational analysis. No wonder *Heat and Dust* radiates little warmth: it is, after all, a private act of defiance. Here is Ruth Jhabvala herself again, writing - explicitly - about her own experience of India:

> To live in India and be at peace one must to a very considerable extent become Indian and adopt an Indian personality. But how is this possible? And even if it were possible - without cheating oneself - would it be desirable? Should one want to try to become something other than what one is? . . . Sometimes it seems to me how pleasant it would be to say yes and give in . . . and be meek and accepting and see God in a cow. Other times it seems worthwhile to be defiant and European and - all right, be crushed by one's environment, but all the same have made some attempt to remain standing. Of course, this can't go on indefinitely and in the end I'm bound to lose . . . . [82]

Ruth Jhabvala, we know, lost this protracted battle shortly after she completed *Heat and Dust*: she decided, finally, to leave India. And this is perhaps the most affecting thing about this cold, cerebral novel: it masks a real-life drama; it is Ruth Jhabvala's own doomed, brave, attempt to remain standing.

---

[82] "Myself in India", p.21.

CONCLUSION

Paul Scott, J.G. Farrell and Ruth Prawer Jhabvala were first linked in the public perception by the award, to each of them, of the Booker Prize in the 1970s. Beyond that accident of history they may seem to have little in common. Scott had created in *The Raj Quartet* a densely textured work on a monumental scale; J.G. Farrell's *Siege of Krishnapur* seems almost slight by comparison, even though it, too, is anchored in a literary project of ambitious dimensions; Ruth Jhabvala's *Heat and Dust*, lastly, - self-contained, light and slim - sits almost uncomfortably next to them. The impression of wide heterogeneity increases still further if one looks a little closer. Even the notion that these three authors share an interest in the Raj proves to have been somewhat misleading. For they approach it from sharply differing angles: Scott revisits in the Raj the land of his war-time years; J.G. Farrell delves into the history books and creates a world in the image of the Albert Memorial; Ruth Jhabvala examines literary evidence from the time of the Raj - rather than of the Raj itself. Nor are the periods they write about identical: Scott is concerned principally with the final years of the Indian Empire; Farrell goes back almost a century earlier, to Company days and the time of the Mutiny; and Ruth Jhabvala divides her time between present-day India and the year 1923. Yet, for all that, a close look at the six books here examined does reveal parallels.

What underlies all of them is a sense of unease. In each of the three writers this shared unease has an individual slant to it and thus, as it were, a personal flavour. But all three are moved by a feeling of dismay about the state of the contemporary world. This may sound like an exercise in nostalgia; and indeed this is a charge routinely and collectively levelled at what is termed 'Raj-revivalism'. That accusation, as has been shown, is both unfair and misleading. Farrell's vision of the Raj drips with sarcasm, as he sets about burying the notion that the past was somehow better, nobler or more honourable than the present. Ruth Jhabvala's approach, though free of Farrell's political intent, is also heavily ironizing; and even Scott, who can at times be susceptible to mild nostalgia, shows himself in Brigadier Reid's 'Memoirs' capable of biting satire at the expense of the Raj and its upholders.

Scott's interest in the Raj is deeper and more complex than that of either Farrell or Ruth Jhabvala, and it contains, perhaps because of personal memories, a considerable emotional investment. The Raj for him is a private as well as a public land, in which and with which he has lived for much of his life. As a result, his evocation of it comes remarkably alive for the reader. This is in marked contrast to either Farrell or Ruth Jhabvala, whose picture of the past remains essentially one-dimensional. Yet Scott, too, sees in the Raj ultimately a means to a literary end. It provides him with a ready metaphor for the development of Western thought. He traces in the tumultous final years of the Indian Empire the old conflict between two, rival, Western ideologies: the conservative paternalism that seeks to preserve empire and the liberal humanism that strives to abolish it. The latter triumphs over the former but is itself quickly buried in the rubble of history. This leaves the Western world drifting without sense of direction or even of clearly defined identity. The Raj, then, - to paraphrase Scott's resonant phrase - is the time and the place where the West came to 'the end of the way it was'.

J.G. Farrell shares with Scott an awareness of history that goes beyond the literary norm. And like Scott, he sees in the fate of the Raj a reflection of the fate of the West in general. The *Siege of Krishnapur* is only one in a series of books in which he charts the Western decline and the gradual loss of purpose and confidence that accompanied it. The Indian Mutiny represents for Farrell a mile stone in this process, and it does so in several ways: it marks the end of the modernizing, expanding, phase of empire, which gives way to the era of retrenchment and defensiveness; this coincides with a range of scientific and technical break-throughs which will ultimately shatter the old order. The sepoy mutiny can be suppressed, but the 'March of Progress', ironized by Farrell, is shown to be out of step with the morality which it claims to embody: Darwinism inevitably goes on to destroy the traditional ordered universe, and the religious and moral convictions on which it was founded. By the end of Farrell's novel, as the layers of civilization have been peeled away by the siege, we see - in anticipation of wider twentieth century experience - life reduced to a crude struggle for survival.

Ruth Jhabvala lacks entirely the interest in history that informs the works of Scott and Farrell. But she shares their conviction that the passing of the Raj marked the end also of a clearly defined European identity. This question of identity assumes for her an immediate personal urgency because of her own early deracination. Both Scott and Farrell, for all their differing approaches and attudes towards the past, are somehow still personally anchored in the experience of Empire of their youth and childhood. In Scott these are straightforward personal memories; in Farrell the influence of boyhood tales of imperial adventure, to which he pays ironic tribute in his fiction. Ruth Jhabvala must seek to reclaim the past in another way. She does so through the various literary testimonials of the India of the 1920s. But, as it were, with the benefit of hindsight, she can provide an ironic gloss to them.

Finally, what unites these six novels on the Raj is that they are all somehow the reaction of a disenchantment of their writers with other novels or novelists. In Scott's and Farrell's cases this is an explicit determination to turn away from the narrow concerns of the post-war British novel, and to attempt, on a larger scale, a larger theme. In Ruth Jhabvala the unease is, again, more personal. Just as her own private life had reached by the mid-seventies a critical juncture, so her writing had reached something of an 'impasse'. *Heat and Dust* is, therefore, an attempt to break the mould. And breaking the mould is something all three writers have also achieved collectively: together they have rescued from obscurity the small world of the Anglo-Indian novel, have widened its concerns and perceptions, and have secured for it a place in the mainstream of English letters.

BIBLIOGRAPHY

PAUL SCOTT

Scott, Paul Mark: *The Jewel in the Crown.* London 1966.

The Day of the Scorpion. London 1968.

The Towers of Silence. London 1971.

A Division of the Spoils. London 1975.

Republished in one volume as: *The Raj Quartet.* London 1976.

Johnnie Sahib. London 1952.

The Alien Sky. London 1953.

A Male Child. London 1956.

The Mark of the Warrior. London 1958.

The Chinese Love Pavilion. London 1960.

The Birds of Paradise. London 1962.

The Bender. London 1963.

The Corrida at San Feliu. London 1964.

Staying On. London 1976.

"An Idealist in Action: Review of 'Indira Gandhi'" by Zareer Masani. *Country Life* 19 June 1975, p.1643.

"How Well Have They Worn?: 'A Passage to India'". *The Times* 6 January 1966.

India: A Post-Forsterian View". *Essays by Divers Hands: Being the Transactions of the Royal Society of Literature.* New Series 36 1970, pp.113-132.

Republished in: *My Appointment with the Muse: Essays 1961-1975.* (edited and introduced by Shelly C. Reece) London 1986.

"The Raj". In: Frank Moraes and Edward Howe (eds.): *John Kenneth Galbraith Introduces India.* London 1974, pp.70-88.

Ableman, Paul: "Paul Scott: A Comic Vision". *Books and Bookmen* 24 (2) November 1978, pp.48-9.

Ali, Tariq: Untitled article. *Time Out* 5-11 April 1984, p.13.

"Fiction as History, History as Fiction". *Illustrated Weekly of India* 8 July 1984.

Anon.: "Decline and Fall". *The Times Literary Supplement* 8 October 1971, p.1197.

"Mighty Opposites". *The Times Literary Supplement* 12 September 1968, p.975.

The Making of 'The Jewel in the Crown'. London 1983.

"The Rape of India". *The Times Literary Supplement* 21 July 1966, p.629.

Appasamy, S.P.: "The Withdrawal: A Survey of Paul Scott's Trilogy of Novels on India". In: K.P.K. Menon, M. Manuel & K. Ayyappa Paniker (eds.): *Literary Studies: Homage to Dr. A. Sivaramasubramonia Ayer.* Trivandrum 1973, pp.58-69.

Baker, John F.: "Interview with Paul Scott". *Publisher's Weekly* 208 (11) 1975, p.7.

Bannerjee, Jacqueline: "A Living Legacy: An Indian View of Paul Scott's India". *London Magazine* New Series 20 (1,2) April/May 1980, pp.97-104.

Barnes, Julian: "Farewell to the Jewel". *The Observer* 18 April 1984.

Beloff, Max: "The End of the Raj: Paul Scott's Novels as History". *Encounter* 46 (5) 1976, pp.65-70.

BIBLIOGRAPHY

PAUL SCOTT

Scott, Paul Mark: *The Jewel in the Crown.* London 1966.

The Day of the Scorpion. London 1968.

The Towers of Silence. London 1971.

A Division of the Spoils. London 1975.

Republished in one volume as: *The Raj Quartet.* London 1976.

Johnnie Sahib. London 1952.

The Alien Sky. London 1953.

A Male Child. London 1956.

The Mark of the Warrior. London 1958.

The Chinese Love Pavilion. London 1960.

The Birds of Paradise. London 1962.

The Bender. London 1963.

The Corrida at San Feliu. London 1964.

Staying On. London 1976.

"An Idealist in Action: Review of 'Indira Gandhi'" by Zareer Masani. *Country Life* 19 June 1975, p.1643.

"How Well Have They Worn?: 'A Passage to India'". *The Times* 6 January 1966.

India: A Post-Forsterian View". *Essays by Divers Hands: Being the Transactions of the Royal Society of Literature.* New Series 36 1970, pp.113-132.

Republished in: *My Appointment with the Muse: Essays 1961-1975.* (edited and introduced by Shelly C. Reece) London 1986.

"The Raj". In: Frank Moraes and Edward Howe (eds.): *John Kenneth Galbraith Introduces India.* London 1974, pp.70-88.

Ableman, Paul: "Paul Scott: A Comic Vision". *Books and Bookmen* 24 (2) November 1978, pp.48-9.

Ali, Tariq: Untitled article. *Time Out* 5-11 April 1984, p.13.

"Fiction as History, History as Fiction". *Illustrated Weekly of India* 8 July 1984.

Anon.: "Decline and Fall". *The Times Literary Supplement* 8 October 1971, p.1197.

"Mighty Opposites". *The Times Literary Supplement* 12 September 1968, p.975.

The Making of 'The Jewel in the Crown'. London 1983.

"The Rape of India". *The Times Literary Supplement* 21 July 1966, p.629.

Appasamy, S.P.: "The Withdrawal: A Survey of Paul Scott's Trilogy of Novels on India". In: K.P.K. Menon, M. Manuel & K. Ayyappa Paniker (eds.): *Literary Studies: Homage to Dr. A. Sivaramasubramonia Ayer.* Trivandrum 1973, pp.58-69.

Baker, John F.: "Interview with Paul Scott". *Publisher's Weekly* 208 (11) 1975, p.7.

Bannerjee, Jacqueline: "A Living Legacy: An Indian View of Paul Scott's India". *London Magazine* New Series 20 (1,2) April/May 1980, pp.97-104.

Barnes, Julian: "Farewell to the Jewel". *The Observer* 18 April 1984.

Beloff, Max: "The End of the Raj: Paul Scott's Novels as History". *Encounter* 46 (5) 1976, pp.65-70.

Beretz, Evelyn: "Subplot bei Paul Scott". 'Staatsarbeit' Cologne 1978.

Bonheim, Jill: *Paul Scott: Humanismus und Individualismus in seinem Werk.* (Neue Studien zur Anglistik und Amerikanistik 23) Frankfurt/Main 1982.

Boyer, Allen: "Love, Sex, and History in 'The Raj Quartet'". *Modern Language Quarterly* 46 (1) 1985, pp.64-80.

Burgess, Anthony: "Hard Work and Gin in the Evening of Empire". *The Independent* 12 October 1990.

Burjorjee, Dinshaw M.: "K. Bhaskara Rao's 'Paul Scott': A Tribute to Forster's Successor". *Chandrabhaga: A Magazine of World Writing* 4 1980, pp.73-76.

Copley, Antony: "The Politics of Illusion: Paul Scott's 'The Raj Quartet'". *Indo-British Review: A Journal of History* 11 (1) December 1984, pp.58-73.

Cruise O' Brien, Connor: "Why the Wailing Ought to Stop". *The Observer* 3 June 1984.

Dawson, P.N.S.: "Race, Sex and Class in Paul Scott's 'Raj Quartet'". In: Bart Moore-Gilbert (ed.): *Literature and Imperialism.* Proceedings of the Conference at the Roehampton Institute of Higher Education in February 1983. London 1983, pp.170-180.

Degi, Bruce J.: "Paul Scott's Indian National Army: 'The Mark of the Warrior' and 'The Raj Quartet'". *Clio: A Journal of Literature, History and the Philosophy of History* 18 (1) Fall 1988, pp.41-54.

Desai, Anita: "The Rage for the Raj". *New Republic* 25 November 1986, pp.26-29.

Dick, Kay: "Shades of Kipling". *The Spectator* 22 July 1966, p.127-128.

Farrell, J.G.: "Indian Identities". *The Times Literary Supplement* 23 May 1975, p.555.

Gooneratne, Yasmine: "Paul Scott's 'Staying On': Finale in a Minor Key". *Journal of Indian Writing in English* 9 (2) 1981, pp.1-12.

Goonetilleke, D.C.R.A.: *Images of the Raj: South Asia in the Literature of Empire.* London 1988.

Green, Benny: "Lost Jewel: 'The Raj Quartet'". *The Spectator* 23 July 1977. p.28.

Green, Martin: *The English Novel in the Twentieth Century: The Doom of Empire.* London 1984.

Gurko, Leo: *Joseph Conrad: Giant in Exile.* (Second edition with a new introduction) New York 1979.

Hanquart, Evelyne: "'Hari Kumar ou Harry Coomar?' Education et empire dans 'The Raj Quartet'". *Migrations.* Centre d'Histoire des Idées dans les Iles Britanniques, Université de Paris IV - Sorbonne 6. 1986, pp.140-152.

Hitchins, Christopher: "A Sense of Mission: 'The Raj Quartet'". *Grand Street* 4 (2) Winter 1985, pp.180-199.

Hoffmann, Barabara: *Paul Scott's "Raj Quartet": Fiktion und Geschichtsschreibung.* (Europäische Hochschulschriften, Reihe 14: Angelsächsische Sprache und Literatur 101) Frankfurt/Main 1982.

Kleinstück, Johannes: "Paul Scott und sein 'Raj Quartet'". *Anglia* 105 (1,2), pp.94-114.

Kohli, Indira: *Paul Scott: His Art and Ideas.* Ghaziabad 1987.

James, Richard Rhodes: "In the Steps of Paul Scott". *The Listener* 101, pp.359-361.

Johnson, Richard M.: "'Sayed's Trial' in Paul Scott's 'A Division of the Spoils': The Interplay of History, Theme, and Purpose". *Library Chronicle of the University of Texas* 37 1986, pp.77-91.

Lewis, Margret B.: "Paul Scott". In: *British Novelists Since 1960.* (Dictionary of Literary Biography 14: 2) Detroit 1983, pp.638-645.

Mahood, M.M.: "Paul Scott's Guardians". *The Yearbook of English Studies: Colonial and Imperial Themes* Special Number 13 1983, pp.244-258. Reprinted in: *Indo-British Review: A Journal of History* 11 (1) December 1984, pp.74-86.

McBratney, John Stuart: "East-West Meetings under the Raj: Rudyard Kipling, E.M. Forster and Paul Scott". Unpublished thesis. University of California at Berkeley 1987.

"The Raj Is All the Rage: Paul Scott's 'The Raj Quartet' and Colonial Nostalgia". *North Dakota Quarterly* 55 (3) Spring 1987, pp.204-209.

Mellers, John: "Raj Mahal: Paul Scott's India Quartet". *The London Magazine* 5 (2) 1975, pp.62-67.

Mehta, Gita: "Class and Crown". *The Spectator* 11 February 1984, pp.16-17.

Moore, Robin: *Paul Scott's Raj*. London 1990.

Moorhead, Caroline: "Getting Engrossed in the Death-Throes of the Raj". *The Times* 20 October 1975.

Narayanan, Gomathi: "Paul Scott's Indian Quartet: the Story of a Rape". *Literary Criterion* 13 (4), pp.44-53.

Parry, Benita: "Paul Scott's Raj". *South Asian Review* 8 1975, pp.359-369.

Petersone, Karina: "The Concept of History in Paul Scott's Tetralogy 'The Raj Quartet'". *Zeitschrift für Anglistik und Amerikanistik* 37 (3), pp.228-233.

Pollard, Arthur: "Twilight of Empire: Paul Scott's 'Raj Quartet'. In: Daniel Massa (ed.): *Individual and Community in Commonwealth Literature*. Malta 1979, pp.169-177.

Rao, Bhaskara K.: *Paul Scott*. (Twayne English Authors Series) Boston 1980.

Ringold, Francine: "A Conversation with Paul Scott". *Nimrod* 21 (1) Fall / Winter 1976, pp.16-32.

Rushdie, Salman: "The Empire Writes Back with a Vengeance". *The Observer* 1 April 1984, p.19.

"Outside the Whale". *Granta* 11, pp.123-141.
Reprinted in: *Imaginary Homelands: Essays and Criticism 1981-1991*. London 1991, pp.87-101.

Scanlan, Margret: "The Disappearance of History: Paul Scott's 'Raj Quartet'". *Clio: A Journal of Literature, History, and the Philosophy of History* 15 (2) 1986, pp.153-169.

Shahane, Vasant A.: "Kipling, Forster and Paul Scott: A Study in Sociological Imagination". In: S.N.A. Rizvi (ed.): *The Twofold Voices: Essays in Honour of Ramesh Mohan.* Salzburg 1982, pp.195-208.

Sharrad, Paul: "The Books Behind the Film: Paul Scott's 'Raj Quartet'". *East-West Film Journal* 1 1987, pp.78-90.

Spurling, Hilary: *Paul Scott: A Life.* London 1990.

"In the Footsteps of Paul Scott". *The Sunday Times* 21 October 1990.

Srinavasta, Aruna: "The Pageant of Empire: Paul Scott's 'Raj Quartet' and Related Versions of Imperialism in the Anglo-Indian Novel". Unpublished thesis. McMasters University (Canada) 1989.

Swinden, Patrick: *Paul Scott: Images of India.* London 1980.

Paul Scott. (Writers and their Work) Windsor 1982.

Tedesco, Janis: "'Staying On': The Final Connection". *Western Humanities Review* 39 (3) 1985, pp.195-211.

Tedesco, Janis and Jane Popham: *Introduction to 'The Raj Quartet'.* Lanham MD 1985.

Weinbaum, Francine S.: "Aspiration and Betrayal in Paul Scott's 'Raj Quartet'". Unpublished thesis. University of Illinois at Urbana-Champaign 1976.

Paul Scott: A Critical Study. Austin, Texas 1992.

"Paul Scott's India: 'The Raj Quartet'". *Critique: Studies in Modern Fiction* 20 (1), pp.100-110.

"Psychological Defences and Thwarted Union in 'The Raj Quartet'". *Literature and Psychology* 31 (2) 1981, pp.75-87.

West, Richard: "Rushdie and the Raj". *The Spectator* 7 April 1984, pp.18-19.

Wijesingha Rajiva: "Women in Colonial Fiction: in the Novels of Conrad, Kipling, Forster and Paul Scott". *Navasilu* 5, pp.88-94.

Wood, Michael: "'The Day of the Scorpion'". *The Times* 7 September 1968.

Woodcock, George: "The Sometime Sahibs: Two Post-Independence British Novelists of India". *Queen's Quarterly* 86 (1979), pp.39-49.

Zorn, Jean: "Talk with Paul Scott". *The New York Times Book Review* 21 August 1977, p.37.

J. G. FARRELL

Farrell, James Gordon: *The Siege of Krishnapur*. Harmondsworth 1973.

Troubles. London 1969.

The Singapore Grip. London 1978.

The Hill Station. London 1982.

"An Indian Diary". Published in: *The Hill Station.* London 1982, pp.208-255.

"No Matter". *The Spectator* 29 August 1970, p.217.

Anon.: "Down to the Bone: 'The Siege of Krishnapur'". *The Times Literary Supplement* 21 September 1973, p.1074.

Balutowa, Bronislawa: "J.G. Farrell's 'The Siege of Krishnapur': A Pattern of Reversal". In: Irena Janicka-Swiderska (ed.): *Studies in English and American Literature: in Honour of Witold Ostrowski.* Warsaw s.a., pp.15-20.

Bergonzi, Bernard: *The Situation of the Novel.* (2nd edition) London 1979.

Binns, Ronald: *J.G. Farrell.* (Contemporary Writers) London 1986.

"J.G. Farrell: A Note". *Malcolm Lowry Newsletter* 7 1980, p.19.

"The Fiction of J.G. Farrell". *Malcolm Lowry Newsletter* 5 1979, pp.22-24.

"The Novelist as Historian". *Critical Quarterly* 21 (2) 1979, pp.70-72.

Bowen, Elizabeth: "Ireland Agonistes". *Europa* 1 1970, pp.58-59.

Bristow-Smith, Laurence: "Tomorrow Is Another Day: The Essential J.G. Farrell". *Critical Quarterly* 25 (2) 1983, pp.45-52.

Brock, George: "Epitaph for the Empire". *The Observer Magazine* 24 September 1979, pp.73-74.

Dean, Malcolm: "A Personal Memoir". Published in J.G. Farrell: *The Hill Station*. London 1982, pp.192-205.

"Grip of Empire". *The Guardian* 13 September 1978, p.10.

Drabble, Margaret: "Things Fall Apart". Published in J.G. Farrell: *The Hill Station*. London 1985, pp.178-191.

Glendinning, Victoria: "Farrell's Last Words". *The Listener* 105, pp.548-549.

Greenberger, Allen J. and Edith L. Piness: "J.G. Farrell's 'The Siege of Krishnapur'". *Indo-British Review: A Journal of History* 11 (1) December 1984, pp.112-117.

Hartveit, Lars: "Affinity or Influence? Sir Walter Scott and J.G. Farrell as Historical Novelists". In: J.H. Alexander (ed.): *Scott and His Influence: Papers of the Aberdeen Scott Conference 1982*. Aberdeen 1983, pp.414-420.

"Ideological Stocktaking in J.G. Farrell's Historical Fiction". In: *Essays in Honour of Kristian Smidt*. Oslo 1986, pp.251-262.

Mahon, Derek: "J.G. Farrell 1935-1979". *New Street* 98, p.313.

Pykett, Lyn: "The Century's Daughters: Recent Women's Fiction and History". *Critical Quarterly* 29 (3), pp.71-77.

Shrimpton, Nicholas: "Talent for Thought". *New Statesman* 24 April 1981, pp.18-19.

Singh, Francis B.: "Progress and History in J.G. Farrell's 'TheSiege of Krishnapur'". *Chandrabhaga: A Magazine of World Writting* 2 1979, pp.23-39.

Spurling, John: "As Does the Bishop". Published in J.G. Farrell: *The Hill Station.* London 1985, pp. 155-177.

Wilson, A.N.: "An Unfinished Life". *The Spectator* 25 April 1981, pp.20-21.

Winnifrith, T.: "J.G. Farrell". In: *British Novelists Since 1960.* (Dictionary of Literary Biography 14 :1) Detroit 1983, pp.288-291.

RUTH PRAWER JHABVALA

Jhabvala, Ruth Prawer: *Heat and Dust.* London 1976.

To Whom She Will. London 1955.

The Nature of Passion. London 1956.

Esmond in India. London 1958.

The Householder. London 1960.

Get Ready for Battle. London 1962.

Like Birds, Like Fishes. London 1963.

A Backward Place. London 1965.

A Stronger Climate. London 1968.

An Experience of India. London 1971.

A New Dominion. London 1972.

How I Became a Holy Mother. London 1976.

In Search of Love and Beauty. London 1983.

Three Continents. London 1987.

Out of India: Selected Stories. Harmondsworth 1989.

Poet and Dancer. London 1993.

Agarwal, Ramlal: "An Interview with Ruth Jhabvala". *Quest* September/October 1974, pp.33-36.

"Forster, Jhabvala and Readers". *Journal of Indian Writing in English* 3 (2) 1976, pp.25-27.

"Two Approaches to Jhabvala". *Journal of Indian Writing in English* 5 (1) 1977, pp.24-27.

Chadha, Ramesh: "'Heat and Dust' and 'The Coffer Dams': A Comparative Study". *Journal of Indian Writing in English* 10 (1,2) 1982, pp.24-30.

Chew, Shirley: "Fictions of Princely States and Empire". *Ariel: A Review of International English Literature* 17 (3) 1986, pp.103-117.

Crane, Ralph J.: "Ruth Prawer Jhabvala: A Checklist of Primary and Secondary Sources". *Journal of Commonwealth Literature* 20 (1) 1985, pp.171-203.

Cronin, Richard: "'The Hill of Devi' and 'Heat and Dust'". *Essays in Criticism* 36 (2) 1986, pp.142-159.

Desai, Anita: "Jhabvala: A Sure Winner". *The Illustrated Weekly of India* 7 March 1976, p.32.

Ezekiel, Nissim: "Two Readers and Their Texts". In: Guy Amirthanayagam (ed.): *Asian and Western Writers in Dialogue: New Cultural Identities.* London 1982, pp.137-141.

Freedland, Jonathan: "Heat, Dust and a Woman with a New York View".

The Independent 1 May 1993.

Gooneratne, Yasmine: "Film into Fiction: The Influence upon Ruth Prawer Jhabvala's Fiction of Her Work in the Cinema 1960-1970". *World Literature Written in English* 18 1979, pp.368-386.

"Irony in Ruth Prawer Jhabvala's 'Heat and Dust'". *New Literature Review* 4 1978, pp.41-50.

"Literary Influences on the Writing of Ruth Prawer Jhabvala". In: Satendra Nandan (ed.): *Language and Literature in Multicultural Context.* University of South Pacific Suva, Fiji 1983, pp.141-168.

"Ruth Prawer Jhabvala: Generating Heat and Light". *Kunapipi* 1 (1) 1979, pp.115-129.

Silence, Exile and Cunning: The Fiction of Ruth Prawer Jhabvala. London 1983.

Hayball, Connie: "Ruth Prawer Jhabvala's India". *Journal of Indian Writing in English* 9 (2) 1981, pp.42-57.

Jussawalla, Feroza F.: *Family Quarrels: Towards a Criticism of Indian Writing in English.* (American University Studies. Series 4: English Language and Literature 17) New York 1985.

Kaveri, Bose: "Margret Laurence and Ruth Jhabvala". In: R.K. Dhawan (ed.), *Commonwealth Fiction* 3. New Delhi 1988, pp.198-209.

King, Bruce A.: "Recent Commonwealth Fiction". *Sewannee Review* 85 Winter 1977, pp.126-134.

"Three Novels and Some Conclusions: 'Guerillas', 'The Adaptable Man' and 'Heat and Dust'. In: Bruce King: *The New English Literatures: Cultural Nationalism in a Changing World.* London 1980, pp.215-231.

Kohli, Devindra: "More Talking of 'Heat and Dust'". *The Indian Literary Review* 1 (2) 1978, pp.35-39.

Kumar, S.N.: "Heat and Dust". *Literary Criterion* 12 (2, 3) 1976, pp.226-228.

Lall, J.S.: "No Heat, Little Dust". *The Illustrated Weekly of India* 8 February 1976, pp.35.

Moorhead, Caroline: "Interview with Ruth Prawer Jhabvala". *The Times* 20 November 1975.

Mukherjee, Meenakshi: "Journey's End for Jhabvala". In: Rajinder Kumar Dhawan (ed.): *Explorations in Modern Indo-English Fiction*. New Delhi 1982, pp.208-213.

"Inside the Outsider". In: C. D. Narashimaiah (ed.): *Awakened Conscience: Studies in Commonwealth Literature*. Delhi 1978, pp.86-91.

Mukherjee, Nirmal: "'Heat and Dust': A Tale of Two Women". *Kakatiya Journal of English Studies* 8 (1) 1978, pp.120-139.

Nahal, Chaman: "Cross-Cultural Tensions: E.M. Forster and Ruth Jhabvala". In: *The New Literatures in English*. New Delhi 1985, pp.65-87.

Naik, M.K.: "Post-Independence Indo-English Fiction". In R.K. Dhawan (ed.): *Commonwealth Fiction* 1. New Delhi 1988, pp.62-69.

Narayan, Shyamala A.: "India". *Journal of Commonwealth Literature* 11 (2) 1976, pp.82-94.

Nirupa, Rani K.: "India in the Fiction of Ruth Prawer Jhabvala". *Commonwealth Quarterly* 3 December 1978, pp.112-127.

Pradhan, Narindar S.: "The Problem of Focus in Jhabvala's 'Heat and Dust'". *The Indian Literary Review* 1 (1) 1978. pp.15-20.

Price, James: "Victors and Victims: More New Fiction". *Encounter* 46 (2) 1976, pp.65-66.

Pritchett, Victor S.: "Ruth Prawer Jhabvala: Snares and Delusions". In: *The Tale Bearers: Essays on English and American and Other Writers*. London 1980, pp.206-213.

Raghavan, Ellen Weaver: "Irony in the Works of Ruth Prawer Jhabvala". Unpublished thesis. University of Houston 1984.

Ramsharma, Aima: "Review of Ruth Prawer Jhabvala's 'Heat and Dust'". *Indian Literature* 19 (5) 1976, pp.153-157.

Rubin, David: "Ruth Jhabvala in India". *Modern Fiction Studies* 30 (4) 1984, pp.669-683.

Rutherford, Anna and Kirsten Holsten Petersen: "'Heat and Dust': Ruth Prawer Jhabvala's Experience of India". *World Literature Written in English* 15 (2) 1976, pp.373-378.

Shanane, Vasant A.: "An Artist's Experience of India: Ruth Prawer Jhabvala's Fiction". *Literary Criterion* 12 (2,3) 1976, pp.47-62.
Also published in: M. Manuel and K. Ayyappa Paniker: *English and India: Essays Presented to Professor Samuel Mathai on His 70th Birthday.* Madras 1978, pp.1-15.
Reprinted in: R.K. Dhawan (ed.): *Commonwealth Fiction* 1. New Delhi 1988, pp.228-244.

"Jhabvala's 'Heat and Dust': A Cross-Cultural Encounter". In: M.M. Naik (ed.): *Aspects of Indian Writing in English: Essays in Honour of Professor K.R. Srinivasan Iyenagar.* Madras 1979, pp.222-231.

Ruth Prawer Jhabvala. (Indian Writers Series 11) New Delhi 1976.

"Ruth Prawer Jhabvala and the Indian Scene". *Journal of Indian Writing in English* 4 (2) 1976, pp.21-24.

Singh, Brijraj: "Ruth Prawer Jhabvala: 'Heat and Dust'". In: Narinder S. Pradhan (ed.): *Major Indian Novels: An Evaluation.* New Delhi 1985, pp.192-222.

Sohi, Harinder: "Ruth Jhabvala's Passage to India". *Panjab University Research Bulletin (Arts)* 16 (1) 1985, pp.3-15.

de Souza, Eunice: "The Blinds Drawn and the Air Conditioner on". *World Literature Written in English* 17 (1) 1978, pp.219-225.

"The Expatriate Experience". In: C.D. Narasimhaiah (ed.): *Awakened Conscience: Studies in Commonwealth Literature.* New Delhi 1978, pp.339-345.

Sucher, Laura Elizabeth: "Quest and Disillusion: The Fiction of Ruth Prawer Jhabvala". Unpublished thesis. State University of New York at Stony Brook 1985.

Sucher, Laurie: *The Fiction of Ruth Prawer Jhabvala: The Politics of Passion.* London 1989.

Summerfield, Henry: "Holy Women and Unholy Men: Ruth Prawer Jhabvala Confronts the Non-rational". *Ariel: A Review of International English Literature* 17 (3) 1986, pp.85-101.

Updike, John: "Raman and Daisy and Olivia and the Nawab". In: *Hugging the Shore: Essays and Criticism.* London 1984, pp.710-716.

Varma, P.N.: "A Note on the Novels of Ruth Prawer Jhabvala". *University of Rajasthan Studies in English* 5, pp.87-96.

Williams, Haydn Moore: *The Fiction of Ruth Prawer Jhabvala.* Calcutta 1973.

"Mad Seekers, Doomed Lovers and Cemetries in India: On R. Prawer Jhabvala's 'Heat and Dust' and 'A New Dominion'". *New Literature Review* 15, pp.11-20.
Reprinted in: *Galaxy of Indian Writing in English.* Delhi 1987, pp.76-89.
Also in R.K. Dhawan (ed.): *Commonwealth Fiction* 1. New Delhi 1988, pp.253-267.

Winterberg, Inge: "'An Experience of India': Zu den Indienromanen von Ruth Prawer Jhabvala". *Arcadia* 17 (2) 1982, pp.171-194.

GENERAL and BACKGROUND

Ackerley, Joe Randolph: *Hindoo Holiday: An Indian Journal.* London 1932.

Anon: "Sex and the Indian Novel". *Cencrastus: Scottish and International Literature, Arts and Affairs* 25 Spring 1987, pp.34-40.

Ballhatchet, Kenneth: *Race, Sex and Class under the Raj: Imperial Attitudes and Policies and Their Critics, 1793-1905.* London 1980.

Batliwala, Rashna: "Delusion and Distortion: A Study of Some Anglo-Indian Fiction". Unpublished thesis. University of Massachusetts 1977.

Burgess, Anthony: "On Lengthy Matters". *The New York Times Book Review* 14 December 1975, p.39.

Candler, Edmund: *Abdication.* London 1922.

Siri Ram: Revolutionist. London 1912.

Chaudhuri, Nirad C.: "India in English Literature". *Essays by Divers Hands: Being the Transactions of the Royal Society of Literature.* New Series 40 1979, pp.15-33.

"Passage to and from India". In: Andrew Rutherford (ed.): *Twentieth Century Interpretations of "A Passage to India".* New York 1970, pp.68-78.

Thy Hand Great Anarch! : India 1921-1952. London 1987.

Conrad, Joseph: *Heart of Darkness.* London 1960.

Lord Jim. London 1978.

Darling, Malcolm: *Apprentice to Power: India 1904-1908.* London 1966.

Dhawan, Rajinder Kumar: "The Artist as Historian: Some New Writers". In: R.K. Dhawan (ed.): *Commonwealth Fiction* 3. New Delhi 1988, pp.238 268.

Edwardes, Michael: *Bound to Exile: The Victorians in India.* London 1969.

The Last Years of British India. London 1963.

Eliot, Thomas Stearns: *The Complete Poems and Plays.* London 1969.

Emerson, Ralph Waldo: *Essays and Lectures.* New York 1983.

Ezekiel, Nissim: "Cross-Cultural Encounter in Colonial Literature". *Indian PEN* 43 (11,12) 1977, pp.4-8.

Forster, Edward Morgan: *The Hill of Devi: Being Letters from Dewas State Senior.* London 1953.

A Passage to India. (Abinger Edition 6) London 1978.

Fowles, John: "Notes on an Unfinished Novel". In: Malcolm Bradbury (ed.): *The Novel Today.* London 1977, pp.136-151.

Green, Martin: *Dreams of Adventure, Deeds of Empire.* London 1980.

Grella, George: Preface to: Brijen K. Gupta (ed.): *India in English Fiction: An Annotated Bibliography.* Metuchen N.J. 1973, pp.vii-xiii.

Hitchins, Christopher: "Busted Blue: 'A Passage to India'". *Grand Street* 4 (3), pp.215-219.

Howe, Susanne: *Novels of Empire.* New York 1949.

Hutchins, Francis: *The Illusion of Permanence.* Princetown 1967.

Hyam, Ronald: "Empire and Sexual Opportunity". *The Journal of Imperial and Commonwealth History* 14 (2) 1986, pp.34-89.

Empire and Sexuality: The British Experience. (Studies in Imperialism) Manchester 1990.

Ingram, Edward: "The Raj as Daydream: The Pukka Sahib as Henty Hero in Simla, Chandrapore and Kyauktada". In: Gordon Martel (ed.): *Studies in Imperial History: Essays in Honour of A.P. Thornton.* London 1986, pp. 159-177.

Kermode, Frank: "Coming up for Air". *New York Review of Books* 15 July 1976, pp.42-44.

Khattak, Zahir Jang: "British Novelists Writing About India-Pakistan's Independence: Christine Weston, John Masters, Ruth Prawer Jhabvala and Paul Scott". Unpublished thesis. Tufts University 1987.

Kim, Suzanne: "Histoire et Roman". *Etudes Anglaises* 36 (2,3) 1983, pp.168-180.

Kipling, Rudyard: *Plain Tales from the Hills.* London 1900.

Lascelles, Mary: *The Story-Teller Retrieves the Past: Historical Fiction and Ficticious History in the Art of Scott, Stevenson, Kipling and Some Others.* Oxford 1980.

Lago, Mary and P.N. Furnbank: *Selected Letters of E.M. Forster.* London 1985.

Lukács, Georg: *The Historical Novel.* London 1962.

Mahood, M.M.: *The Colonial Encounter.* London 1977.

Mannoni, Octave: *Prospero and Caliban: The Psychology of Colonization.* New York 1964.

Meyers, Jeffrey: *Fiction and the Colonial Experience.* Ipswich 1973.

"The Hero in British Colonial Fiction". Unpublished thesis. University of California at Berkeley 1967.

Mukherjee, Sujit: "The Overaching Sky: Forster and the Tradition of Anglo-Indian Fiction". *Cahiers d'études et de recherches victoriennes et édouardiennes* 4 (5), pp.161-173.

Murdoch, Iris: "Against Dryness: A Polemical Sketch". In: Malcolm Bradbury (ed.): *The Novel Today: Contemporary Writers on Modern Fiction.* Manchester 1977, pp.23-32.

Nehru, Jawarharlal: *An Autobiography.* London 1936.

Orwell, George: *Burmese Days.* London 1961.

Collected Essays. London 1961.

Rubin, David: *After the Raj: British Novels of India Since 1947.* Hanover NH 1986.

Schmid, Olga Carmelita: "Effects of Colonialism on Colonizers in Imaginative Writing". Unpublished thesis. US-International University 1979.

Sencourt, Robert: *India in English Literature.* London 1925.

Shamsul, Islam: *Chronicles of the Raj: A Study of the Imperial Idea towards the End of the Raj.* London 1979.

Suleri, Sara: *The Rhetoric of English India.* Chicago 1992.

Taylor, D.J.: *A Vain Conceit: British Fiction in the 1980s.* London 1989.

Vinson, James: *Contemporary Novelists.* London 1972.

Walsh, William: "India and the Novel". In: Boris Ford (ed.): *The Present* (The New Pelican Guide to English Literature 8) London 1983, pp. 245-260.

Williams, R.J.P.: "Presenting the Raj: The Politics of Representation". Unpublished thesis. University of Nottingham 1988.

Woodcock, George: *Who Killed the British Empire? : An Inquest.* London 1974.

Woolf, Leonard: *Growing: An Autobiography of the Years 1904-1911*. London 1961.